Hartland to Capitol Hill

Hartland to Capitol Hill

The Journey of a Wounded Healer

Mary Gunderson

Co-written by
Ernie Gunderson

NORTH STAR PRESS OF ST. CLOUD, INC.
St. Cloud, Minnesota

Copyright © 2011 Ernie Gunderson

All rights reserved.

ISBN: 978-0-87839-578-1

Printed in the United States of America

Published by
North Star Press of St. Cloud, Inc.
P.O. Box 451
St. Cloud, Minnesota 56302

northstarpress.com

Table of Contents

Foreword		vii
Chapter 1	The Train to New York	1
Chapter 2	Hartland, 1931	4
Chapter 3	Grand Central Terminal	19
Chapter 4	The Promised Land, 1936	23
Chapter 5	Hartsdale Corners	39
Chapter 6	Higher Education	43
Chapter 7	Dinner with Erna	56
Chapter 8	Giffin School, 1946	60
Chapter 9	St. Patrick's Cathedral	73
Chapter 10	LBI and the Men of My Dreams	78
Chapter 11	St. Thomas Church	95
Chapter 12	Marriage and Family, 1949-1958	98
Chapter 13	Bread and Wine	113
Chapter 14	Blessed and Cursed, 1958-1973	116
Chapter 15	Ellis Island	135
Chapter 16	Broadening Horizons	139
Chapter 17	Choral Evensong	156
Chapter 18	Psychotic Relapses	159
Chapter 19	A Stroll down Fifth Avenue	173
Chapter 20	Blessed are Those Who Mourn	176
Chapter 21	White Plains	188
Chapter 22	A Time to Dance, A Time to Speak Out	191
Chapter 23	Last Evening in Hartsdale	205
Chapter 24	Capitol Hill	208
Chapter 25	The Journey Home	217
Epilogue		221
Acknowledgements		225
Bibliography		227

Foreword

The term *wounded healer,* coined by Carl Jung and the title of a book by Henri Nouwen, is derived from the Greek legend of Asclepius, the physician. In the process of identifying and healing his own wounds, Asclepius created a sanctuary for healing others. Many historical and present day figures are identified with this archetypal character. The best-known example of a wounded healer, according to Nouwen, is Jesus Christ, whose resurrected body became an enduring symbol of hope and faith for the persecuted masses. Most wounded healers, however, are regular folks who lived or are living among us with some kind of personal hardship or tragedy, using their knowledge and energy to help others similarly wounded.

This story, written like a memoir, is about one of those regular folks. It is the inspirational narrative of Mary Gunderson's life journey, her personal development, a family tragedy, and the healing power of prayer, grief work, and self disclosure. After revealing her tragic story before a crowded forum of mental health professionals, Mary was invited to Washington, D.C., to share it with elected officials and the world. In the process of healing herself, Mary became a committed organizer and advocate for mental health causes and for others who suffered from mental illnesses.

The daughter of Danish immigrants, Mary was born in 1926 and given the name Marie Mikaelsen. She lived nearly her entire life on farms in Minnesota and Iowa, first as a farmer's daughter and then as a farmer's wife. Other than raising eleven children, losing two to mental illness and suicide, and going to Washington to tell about it, there was nothing particularly unusual about Mary, except for one thing. She was a prolific writer. What is remarkable about Mary is that she recorded her whole life

Foreword

in diaries, journals, articles, letters, and an unpublished memoir. She preserved her photos and memorabilia in dozens of albums and scrapbooks, labeled everything, and managed to save it all. Regarding her Danish family of origin, the Mikaelsens, theirs was a story experienced by countless other immigrant and farm families who survived the times and forged successful lives from the ash heap of the Great Depression.

After Mary died of cancer in 2000, her written legacy survived a farm sale and two moves, finding safe storage in the homes of her survivors, who saved and protected her things as living remnants of their beloved mother and partner. Before starting this publication of Mary's memoirs, Ernie collected, catalogued, and indexed over 6000 pages of her written records and memorabilia. In a bequest he found in this collection, Mary had written, "If I've created problems by being a packrat, forgive me. I will appreciate it if what has been important to me will survive and not be tossed into a scrap heap without due consideration." Ernie's previous publication of Mary's five-year *Diary of a Young School Teacher* and this publication of her memoirs are the due consideration of the things important to Mary Gunderson.

This story is based entirely on Mary's written records except for historical details gathered from the following sources: various books and websites (see bibliography), letters and memoirs written by Mary's relatives, Ernie's recollections and observations, and recollections from Gordon, Mary's children, and her relatives and friends, several of whom Ernie interviewed. Some of the stories and descriptions are taken verbatim from Mary's journals and memoirs, but most of the book is Ernie's edited version of her story, organized and integrated into a cohesive narrative with dialogue and details added for effect. Mary's seven day trip to Capitol Hill and Hartsdale, New York, in 1990 is the setting and framework within which she tells the story of her life. This book preserves that story and the life work of Mary Gunderson, who suffered from wounds of stigma and loss, who succeeded in healing herself through faith, grief work, and giving support to others who suffered from illnesses of the mind.

1

The Train to New York

In 1990 I was invited to Washington, D.C., to share my testimony with congressional delegates on Capitol Hill. My hosts, NAMI (National Alliance for the Mentally Ill) and the National Institute of Mental Health, paid for the entire trip. I stayed in the Comfort Hotel in Arlington, Virginia, down the street from NAMI headquarters. The people at NAMI wanted me to appear on the *Today Show*, too. They asked me to go to New York while they negotiated with NBC studios.

On the morning of April 28, I took a taxi to Union Station. It was clear and steamy that day with temperatures headed for the nineties. I paid the driver and toted my luggage into the grand waiting hall. The place is huge! Saturday morning travelers were lined up in the ticketing area. I purchased my ticket, took a seat in the waiting area, and settled in for the half hour wait. While inspecting my luggage, I heard a friendly voice.

"Weren't you one of the lobbyists at mental health day?"

I turned and met the gaze of a familiar looking man. He was tall, a little stooped, and very congenial. "Yes, I was," I replied. "Didn't we meet at the reception?"

"Yeah, you're the lady from Minnesota, right?"

I remembered talking to him at the reception but I couldn't remember his name. "That's right," I replied. "I'm Mary Gunderson from Mora. And aren't you from Iowa?"

"Well, I grew up there. Now I live in Chicago. The name is Lindberg, Don Lindberg. How did it go on the Hill?"

"Very well, very interesting. Thank you. We met with four of my congressmen. I hope my testimony was effective."

"What was your testimony about?"

"I was asked to tell about my son and daughter who both suffered from mental illness and committed suicide. The APA—American Psychiatric Association—was looking for people who could highlight the gaps in mental health services."

"I'm sorry. I shouldn't have pried," he said.

"Oh it's okay. Thank you for asking. I've told the story many times by now."

"Are you taking the train back to Minnesota?" he asked.

"No. I'm going to New York City to visit my cousin. She lives in Hartsdale, a northern suburb. NAMI and the National Institute of Mental Health are trying to get me a spot on the *Today Show* next week. They want me to tell my story to the whole country."

"Well, good for you. I'll have to keep an eye on the *Today Show*."

"How about you, are you heading home to Chicago?"

"Yeah, I enjoy riding the train," he said.

A line was forming at gate E when the announcement came: "Train 174 to New York Penn Station now boarding on track twenty." I said good-bye to Don and took my place in a short line. At the gate, I showed my ticket and asked, "Does it matter which car I get on?"

"Rear five coaches, ma'am, track twenty."

The tracks and platforms stretched out ahead. Several trains stood waiting. At track twenty, I strolled up a short ramp to the platform alongside a sleek silver train. I passed two cars labeled "coach" and entered the third through open doors. Halfway down the center aisle, I hoisted my suitcase into the overhead rack and lowered myself into a contoured seat next to the window. I studied the surroundings as other passengers trickled in. The interior of the coach was luxurious and clean with nicely upholstered seats.

I was still glowing from the kind treatment I received in Washington and the warm reception I got during my day of lobbying on Capitol Hill. But I was also glad to be on my way to Hartsdale to meet my second cousin Erna.

Erna Christensen was a retired professor. What little I knew about her, I learned from a newspaper article shown to me by relatives in

Denmark. The article told about Erna's trip in 1961 to escort her ninety-year-old mother Christine on a tour of Denmark. They visited Christine's hometown seventy-two years after she immigrated to America. I hand copied the article and saved it, hoping to meet Erna someday. When the opportunity arose to appear on the *Today Show*, I jumped at the chance to extend my trip. I contacted Erna and arranged to stay with her.

A voice came over the intercom announcing the train's departure. At 9:25 the train quivered slightly and rolled slowly forward. Through polished windows, I watched the streets and buildings pass by as the train rolled north and gradually accelerated through a warehouse section of the nation's capital. Cruising speed for the Amtrak is eighty miles per hour, and it wasn't long before the train approached that speed. It would be three more hours, with stops in Baltimore, Wilmington, Philadelphia, and Newark before arriving at Penn Station in New York City. The northern suburbs of Washington soon gave way to pines, marshland, and hardwoods beginning to show a tinge of spring green. North of Baltimore the forests yielded to scattered farmland.

The gentle motion and occasional muffled whistles reminded me of train rides long ago in Minnesota. Passenger trains were still common in the Midwest during my youth, before automobiles became the main mode of transportation and freeways the main arteries. I loved riding the Rocket to Austin and Albert Lea to visit my cousins, the Nielsens. In fact, Else Nielsen was a younger sister of the elderly Christine Christensen featured in the Danish news. Else, her husband Chris, and their children were waiting at the train depot in Albert Lea when my parents, Hans and Anna Mikaelsen, and my three siblings arrived from Denmark in January 1926. I was a stowaway in Mother's womb, not due until June. The Nielsens had agreed to sponsor the immigrant Mikaelsen family, and Else, formerly a Mikaelsen herself, later became my godmother.

Unable to gain a financial foothold before the Depression started, my parents spent the first ten years in America wandering about, subsisting on rented farms and borrowed money. I don't remember the early years, but I heard plenty of stories about them. My earliest memories are from the farm we rented near Hartland.

2

Hartland, 1931

I was only four years old, but I will never forget our first trip to the Jensen's. It was late on a Sunday morning in February. The sleigh was ready. Papa had the horses hitched, and Mama carried the hot bricks. A heavy horsehair blanket covered all but my face, and a scarf was wrapped twice around my head. The whole family piled into the sleigh. My three older siblings, John, Martin, and Esther were laughing and talking, but I sat quietly by Mama. The sleigh glided easily over glistening snow as the horses trotted up the lane and east on the road to Ellendale. Martin warmed his harmonica, and soon the only sounds were the steady drumbeat of hooves and old familiar tunes.

Several miles later we turned down a snowy driveway and stopped in front of the Jensens' house. They were Danes also and still spoke Danish in their home like we did. I was carried into the house and deposited among several children. Edith was six, the same age as Esther. Ardis was my age and exactly my size. She smiled, took my hand, and led me to her room. I stood wide eyed in amazement, looking at her dolls and playthings.

"Would you like to have a tea party?" she asked.

I nodded and replied, "I like tea parties."

"You can sit here," she said, showing me to a small table with two little chairs. In the other room a lot of talking and laughing could be heard, but we were absorbed in our own play. Annabel and Alice, the two rag dolls, were clothed in creamy white gowns and tucked into a wooden cradle. Sitting in miniature high chairs were two larger walking dolls with real hair and beautiful blue eyes that opened and closed.

"This one is Olive," said Ardis, "and this one is Priscilla. We won Priscilla at the Christmas raffle. Do you have any dolls?"

"No," I replied. A lump rose in my throat.

"Why not?"

Hesitating, I pulled one of the larger dolls closer to the table and replied, "Papa said we don't have enough money for dolls."

"Then you should come over more often to play with my dolls," she said. And that was the beginning of a long friendship which lasted throughout my childhood years.

Later, back in our own drab home, the stillness was pierced by a knock at the door. I followed my mother to find Nick Jensen standing outside with a package wrapped in newspaper.

"I brought you some frozen fish," he said, smiling.

I only stared.

"Come in, come in," Mama insisted. I continued staring as he wiped his shoes and entered the kitchen.

Placing the package on the table, Nick looked at me. "Would you like to open it, Marie?" he asked.

After much hesitation and with encouragement from the rest of my family, I dared cautiously to pull back the newspaper. There lay not a frozen fish but a beautiful walking doll with real hair.

"It's for you," said Nick. "Ardis wanted you to have it."

I was so thrilled to see that doll, it did not occur to me until later to thank him. A ray of hope and happiness came into our home that day and lit up the gloom. I played with that doll for years until it was tattered and torn.

This memorable event took place at the Freemo farm near Hartland, Minnesota. We moved there the previous spring when I was still named Marie or Mia, my nickname. I was born on Rusley's farm three miles north of Albert Lea only five months after my family immigrated.

Mama hated leaving Denmark. She got pregnant and resisted the sale of their property and belongings, but Papa was undeterred. When it came time to leave, she refused to pack, so Papa did all the packing. Mama failed at every attempt to change his mind because Papa was greatly inspired by the stories of success coming from other Danish settlers in America. The Danes called this "America Fever." He wanted to go to America, and that was that.

Mama ultimately boarded the ship, but she never got on board with Papa's desire to settle in America. One way Mama expressed this resistance was by refusing to yield to the foreign tongue. She never learned to speak English, a deficiency that had lasting repercussions. At my birth, for example, Mama intended my name to be Else Marie, her sister's name. But somehow the doctor misinterpreted her request and recorded only "Marie" on the birth certificate: Marie Mikaelsen with no middle name.

Another lasting symbol of Mama's language handicap occurred on my first day of school, two and a half years after we moved to the Freemo farm. I walked with my sister and brothers a mile south to the village of Bath, which was more a crossroad than a town. St. Riden's Catholic Church and a cemetery occupied a hill to the left. On the right stood a store and the creamery where Papa sold his cream. Across the road was the District 103 school house, which we entered upon arrival. The teacher smiled at me and said, "Hello. Welcome to Bath School. I'm Magella Ferry. What is your name?"

I was not yet conversant in English. Recognizing the word *name*, however, I vaguely understood what she was asking and replied, "Mia."

Miss Ferry frowned, a little bemused, and said, "I haven't heard that name before." She shrugged and then continued, "Our toilets are in the yard behind the school. You may use them when needed. If you raise one finger I will know you wish to go. If no one else has left the room, I will give you permission to leave."

Comprehending none of what she said, I stood perplexed and looked around. A group of children had gathered and were staring at me.

"Do you wish to go now?" Miss Ferry asked.

I looked at Martin, not knowing what to say. He was in seventh grade and fluent in English by then.

He looked at Miss Ferry and said, "She hasn't learned any English yet." Then he turned to me and said, *"Hun kan ikki forstaa var dit navn er."* (She cannot understand what your name is.)

"Marie," I said, louder this time.

Puzzled, Miss Ferry turned to Martin and said, "I do not understand what she said. Can you tell me what her name is?"

"We call her Mia."

"May I?" she replied. This was how my nickname sounded in Danish.

"No, Mia," he repeated.

Miss Ferry still did not understand and looked frustrated. The other children were giggling and broke into open laughter. It seemed very funny, so I laughed too. Miss Ferry gave up for the moment and decided to call on us at home that evening, whereupon she asked Mama the same question, "What is her name?" My brother John translated.

Mama replied, *"Hun er navned eften den ungfru Maria."*

"Den ungfru Maria?" Miss Ferry said, even more puzzled.

Papa, who was fluent in English, said, "She is named after the Virgin Marie."

"Oh, her name is Mary," Miss Ferry concluded, and in that moment my name was changed forever. I have been called Mary ever since. If Mama or Papa had thought to spell it out on paper for Miss Ferry, I might still be Marie.

I attended Bath School for the next four years and learned to read and write and speak English. There were over thirty children in attendance there. Much to my dismay, some of the children began to call me "May I," which hurt and angered me. I came to loathe that name and begged my mother to call me Mary instead, which she was not able to pronounce. The best she could do was "Maa-ree," rolling the "r." She called me *lille Maaree* (little Mary).

In addition to the name Marie and my nickname Mia, I came to loathe my foreignism as well. I shed tears over having to wear long underwear with black stockings and high-top lace-up shoes. From the beginning, I got the feeling that other children laughed behind my back. This was deeply humiliating for me and one cause, perhaps, for the melancholy I suffered in childhood.

Because my family was poor, my siblings and I were not able to buy clothing. Instead we wore second-hand clothes from our friends and relatives in Albert Lea, like the Nielsens. Mama, who was not the best seamstress, modified these to fit us. Because her sense of fashion had not changed since she left the old country, my sister and I were sent off to school in jumpers worn over long underwear. Esther and I rolled up our long underwear on the way to school and folded our long stockings down so we would not look so different. Of course, on the way home we reversed this process so as not to disturb our parents. Papa encouraged Mama's old-fashioned sense of style because he thought it would help prevent in us the moral decay he perceived in popular fashions and culture, not to mention that it was easier on his pocket book.

A few months after my grandmother Maren died in Denmark, her heavy black community costume arrived in the mail. A few years later Mama decided to alter it for me to wear as a school outfit. She converted it to a jumper which hung crooked below my knees. I am sorry to say this now, but I was embarrassed to wear it.

All these memories were from our early years on the Freemo farm, which we rented near Hartland, Minnesota, twelve miles north of Albert Lea. We moved there in 1930 after shifting around several years from place to place, failing to gain a financial foothold. Papa didn't want to remain on the Rusley farm, where I was born, because it was only forty acres. We stayed there just one year. Unable find a larger farm near Albert Lea, he began to consider other communities.

One day Papa received a letter from his friend in Luck, Wisconsin, telling him there were farms available. A few weeks later, Papa drove up there in his Model T Ford. He found a small farm on the east shore of Bone Lake. Not only did Papa sign a lease, he also bought machinery and livestock at the auction with money loaned to him by his old friends. Much to Mama's dismay, we moved there in the spring of 1927. That move turned into a bitter failure. The crops were poor two summers in a row, and the cows got a persistent mastitis. Worse, on the eve of the Great Depression, the prices for most farm products had already begun to collapse. When he sold out, Papa got little in return for his cattle and machinery.

After failing to realize his dream in the Midwest, Papa decided to move our family to California, having heard promising news about farming in the Central Valley. In the fall of 1928, we packed all our belongings into the Model T and a trailer Papa made from an old chicken coop. Nearly out of money, we stopped in Albert Lea on our way to California. Papa pleaded with our relatives for a loan so we could continue our journey. By then they were probably strapped financially themselves or tired of loaning money to Papa for his ill-fated adventures. Moreover, our relatives thought we were crazy to drive that old Ford and ramshackle trailer over the mountains, particularly in the wintertime. In any case, the answer was uniformly, "No." John Steinbeck may have confirmed their prescience ten years later with *The Grapes of Wrath,* which immortalizes the sorry fate of those who actually made it to California during the Depression. We could have easily ended up like the hapless Joad family!

We spent the winter of 1929 in a tiny upstairs apartment in Albert Lea living on handouts from relatives and church friends. Papa got a job at Wilson Packing Company and worked for a few weeks until he broke out with an allergic rash, an apparent reaction to the salt brine preservatives, and that was the end of his job. How we survived that winter, I do not know.

In the spring we got another loan from our relatives to buy some cattle and rent a small farm six miles northeast of Albert Lea near the town of Lerdahl. We moved on the first of March. By my third birthday, in June, Papa had all the crops planted and a barn full of cows.

At Lerdahl Mama and Papa received sad news. Two of my grandparents, Mama's father Johannas and Papa's mother Maren, died that year in Denmark. Having never met any of my grandparents, I had no concept of who they were.

The farm at Lerdahl was too small. We stayed there just one season before Papa found the Freemo farm available near Hartland. The following spring we moved again. It was twelve miles to the Freemo farm, and we could not afford to hire a truck to haul the cattle. Starting early one morning, Papa and my brothers herded the cows west down the road. Esther and I walked some, too, but mostly we rode with Mama, who followed behind in the Model T. We stopped for lunch near a grove of trees and let the cows graze in the ditches. Then we turned north and walked the rest of the day. By sunset that evening we arrived at the Freemo farm, tired but grateful. The cows seemed weary and bewildered, but they went happily into the barnyard where there was fresh hay. That was an exciting day for us children and one of my earliest memories.

Mrs. Freemo owned the 160 acre farm we rented. We stayed on that farm for six years. It was the first period of relative stability for our family since leaving Denmark. Upon our arrival at the Freemo farm, Papa was 45, Mama was 40, John was 12, Martin was 10, Esther was 5, and I was 3. Most of my early memories begin there. Hartland, our mailing address, was six miles to the southwest and the nearest town with a post office. Papa was able to get a loan from the bank in Hartland and used that money to pay off older debts and acquire more cattle, horses and machinery to accommodate the larger acreage. He bought everything second hand at auction sales from farmers who were going out of business.

It seemed like 1930 was going to be a better year for us. Progress appeared to be just around the corner, but economic conditions worsened, and prices for farm products kept falling. The price for a bushel of corn fell that year to 80 cents, as compared to $1.10 per bushel in 1926. By 1932 the price of corn dropped to 25 cents a bushel, hogs sold for 3 cents a pound, milk for 2 cents a quart, and eggs for 12 cents a dozen. The late 1920s and early 1930s were desperate years for farmers. Uncle Andy said it was because there were too many farmers producing too many goods, just trying to survive. Always there were some willing to sell for less, which perpetuated the downward pressure on prices.

But not all was doom and gloom. As a family, we had several things going for us, if not luck. We were able and industrious workers, resourceful and at times ingenious. When Papa bought a used Model A Ford, for example, John and Martin converted the old Model T into a tractor. Papa still used horses, but the boys were proud of their tractor and used it for all kinds of field work. Beyond ingenuity and hard work, we stayed together, supported each other, and kept our faith in God that all things would work out.

Though Papa loved America, he never grew to like our neighbors at the Freemo farm. The Sullivans across the road went to the Catholic church. South on the way to Bath there were two other farms. On one lived a young couple from Russia who had recently immigrated. On the other was a Danish couple without children. Going north there was a tee in the road. To the left was a farm with a Norwegian family; to the right was another Danish family with two adolescent children. These Danes were also recent immigrants and the only neighbors with whom Papa and Mama socialized other than the Jensens, near Ellendale.

Papa had plenty of reasons for not associating with the neighbors. He was not comfortable with Catholics because they believed that people could be saved by doing good works. He did not trust the Russian couple because they might be communists. The Danish couple down the road were okay, but they did not have children. The Norwegian family seemed like good folks, but the father was college educated and knew how to say the right words without really meaning them. Worse yet, they went to a Norwegian Lutheran church, which didn't have midweek prayer meetings. So we did not socialize much with our closest neighbors and lived mostly in our own little world.

The Freemo farm was an idyllic place for a growing child. The buildings were set into a grove of trees at the end of a long sloping driveway, barely more than two tire ruts across the field. Besides the handsome red barn, there was a hog house, a chicken house, a small brooder house, and a granary, all clustered around the turnabout at the end of the driveway. A tall windmill next to the barn pumped clear cool water into a large cow tank, where Esther and I dunked ourselves on hot summer days.

Near the driveway was a spacious two-story farmhouse with an open porch. Upstairs were three bedrooms and a hall. A stairway led down to the sitting room, dining room, and kitchen, where a wooden telephone hung on the wall. In those days, the living room was called a parlor or sitting room. A sidewalk in the back yard led to a summer kitchen, where we did our laundry and cooking during hot weather.

Around the farm buildings rows of ash, elm and spruce trees protected us from the winter winds. Esther and I loved playing in the trees. A pasture led from the trees to the far end of the property, where we went with our brothers to fetch the cows and horses.

Across the driveway south of the house stood a fine grove of apple and plum trees. We enjoyed the bounty of these fruits and garden vegetables, which Mama canned and preserved for use during the long winter and spring months. In addition to doing all the cooking, canning, gardening, and housework, Mama helped Papa with the farm work whenever she could. Socially, however, she never became comfortable in the community and never spoke in the English tongue even after she began to understand it.

A few years after we moved to the Freemo farm, Papa received his citizenship papers. Mama began to give up hope of returning to Denmark, of ever seeing her mother and sisters again. Her smile faded away and her mental health began to fail. She began to lash out at Papa in verbal tirades for bringing her to this godforsaken country. As our financial situation grew more desperate, these tirades became more frequent. They were often triggered by the slightest provocation.

One day Papa went to an auction sale and returned with a pump organ he purchased for seven dollars. In Denmark Mama had an organ, and she often lamented the absence of music in her home in America. She seemed somewhat appeased when Papa and the boys moved the organ into the living room. At first she ignored it, but eventually she sat down and began to play beautiful music, which I had not heard before in our home. I watched in wonderment and noticed her smile and a tear running down her cheek. Mama knew the old Danish hymns from memory, which she had learned to play by ear. She knew all the words and sang while she played.

Two things changed after that: Mama's mood improved and we began singing in our home. In the evenings after sending us to bed, she sat down and played the organ. While drifting off to sleep, I loved listening to the sound of her music. I was fascinated with the keys and the pumping mechanism, and before long I learned to play it too. Mama taught me how to play music by ear, like she did.

Papa was irrepressible in his religious zeal. On Sunday we held church in our home or outdoors in the summertime. Mama began by playing hymns. We all sang along, and Papa read the liturgy and preached a sermon. Once a month we drove to Albert Lea to attend Trinity Lutheran, where I was baptized and where a Danish language church service was offered once a month. Afterward, we often went to the Nielsens for Sunday dinner. Else Nielsen, my godmother, was Papa's cousin from Denmark.

Her husband Christian was a house painter. They had immigrated several years before we did and sponsored us when we arrived. I loved visiting them because their daughters, Minnie, Lilly, and Lydia, who had already graduated from high school, all took an interest in doting on me.

Papa was irrepressible in his work too. He could spend entire days working in the fields with his team of Percherons pulling the plow or the other machines utilized in planting and harvesting the crops. John and Martin were old enough to work alongside Papa, and they began to take over many of the chores, like milking the cows by hand. By the time we moved to the Freemo farm, John and Martin were each milking four cows, Esther was just learning how, Mama milked as many as she could, and Papa milked the rest. We had sixteen milk cows. The first two years there, I was too little to help, but I went along to the barn with everyone else so I wouldn't have to stay alone in the house.

One evening, however, during our first winter on the Freemo farm, I was ill and could not go to the barn as usual. Mama told me to stay put while she went out to help milk the cows. I was lying in the living room where she had left the oil lamp burning. Before leaving, she asked, "Will you be okay, lille Maaree?"

"I'm not afraid," I said, and she went out. After she left, I stared at the bright flame in the lamp. It began to flicker some, and I noticed the light dancing on the walls along with the shadows. My imagination went to work, and I became more and more frightened. Finally, I tiptoed over to the lamp and blew across the top the way my parents did to put out the flame. The light went out and the shadows stopped, but suddenly it was pitch dark, and I became even more frightened. The dreadful darkness permeated my every fiber as I sat there trembling for what seemed like hours. Finally Mama came in from the barn with Esther and exclaimed, *"Hvor sidde du her i mork? Hvordan ga eys ud?"* (Why are you sitting in the dark? How did the light go out?)

I was ashamed to admit what I had done, so I kept silent. When Papa and the boys came in from the barn, Mama told them what happened. And suddenly I exclaimed, *"Tak Skabaren!"* (Thank God the creator!) Then everyone laughed, and I did too.

Hartland, 1931

Every few days, Papa hauled the cream to the creamery in Bath. We had a separator in the barn that separated the cream from the milk. It was John and Martin's job to turn the crank on the separator, which had two spouts, one for the milk and another for the cream. We used some of the milk for our own consumption and fed the remainder to the pigs, the dog, and the cats. The cream was put into ten gallon cans, which Papa loaded into a two-wheel trailer and pulled behind the car to the creamery. In the winter he used the horses and bobsled. Mama always sent along a crate full of eggs, which Papa traded at the store for necessities. Usually he went by himself while the rest of us worked at home, but occasionally he let us ride along, and this was a great joy for me. On our birthdays we were treated to ice cream cones, which they made at the creamery.

Esther and I helped Mama in the house and garden. We worked in the house or summer kitchen much of the day cooking, cleaning, and canning. It was necessary to use the summer kitchen on hot summer days to avoid heating up the house with the wood-burning cook stove. Besides cooking in the summer kitchen, Mama used a kerosene burner there for heating large kettles of wash water to do laundry. When the water was hot, she poured it into the wooden washing machine, which had an agitator attached to a lever. Esther and I took turns pumping the lever, which turned the agitator. After the chores were completed in the evening, Mama toiled in the garden. We all helped her when we could, but mostly the garden was her affair and she was very good at it.

In addition to her gardening expertise, Mama was also a good cook. Before she got married in Denmark, she was a housemaid and did all the cooking for a wealthy family in Copenhagen. Chickens were one of her specialties, both raising them and cooking them. Beside the granary stood a little round-roofed brooder house in which the little chicks were protected and raised to adulthood. Once the chicks were mature enough, they mingled with the adult chickens. It was not uncommon to see two hundred chickens, many of them laying hens, roaming about our farmyard.

When it was time to butcher a chicken, Mama caught a rooster and chopped off its head. This was a little gruesome to watch, especially when the chicken jumped up and ran around after its head was cut off. She plopped the dead chicken into a pail of scalding water for one minute, which made it easy to pull out the feathers. The downy under-feathers were singed off over an open fire. Next, she carved a slit at the base of the throat and pulled out the gizzard, cleaning out its contents and saving the meaty part. Then she carved a larger opening around the chicken's rear end, slid her hand into the interior and scooped out the innards.

Mama sliced the carcass into pieces: two drumsticks, two wings, the breast bone, two thighs, the tail bone, the liver, heart and gizzard. She browned these in butter in a large frying pan and placed them into a roaster along with potatoes, carrots and onions. Then she rinsed the frying pan and poured the rinse-water over the contents. Finally the lid went on the roaster, which went into the hot oven for one hour.

When the meat was tender, Mama put the contents on a platter in the center of the table. She tossed some flour on the drippings in the empty roaster, added the boiled pea water, and mixed this into a thick gravy. Served with the potatoes, onions, peas, and carrots, the chicken and gravy made a delicious meal.

Mama and Papa had very different personalities. Papa was always optimistic, and Mama was a worrywart. Years later, we learned this definition of a worrywart: one who is intimately familiar with an optimist. This seemed to fit my parents well. Papa always believed success was just around the corner, and Mama had learned that around each corner was another failure waiting to happen. To soothe her frayed nerves, she prayed often and played Danish hymns on her organ. She also kept up steady correspondences with her parents and four younger sisters in Denmark, a connection and coping strategy that continued throughout her life. Mama's youngest sister Ingeborg, as a newlywed, had also immigrated in 1926 with her husband Anders. They lived and worked four years in Albert Lea, saved money to get started in farming, and then rented a farm. Papa was concerned about Ingeborg because she had cut her hair short and worked at a job away from home. This went against our pietistic beliefs, so we often prayed for Ingeborg.

During the years we lived on the Freemo farm, our language patterns gradually evolved. At the beginning, we all spoke exclusively in

Danish, except in school. By second grade I was fluent in English, and we siblings began speaking to each other in English at home while Mama and Papa continued speaking to each other and to us kids entirely in Danish. We would answer back in English when they spoke to us in Danish. Likewise, when we visited our Danish friends, it was all Danish between the older adults and all English between the children. Whereas Mama never learned to speak English, Papa was fluent before we arrived in 1926 and continued to improve year after year.

The one constant during the lean years was the strength of our religious belief. What we lacked in material wealth and financial security, we made up for with religious devotion, which was another sort of lifeline as the farming economy collapsed further. Praying together, we somehow believed that God would protect us from financial ruin and the humiliation of another failure.

Just when we thought the times couldn't get worse, they did. When our loan came due at the Hartland bank in the fall of 1935, Papa did not have enough money to pay the interest. The bankers wanted their money and refused to renew the loan. After fall harvest they initiated a forced sale of our assets. Ten years of hard labor trying to gain a foothold in America, and we had failed again. During the auction, we watched helplessly as the accumulation of six-years' labor on the Freemo farm was sold away before us. All the animals were sold except a few dozen chickens and young pigs.

The utter despair brought on by repeated failures finally caught up with Papa's optimism. A defeated man on the eve of the auction, Papa fell to his knees in the living room. It was the only time I ever saw him weep. The rest of us gathered around him and got down on our knees in sympathy. Martin put his hand on Papa's shoulder and said, "Don't you remember what you said about trusting in God?" In that moment a family tradition began. We kneeled together while Papa prayed:

> Dear Heavenly Father, forgive us for our sins and our failures. The present and future are a great mystery now, but we trust that you will deliver us from evil and lead us out from the shadow of death into green pastures. We ask you to watch over us and provide for us a new home and a good Christian community . . .

The sale went better than expected. The horses and cattle brought more than the going rate, which wasn't much. Most of the machinery went dirt cheap, which was probably about what we had paid for it. The auction raised enough money to pay off the entire bank loan with several hundred dollars left over.

Not long after the sale, Papa learned about a new government program initiated by another savior of sorts, Franklin D. Roosevelt. Just that year Roosevelt had created the Farmers Home Administration and the Federal Land Bank, which made loans to displaced farmers who were not able to secure bank financing. Papa submitted an application and soon got word that we qualified for an FmHA insured farm mortgage with only a $200 down payment. With that news, Papa's spirits lifted and he began looking for another farm.

Not wanting to stay in the Hartland community, Papa went looking for farms in northwest Iowa near the town of Ringsted, a Danish settlement in the heart of the Corn Belt. One day he drove down there and before long returned with good news. He had signed an agreement to purchase a 120 acre farm, and we could move in on the first of March 1936. March first was moving day for farmers because the dirt roads in those days were often impassable later in the spring, and farmers needed to be settled in before spring planting season.

With much anticipation about the upcoming move, we endured the most severe winter in modern history. Across the northern plains in January and February, heavy snowfall accompanied the coldest temperatures on record. The thermometer dropped below zero (-15 Celsius) 36 days straight in Minneapolis, a record that still stands. In Albert Lea, 18 of the 31 days beginning on January 20 never went above zero Fahrenheit. Usually Esther and I walked to school, but Mama insisted we ride with the Sullivans, who took their kids in the bobsled on the coldest days. We told Miss Ferry, our friends, and our schoolmates that we would be leaving on March first and began preparing for the move. Esther was in sixth grade; I was in fourth. John and Martin had already graduated from eighth grade and were working for neighbors. John had also enrolled in a correspondence course to learn how to build and repair radios.

Hartland, 1931

The day before the move, we got six inches of new snow, and then it started to blow. Papa had hired a trucker with money left over from the sale. On the afternoon of February 29, the truck came rumbling down the driveway through drifting snow, and we began the process of loading. The trucker stayed at our house that night, as we needed to leave early the next morning.

The morning of March first dawned cloudy and cool, the temperature just below freezing. We ate breakfast and loaded the remaining furniture and food into the truck. All the remaining vegetables and canned goods were crated and packed. The young pigs and chickens were loaded last in crates constructed ahead of time. When everything was packed and loaded, we took one last look at the home of bittersweet memories.

"I'm gonna miss this place," Esther said.

"Not me," said Papa. "I never liked dealing with Mrs. Freemo."

"Let's get on with it," said Mama. "I don't care if I ever see this place again."

"Can we please take Fido?" I begged. Fido had been our dog as far back as I could remember.

"No," said Papa. "I told you, Fido is too old for a trip like this. The Sullivans are going to adopt Fido. We can get another dog in Iowa."

The world I knew seemed to be collapsing around me. I could not remember living anywhere else. I liked the Freemo farm. I liked the one-room school at Bath and my teacher. I liked our friends in the area and our cousins in Albert Lea. To make matters worse, my brothers threw my doll on the scrap heap. "It's all worn out," they said. "Besides you're too old for a doll."

"All right," cried Papa. "Let's head for Iowa."

Esther and I rode in the Model A with Mama and Papa. John and Martin rode in the truck. They got out to push us when the car got stuck in the driveway. Mama, who seemed hyper and nervous before, rode silently. She seemed exhausted and resigned to her fate. As we proceeded out the driveway, we could not hear the phone ringing on the kitchen wall.

3

Grand Central Terminal

Entering Philadelphia, the train began to slow as I watched a changing scene outside the window. Block after block of row houses, apartments, and industrial buildings passed by. At Thirtieth Street Station many more passengers boarded the train and began filling the remaining seats. A woman close to my age stopped by the seat next to me. "Is it okay if I sit here?" she asked.

"By all means, sit down. I could use some company," I replied.

About my height and trim with dark curly hair, the woman wore a stylish navy skirt and gray blazer. She hoisted her suitcase to the overhead bin and sat down. "I'm Phyllis Waters," she said.

"Hi, I'm Mary Gunderson. Are you from Philadelphia?"

"No, actually I'm from Richmond. I just stopped in Philly to visit a friend. Now I'm going to Poughkeepsie to see my mother. Where are you from?"

"Minnesota. Mora, Minnesota. It's about seventy-five miles north of Minneapolis. I'm going to Hartsdale, New York, to visit my cousin."

"Ever been in New York City before?"

"No. I haven't."

"If you don't know your way around, it could be a little overwhelming. Where is Hartsdale?"

"It's north by White Plains. I was told it would take a half hour by commuter train out of Grand Central Terminal."

"I'm going to Grand Central too. Maybe we can take a cab together."

"I would appreciate that, thank you. Do you go this way often?"

"Two or three times a year since my father passed away in eighty-two. Before that, about once a year. My mother is getting old now and needs the help. I was hoping she would move to Richmond, but she doesn't want to. I moved there in the sixties when my husband got transferred. We raised our children there, and now we're accustomed to it. It's home; we like it there. And, how about you?"

"We live on a farm near Mora - been there since seventy-four. It's a great place to live. My husband and I raised eleven children. They're all grown now and gone except Geoff, our youngest son. He's been living at home off and on since high school."

The ride from Philadelphia to New York took about ninety minutes. By the time Manhattan came into view across the Hudson River, I was well acquainted with Phyllis Waters. Although I am comfortable traveling alone, I was happy to have her companionship, if only for a short while.

The train slowed as it crossed the river and then entered an underground tunnel before stopping at Penn Station, the underground remnant of the original Gilded-Age masterpiece. Pennsylvania Station was demolished in 1963. The architectural jewel was replaced by two office towers and a sports arena, Madison Square Garden. What is left of the train station remains entirely below ground. Public outrage over the demolition of this famous landmark and its replacement by such mediocre structures became a rallying cry for the architectural preservation movement in America.

Phyllis and I gathered our luggage and stepped off the train. We took the escalator up a shiny metal tube to the crowded main hall. Penn Station is the busiest train terminal in North America; in 1990, it handled nearly 400,000 passengers per day. Toting our luggage across the main hall, we stepped onto another escalator and exited the station at Eighth Avenue and West 33rd Street. Pedestrians moved in every direction. Streams of taxis, buses and delivery trucks filled the streets. The air was warm and sticky. A hazy blue sky hovered over towering skyscrapers. My single focus was to follow Phyllis, who wove through the pedestrian traffic to the Eighth Avenue curb, where she waved in a yellow cab. It seemed like all the cabs were yellow.

Grand Central Terminal is only a one mile drive from Penn Station, about a ten minute cab ride. There is no rail connection other than a subway link between the two train stations. While Penn Station is now the busiest train terminal, Grand Central is still the largest train terminal in the world, covering 48 acres with 67 tracks terminating at 44 platforms. A decade after Pennsylvania Station was demolished, Grand Central Terminal was saved from a similar fate by the city's new Landmark Preservation Act, upheld by the Supreme Court in 1978 when the owner wanted to demolish the building to make room for a new office tower.

The taxi stopped in front of Grand Central Terminal, which loomed majestically across the street, hemmed in by towering skyscrapers. Splitting the fare, Phyllis and I paid the driver and stepped into the midday din of Manhattan. I gazed at the busy scene while the driver pulled our suitcases and hand bags from the trunk. It was impossible to take the photograph I wanted because of the impatient traffic and crowds of people. When the signal turned, the crowd spilled onto 42nd Street and swept us along.

I followed Phyllis into a corner entrance, down a hallway, and into the immense central concourse, several hundred feet long and a hundred feet high. Commuters and tourists moved about like ants on a sugar cookie. I tried to picture my parents and siblings in the same concourse sixty-four years earlier when they boarded the train bound for Chicago and Albert Lea. I had been there, too, in Mother's womb.

"We better get in line," Phyllis suggested, pointing to a row of ticket windows. "You never know how long it will take." We stood in line and, before long, purchased our tickets. Phyllis looked at mine and pointed across the hall. "Gate 27 is that way," she said, "I'm going to gate 32."

"I was lucky to meet you," I said. "Can I get your address?"

I fumbled for my camera while Phyllis wrote her address on my pad. Then she smiled broadly while I snapped a photo. We said our good-byes, shook hands, and went our separate ways.

At Gate 27, I went down a short ramp and found the Metro-North train, white and shiny, already waiting at the platform. The second car was nearly empty when I took my seat. My parents could have boarded at the same platform, I thought. The scene would have been very different in 1926. Mother said it was after dark when they entered New York, which in

January could have been any time after 5:00 p.m. She said Martin, who was five, got upset because he couldn't see the skyscrapers.

In 1979 a Danish cousin gave me two of the first letters my parents sent home to Denmark in 1926. I was disappointed there was no description of the ocean voyage, the passage through New York, or the train trip to Albert Lea. Ever since my parents passed away, I have been interested in knowing more about these things. All I had to go on were the stories my parents told long ago and the recollections and oral descriptions from my brother John.

When the commuter train began to roll, the lights outside the window receded as the train entered a tunnel to the outside world. The platforms at Grand Central Terminal are deep underground. Dark tunnels leading north disgorge trains into the light of day near the middle of Manhattan Island, where the trains continue north into the Bronx.

Suddenly, I was aware of a man standing next to me.

"May I see your ticket please?" the conductor asked.

"Oh, sure," I said and handed it over.

The man punched my ticket and moved on. I closed my eyes and pictured my parents heading the same direction in 1926. They had gone this way too, I guess, before heading west over the Hudson River. Gradually my thoughts returned to the wintry scene in 1936, when my family departed from the Freemo farm for a better life in Iowa.

4

The Promised Land, 1936

From the Freemo farm, it was roughly a hundred miles southwest to Ringsted. Esther and I played games in the back seat and kept an eye on the truck following behind. As we rolled south through Hartland, Papa snorted some epithets at the bank, but I don't remember what he said. Near Albert Lea we turned west through rolling hills and took the main highway to Fairmont. The landscape was pure white, snow-covered and frozen, dotted only by scattered sheds and barns under low-hanging clouds. Houses were mere shadows on the land. Distant trees hung like etchings on the white expanse. Since moving to Wisconsin this was farthest I had ever traveled.

Heading south into Iowa, we discovered the snowstorm had been much worse down that way. Over twice as much snow had fallen, and because it was more open country, many of the roads were still drifted shut. Even so, we made good progress on plowed roads until our turnoff from Highway 15, two miles east of Ringsted. The gravel road going south was impassable. The approach was blocked by a mountain of snow. Even if we could have shoveled through the snow bank, the mile beyond was covered by a sea of snowdrifts.

A schoolhouse stood near the corner, smoke curling from its chimney. The sign on the front read, "Sunnyside School." While the boys rode with Papa to a nearby farmhouse, Esther and I went with Mama to the schoolhouse. The teacher heard us entering the cloak hall and came to have a look. "Hello, can I help you?" she asked.

Assuming the woman would not understand Mama, Esther said, "Excuse us for interrupting. We're moving to a farm nearby, but the road is closed. Is it okay if we wait inside while our father goes for help?"

The Promised Land, 1936

"Of course, come in. You can sit right over there," she replied, motioning toward a row of chairs in the back of the classroom.

About fifteen children watched curiously as we entered. A girl about my age smiled at me. I smiled back.

"I'm Miss Gladstone," the woman said, "and who are you?"

"Esther Mikaelsen. This is my mother Anna and my sister Mary."

"Where are you moving from?"

"Hartland, Minnesota. It's about a hundred miles from here," Esther replied. Mama, who by now was a nervous wreck, said something to Esther, who translated. "My mother wants to apologize for the intrusion," she said.

"Oh, it's no bother at all. We like to have visitors. You just make yourselves comfortable, and we'll get on with our lessons."

We went to the chairs and sat down. I wondered if this was the school Esther and I would be attending. It certainly seemed pleasant enough, and I liked Miss Gladstone. Only about half the desks were occupied, and several pupils looked about my age.

When Papa and the boys returned a while later we said goodbye to the teacher and the pupils and went back out the door. Papa had good news and bad news. "I spoke to Mr. Sorensen on the phone," he reported. "Sorensens live just down the road from our farm. We can stay at their place. He's coming to get us with a sleigh. Unfortunately, the trucker has another move today and needs to unload the truck. We'll have to pile our things on the road."

Mama looked stunned. "No, we can't leave our belongings on the road," she protested. "What about the canned food, the potatoes, the carrots? They'll freeze. Everything will be ruined!"

"Mr. Sorensen will haul the perishables to the farm," Papa said. "We can put them in the house and haul the pigs and chickens later. They'll be okay if we cover them."

Papa's optimism prevailed once again over Mama's pessimism as he coaxed her into willing participation. Resigned to the circumstances, she followed him grudgingly to the truck, holding me by the hand. I felt so sorry for Mama and prayed that everything would be okay.

Leaving space for a snowplow's approach, we piled our possessions neatly on the shoulder of Highway 15 near the junction of the drifted road, lining up the crated pigs and chickens between pieces of furniture to block the wind. When everything was unloaded, Papa paid the truck driver, who then hurried to his truck and drove away. Papa moved the Model A forward until the bumper was nearly touching the pile, the entire accumulation of our ten years in America.

"Let's go back to the school," he suggested. "It's too cold to wait out here." And once more we headed for the schoolhouse.

"This is turning into a real adventure," Martin quipped. Mama just glared at him. Nothing seemed funny to her at times like this.

Miss Gladstone welcomed us back, and once again we took seats along the back wall. The lessons resumed. We waited quietly, and before long we heard the thudding of hooves on the snow-packed drive.

August Sorensen, a sturdy Dane as kind as he was strong, entered the schoolroom. "I'm here to pick up the Mikaelsens," he said.

We waved goodbye to the teacher and pupils. Three of them were Mr. Sorenson's children, Cora, Arne, and Ruth. They would be walking home later. Outside, Papa introduced us to Mr. Sorensen. "He goes by August," Papa added. Papa's brother in Denmark was also named August.

Mr. Sorensen's sleigh was similar to the one we owned at Hartland. It was a bobsled, a sturdy wagon box with steel-plated runners in each corner like wheels on a wagon. The two runners in front pivoted with the harness pole, allowing the bobsled to turn with the horses. We climbed aboard and headed for our pile of belongings. August helped Papa load the crates of potatoes, carrots, and onions wrapped in quilts to prevent freezing. The rest of us loaded the canned fruits, green beans, corn, and tomatoes. Clucks and grunts came from the nervous animals.

"We'll come back for the animals later," said Mr. Sorensen. Four crates of chickens and three crates of small pigs remained on the roadside. There was no room left in the bobsled. When all the perishables were loaded, we clambered aboard, sitting on the covered crates of vegetables. Mr. Sorensen flicked the reins, urging his team forward. We headed back to the schoolyard and then across the field on the freshly made trail. The

The Promised Land, 1936

horses strained through deep drifts. The bobsled glided along behind, rocking awkwardly as we angled onto the road. Heading south, Mr. Sorensen, turned and asked, "How is everyone doing?"

"Doing fine, August," Papa answered. The rest of us nodded in agreement. Feeling chilled, I pulled my scarf a little tighter around my ears and snuggled closer to Mama, who stared quietly into the distance. The horses trotted slowly south, following sled-tracks on the drifted roadway. After passing two farms on the left, three farms were visible ahead, one to the right, one to the left, and one straight ahead. Papa pointed to the one on the left a quarter mile away and said, "That's our farm over there." Pointing to the farm on the right, he added, "Sorensens live over there."

I could see a crossroad ahead at the bottom of a gentle slope. To the south lay a broad shallow valley. My fears about not liking the place soon evaporated. In fact, I was thrilled at the first sight of our new farm. A white clapboard farmhouse stood on a rise at the end of an arcing driveway. Trees lined the drive and surrounded the house and farm buildings. A small red barn with a gable roof and cupola stood next to the driveway downhill from the house. Several other farm buildings were nestled among the trees to the left and right of the barn. Open fields surrounded the farmstead and sloped to the south where a frozen creek wound its way across the property, flanked on the south by a wooded slope.

"That's Black Cat Creek down there," said Papa, "There's a bridge crossing in the pasture behind the house." At the crossroad Mr. Sorensen turned his team and headed east to the tree-lined lane. We proceeded up the lane to the turnabout as a man and woman emerged from the farmhouse and watched passively as we pulled up.

Mr. Sorensen halted the horses, and stepped into the snow. "Some miserable moving weather!" he exclaimed. "We only brought the vegetables and canned goods. Everything else is still sit'n on the highway." He shook hands with his soon-to-be-departing neighbors, the Pedersens, and introduced us.

"You're welcome to store your food in the house," Mr. Pedersen offered. "We expect the roads to be plowed by morning. Hopefully we'll be out of here shortly after breakfast." A loaded truck and wagon waited in the yard. "Would you like to come in and take a look at the house?" he added. As we climbed out of the bobsled, Mr. Pedersen said, "I tried calling you this morning, but nobody answered. When the snowplow didn't come, I was going to suggest you wait a day or two for the road to open up. But I suppose things will work out anyway."

There seemed to be a tone of sorrow in Mr. Pedersen's voice. Papa told us earlier the Pedersens had failed, too, and were forced by the bank to sell out. Perhaps their loss was our gain, one bankrupt family replacing another to occupy the same land.

We followed the couple to the house. Inside, it was mostly empty except for the kitchen table and chairs and the large wood-burning cook stove. Moving about, we inspected the rooms, surveying the possibilities. Mama was a little concerned about the space. It was smaller than our previous house with no second floor and only two bedrooms. She decided Esther and I would share the larger bedroom with her and Papa while John and Martin would share the other bedroom.

"Can we put our pigs and chickens in the barn?" Papa asked.

"Help yourself," said Mr. Pedersen. "The barn is empty."

"Is it okay to put our vegetables in the root cellar?"

"We still have ours down there, but there's room for more. Stack yours along the empty wall," Mr. Pedersen said.

"How about the pantry?" Papa asked. "Is there room for any canned goods?"

"We still have our things in there," Mrs. Pedersen said, "but you can stack the canned goods along the kitchen wall until tomorrow."

"Where are you moving?" Papa inquired.

"My parents have a farm down by Fenton," said Mrs. Pederson. "They're get'n old and need help. It's the same size as this farm, 120 acres."

"Well good luck," Papa said. "We'll move the food crates now and come back later with the animals." The boys helped Papa and August carry the food crates to the cellar. The rest us carried the canned goods into the kitchen. Then we thanked the Pedersens and said goodbye.

Mr. Sorensen turned the bobsled around, and we all clambered aboard once more. Ten minutes later he turned into his driveway. The horses trotted up the slope toward Sorensens' farmstead, stopping in front of the house. Mr. Sorensen walked us to the door, and Mrs. Sorensen welcomed us into a warm cozy kitchen. She introduced herself as Thyra. In her Danish tongue, Mama introduced Esther and me. Papa and the boys went with Mr. Sorensen to fetch the pigs and chickens from the highway.

Thyra was as nice as August. She hung up our coats and offered us coffee, milk, and cookies. "We'll put the three of you in the girls' room upstairs," she explained in Danish. "Cora and Ruth can sleep in the living room. The Madsens said you could stay down there too. Maybe Hans and the boys could stay at their place. They live just south of here."

"*Mange tak*," Mama replied. "You are so kind. Hans and the boys will be happy for a place to stay."

"How old are your children?" Thyra inquired.

"*Lille* Maaree is nine, Esther is eleven, Martin is fifteen, and Johannes is eighteen."

"Oh, that's very close to our children," said Thyra.

An hour later Cora, Arne, and Ruth came trudging home from school. They had ridden the bobsled along with the crated animals down to the crossroad. Thyra introduced us while they removed their coats and snow-covered boots. Arne was a year older than I, and Ruth two years younger. Cora was a beautiful girl two years older than Esther. Leo, the oldest, was the same age as Martin and a sophomore at Ringsted High School.

Having moved the pigs and chickens into our barn, the men and boys returned and headed straight to the Sorensens' barn to do evening chores. Meanwhile Mama helped Thyra prepare roast chicken and vegetables for twelve. Esther chatted amiably with Cora while I played with Ruth. When the men and boys came in from chores, we all sat down to eat. Papa and Mama said, "*Mange tak,*" again for the fortieth time and reminded the rest of us to thank them too.

As darkness settled over the frozen land, Papa and the boys took the horses and bobsled to the Madsens. Thyra showed us our room, a medium-sized bedroom with one full sized bed, a chest of drawers, and a dresser. The three of us knelt at the bedside while Mama prayed, "Thank you Lord for providing safe travel, generous neighbors, and food that sustains us. We ask you for courage to face the coming days. Be with Grandma Karoline and all my dear sisters and loved ones in Denmark." Finally, we crawled into bed and went to sleep.

In the morning Thyra called us down for breakfast. Steaming coffee, cold milk, toasted buns, hot pork and eggs waited on the table. August, just in from morning chores, reported, "Good news, the snowplow came early this morning and the roads are open." As we ate, Mama began telling about the forced sale, the events of recent days, and the stress of the move. August and Thyra understood her Danish tongue. However, their children looked a little confused at times.

"Most of our neighbors came to the sale," Mama explained. "Some helped prepare lunch food, which we sold to the others. Many people came. It was difficult to watch our cows being sold. They provided us milk and income for six years. But we are accustomed to selling our things and moving. Before we moved to Hartland, we sold out and moved five times in as many years. This will be the first farm we have owned since 1925 when we sold our beautiful home in Denmark." I had not seen Mama so animated in a long time. At Hartland she did not speak to the neighbors like that and only sometimes to our friends who understood her. But here she had been fed and treated like family, which loosened her tongue. The Sorensens listened attentively and seemed genuinely moved.

After breakfast, Papa and the boys returned from the Madsens, eager to get started with the move. They had called the Pedersens and learned they would be leaving by midmorning. August had already offered to help us move and went out to prepare the horses and wagon. Mama thanked Thyra enthusiastically again. Esther and I thanked her, too, as we went out the door. The horses stood harnessed to a large hay wagon. Blessed with mild temperatures and sunny skies, we all climbed aboard.

The horses trotted down the newly plowed road, pulling the hay wagon. The countryside was white and glistening as far as the eye could see, with huge snow banks along the road all the way to the highway. Our belongings were still piled there on the shoulder, apparently untouched. First, Papa and the boys lifted Mama's pump organ onto the hay wagon,

The Promised Land, 1936

covered it with a blanket, and moved it carefully to the back. Then we all loaded the boxes, chairs, the table and the beds, until everything was on the wagon. Papa went over and started the Ford. Mama, Esther and I rode with him. John and Martin hopped on the wagon to ride along with our things. Mr. Sorensen started his team and followed us. At the crossroad ahead, we saw the Pedersens turning south toward Fenton.

The driveway and turnaround had been scraped clear by the snow-plow. Mountains of snow were piled along the edges. Papa parked the car and went straight to the barn to check on the animals. Esther and I ran ahead of Mama to the house and were the first to enter. Inside the front entry was a vestibule with coat hooks and a large wood-box half full of split wood. Mama put a chunk of wood in the parlor stove while Esther and I explored the house. It was empty except for the pot-bellied stove in the parlor and the kitchen cooking stove that came with the house.

A door led from the vestibule into the parlor. To the left was the large bedroom. To the right was the door to the kitchen, which also served as a dining room. The pantry was on one end of the kitchen, and the door to the smaller bedroom was on the other end. A wood telephone with a crank hung on the kitchen wall, the same as our previous home. A back door led from the parlor to an open porch, where a path led to an outdoor toilet.

We started moving boxes and bags into the house. Papa, August, and the boys carried the furniture in and, last of all, the pump organ. When everything was inside, August said goodbye and left. Esther and I helped Mama and Papa assemble the beds and arrange furniture. Mama and Papa put their bed on one side of the larger bedroom, Esther and I put our bed on the other side, and Mama hung a privacy curtain between the two. In the kitchen we put away the dishes, pots and pans. The canning jars and crates of canned goods went on the shelves in the pantry as well as bags of flour, barley and oatmeal. The table and chairs fit nicely into the kitchen with enough room for the day bed on one side. The pump organ stayed in the parlor along with the davenport and rocking chair.

By sundown we were settled into our new home, the pigs in the hog-house were fed and so were the chickens, still loose in the barn. Esther and

I helped Mama prepare dinner. Out the window, an orange glow lit the western horizon. Indoors, two oil lamps cast a warm glow on the table. A fire burned in the cooking stove. It was similar to the one in our previous home, only this one had two overhead warming ovens. When supper was ready, we each took a chair at the table, bowed our heads, and Papa prayed aloud:

> Oh, loving and merciful God. Be Thou near us as we thank You for the many blessings You have bestowed on us, for safe passage, the new home, and the farm that You have provided for us. Forgive us for our sins and restore us to thy kingdom. Guide us by Your Holy Spirit, that we may always pursue Your will. Bless now to us this food. In the name of Jesus Christ, our Lord and Savior, we pray: Our Father who art in heaven, hallowed be Thy name . . .

When we finished reciting the Lord's Prayer—our traditional conclusion to the table prayer—Mama passed the *kartoffel* (mashed potatoes), *kokkenurter* (vegetables), and *frikadelle* (meatballs). It was a memorable meal. Mama's smile was the first I had seen in days, maybe all winter. Papa looked triumphantly around the table and said, "We waited a long time for this. God answered our prayers. What do you think about that?"

"I'm just glad to have a roof over my head," said Mama.

"Papa, when can we get a puppy?" I asked.

"Well, just as soon as we can find one," he replied.

"What are we doing tomorrow, Pa?" asked Martin.

"I need to go to town to find out where we can buy some milk cows, and Mama needs to get some supplies." In addition to loaning us money to buy the farm, the Federal Land Bank had guaranteed us a loan for farm equipment and livestock.

"I need to start looking for a job," said John. "The correspondence school sent me a list of radio repair shops. With God's help, I hope to be working on radios soon." Just before the move, he had completed his radio repair schooling. Though John was a willing helper, he never cared much for farming. Instead, he took to electronics and radios like a cow to a corn field. He seemed determined to chart a new course for himself, which did not involve farming.

The Promised Land, 1936

"You have my blessing, John. I wish you good fortune in your new career, as long as it is in service to God," said Papa, "but I also want your help to get this land in shape for spring planting."

"Until I get a job, I'm all yours, Pa," he replied. In John's absence, Martin would be Papa's main helper on the farm. Martin was more interested in farm work, but he too had hopes of branching off into something different. He liked carpentry, and his building skills had become a real asset to Papa.

"I want to get the chickens set up in the henhouse so we can start collecting eggs again," Mama said.

"Martin and I can help you with that tomorrow after we go to town," Papa replied.

"Can I go too?" pleaded Esther. She was the extrovert who loved to be where the action was.

"You have school tomorrow," said Papa. "You can go to town on Sunday when we go to church. There's a Danish Lutheran Church in Ringsted."

"And Thyra said they have a Danish-speaking Ladies Aid," Mama added.

Changing the subject, she said to me and Esther, "Thyra said you would be going to Pleasant View School a mile south of here. You need to get up early so Papa can take you down there by nine o'clock."

"But Mama, I thought we were going to Sunnyside School with the Sorensens," whined Esther. "It's only one mile up there too."

"If we lived on the north side of the road, then you would go there," said Mama. "But we're on the south side of the road, so you will go to Pleasant View." One-room country schools were placed at two mile intervals to minimize the walking distance for any one family. It was common for children living on opposite sides of the road to attend different schools.

Remembering my unpleasant beginning at Bath School, I was feeling a little apprehensive about starting at the new school. The thought of meeting a new teacher and classmates was exciting, of course, but a little scary too. Where Esther was outgoing, I was quite bashful.

32

We went to familiar beds that night in new and strange quarters. It was sweet sleep for me interrupted only once by a disturbing dream in which I had arrived at school. Upon removing my coat, I was horrified to discover that I had forgotten to put on my clothes. There I stood in my long underwear in front of all my classmates who were laughing at me. It was not the first time I had that dream, nor the last.

The new day broke clear and cold with sunlight streaming through the east windows. I felt warm beneath the heavy featherbed, but the air was so cold I could see my breath. Mama and Papa were already up, and I could hear the clanking of pots and pans in the kitchen. Crawling out of bed, I quickly put on the school clothes I had laid out the night before. I did not mind wearing long underwear, when it was that cold.

"Aren't you getting up, Esther?" I said. She had not moved.

"I think I'm sick," she moaned.

I went to the kitchen and reported this to Mama.

"Stir the oatmeal," said Mama. "I'll check on her."

It was warm in the kitchen with a hot fire burning in the stove. The only heater in that part of the house was the kitchen stove. Starting the fire was task number one for whoever got up first, usually Mama or Papa. It became our practice to keep the door closed to the living room so the kitchen would stay warm, and we built a fire in the parlor stove only when it was really cold or if we were having company. Therefore, it was usually quite cold in our bedroom at the far end of the house.

Mama returned to the kitchen with Esther and tucked her into the day bed. "Esther is running a fever. She'll have to stay home from school today."

"But, Mama, I don't want to go to school alone."

"It'll be okay, *lille* Maaree. Papa will introduce you."

This settled my anxiety only a little.

Papa and Martin came in the door and removed their coats. The pigs and chickens were fed and comfortable, Papa said. It seemed like Papa was always focused on farming business or religious matters. He was much too busy to think about introductions at the new school. That should have been Mama's department. I resented that she could not speak English well

The Promised Land, 1936

enough to go with me to school and support me there. It would have been nice to have that from Mama. She understood my needs and sensitivities much better than Papa did.

"Breakfast ready yet?" Papa asked.

"It'll be ready as soon as you can sit down," Mama replied. "John, come and eat."

"Be there in a minute, Ma," John hollered from his bedroom. "I'm finishing my résumé."

"That shouldn't be too hard," Martin teased.

Soon we were all at the table, except for Esther who lay ill on the day bed. The table was set. Oatmeal steamed in the kettle. Milk from the Sorensens filled the pitcher. A pot of coffee was percolating on the stove. Papa led us in the table prayer, and Mama scooped the oatmeal. It felt good to be dining in our new kitchen and finished with the moving. Then it was time for devotions, which had been our morning ritual for as long as I could remember.

Papa reached for the worn Danish Bible lying ready on the kitchen table, the same one that sustained my family on the voyage to America. A golden string marked the place in the book of Romans where Papa finished his previous reading. He opened to chapter two and began to read in his Biblical reading voice, a kind of monotone chant like that of his elders in Denmark.

Therefore you have no excuse, Oh man, whoever you are, when you judge another; for in passing judgment on him you condemn yourself, because you the judge are doing the very same things. We know that the judgment of God rightly falls upon those who do such things . . .

As he read on, I thought about the judgments Papa made about our neighbors at Hartland, particularly those whom he thought could not be Christians. But I did not dwell long on this discrepancy, for I was still at an age where I thought Papa, like God, could do no wrong.

When he finished the chapter, we slid back our chairs and kneeled, continuing the tradition we began at Hartland. With heads bowed we listened to Papa chant a version of his usual daily prayer, followed by the Lord's Prayer in unison.

34

It was 8:30 and time for me to go to school. Mama stayed home with Esther. Papa started the car, and Martin came running out to join us. I was glad Papa was taking me to school. That only happened on rare occasions, usually when he was already on his way to town. But Pleasant View School was not on his way to town. We drove to the crossroad and turned south. We went over a hill and crossed the bridge over Black Cat Creek, then up another hill past the Madsens, and then over some rolling slopes before approaching the next crossroad.

The schoolhouse stood on the corner with a sign on the front that read, "Pleasant View." Several boys and girls were playing on the high snow banks in the schoolyard as we drove in. A snowdrift climbed west from the road all the way up to the eaves on the far side of the schoolhouse. Papa and Martin escorted me inside, where we passed through a narrow cloak hall to the schoolroom. A piano and bookcases stood against the far wall. Heat radiated from a large cast-iron stove near the back of the room. A black chimney pipe led up and out the back wall. Several rows of desks faced the teacher in front, who stood up to greet us.

"Hello," she said, "I'm Ella Jensen."

"I'm Hans Mikaelsen. This is Mary and Martin. We moved in yesterday up where the Pedersens lived."

"Yes. I heard you were coming. But don't you have two girls?"

"Yeah, Esther is home ill today, and she'll be coming, too, when she gets well."

Turning to me, Miss Jensen smiled and said, "Welcome to Pleasant View School, Mary. What grade are you in?"

"Fourth grade. Esther is in sixth grade."

"What school are you coming from?"

"We went to District 103 in Bath, Minnesota," I replied. "It's up by Hartland."

"Twelve miles north of Albert Lea," Papa added. "I drove Mary here today, but normally she and Esther will be walking to school."

"Thank you for bringing her. It's always good to meet the parents."

"Who is the director here?"

"Thorvald Hansen. He lives on the farm just south of here."

"Thank you," said Papa. "We'll be leaving now."

Miss Jensen was very kind. She showed me around the schoolhouse and introduced me to the other children, ten altogether, who were beginning to take their seats. Each desk was wide enough for two pupils, but because there were only twelve pupils, each one had a desk of his or her own. There were sixteen desks, enough to hold thirty-two children, which was exactly how many attended Pleasant View in 1920 when rural school enrollment was at its peak. All my apprehension about not feeling welcome, or fitting in, soon evaporated. Many of the children had familiar Danish accents. The girls helped me find a seat, and Edna Metz asked if she could sit by me during lunch. She smiled at me every time I looked at her, which put me at ease.

As it turned out, Esther was ill for a whole month. I walked to school alone and became very familiar with the snow-packed road. Each day the sun climbed a little higher in the sky. The snow and ice began melting from the road and Black Cat Creek began to thaw. One day on the way home, water was flowing under the bridge and across the snow-covered valley, a dark ribbon dissecting the white landscape. The snow melt continued for several weeks. The endless white mantle gradually yielded to black soil and tawny brown pastures, and the creek became a swirling torrent under the bridge.

When Esther finally came to Pleasant View, I was well acquainted and thriving in the classroom. The walk to school was more enjoyable, and Esther became very popular with her schoolmates, as usual.

With so many Danes around Ringsted, Mama felt practically at home. The name Ringsted, in fact, came with the original settlers from a larger town in Denmark by that name. Our farm was located in Denmark Township, and many of our neighbors were Danish Americans. Mama thrived at St. Paul's Lutheran Church in Ringsted, where she joined the Danish-speaking Ladies Aid, and Papa liked the evangelical theology. Better yet, the Northern Iowa Inner Mission Society had a strong presence in the area. Papa and Mama belonged to the same pietistic movement in Denmark and were thrilled to find an active Inner Mission group in the Ringsted area. The fellowship meetings were held in private homes on

Friday evenings. Before long we became regulars and even hosted the meetings periodically.

By the time the pastures were green, Papa had filled the barn with milk cows. Much to my delight, he brought a puppy home one day, too, which we named Fido. All that summer and fall, Esther and I walked with young Fido to the far pasture each day to fetch the cows for milking.

We were willing helpers on the farm. When I was big enough, Papa taught me how to milk a cow by hand. By my twelfth birthday, I was milking two cows each morning and evening, the same as Esther. After milking, it was our job to turn the crank on the cream separator and wash it out afterward. It was my job to feed the pigs. I counted fifty ears of corn and tossed them into the feeding trough while Esther fed the chickens. After feeding the animals we collected the eggs.

During the summer months, the chickens wandered the farmyard and roosted wherever they wanted. Before snowfall we moved them into the hen house for the winter. It was easy collecting eggs from the rows of nests in the hen house. The grocery store in Ringsted still allowed eggs in trade for other essentials.

Mama taught Esther and me how to butcher chickens, too. We cringed at chopping off their heads. Although we learned how to kill and clean chickens, we never learned to cook them as well as Mama could. Each year Mama slipped a few duck or goose eggs underneath the hens; the ducks and geese hatched and grew up along with the chicks. On holidays and special occasions we dined on delicious duck or goose meat.

John found a radio repair job in Spring Valley, Minnesota, and learned his trade. A year later, he returned to Ringsted and opened his own radio repair shop. In 1936 the Rural Electrification Administration (REA), a New Deal program, began providing low interest money to extend power lines into rural areas, and farmers were eager to have their farms wired for electricity. Electricians were either nonexistent or in short supply, and before long, John's radio customers were asking him to wire their farms. He wired his first farm in 1938 and quickly learned the trade. With rural electrification moving into high gear, John could not keep up with the demand and soon hired a couple of helpers. Over the next three years, John and his crew wired many of the farms around Ringsted, including ours.

Our new farm produced bumper crops of corn and oats. Prices for farm products began to improve, and soon Papa was repaying the debts he owed to relatives. We made a trip each summer to the Neilsens and Knudsens in Albert Lea so Papa could make the payments in person. The value of our farm tripled in just a few years as the economy strengthened, and Mama began to feel secure again.

5

Hartsdale Corners

Heading north through the Bronx, I observed mile after mile of urban decay. Farther on, Tuckahoe, Crestwood and Scarsdale were tidier towns, and then a voice announced the train's approach to Hartsdale station, the last stop before White Plains. A few miles east of the Hudson River, Hartsdale is an outer ring suburb twenty miles north of Grand Central Station. When the doors opened, I stepped from air-conditioned comfort into the ninety degree heat. A footbridge led to a small depot across the tracks, where at half past three I called Erna.

"Hello Mary. Just sit down and wait," she said. "I'll be there in ten minutes."

I went outside and found a bench in the shade. The train station appeared to be the hub of a small business district along Hartsdale Avenue. Specialty shops, a bank, meat market, and several restaurants lined the street. A row of red taxis waited in the parking lot next to the train station.

A short while later Erna pulled up in her shiny gray LeSabre. She stepped out and greeted me with a smile. "Hello Mary. Welcome to Hartsdale."

"Hello Erna," I replied. "It's a pleasure to meet you. I can't tell you how much I appreciate this." Erna Christensen looked younger than her years. You might have guessed we were the same age, even though she was twelve years older than I. She conducted herself with dignity and poise, a handsome woman with perfect diction and decorum. She reminded me of Lydia, my late cousin and mentor in Minnesota.

I put my suitcase in the trunk and slid into air-conditioned comfort. Erna drove up Hartsdale Avenue, a graceful winding road through wooded hills with six story apartment buildings, one after another, well kept and clean with manicured lawns.

"How big is Hartsdale?" I asked.

"About ten thousand," replied Erna. "Hartsdale is actually a neighborhood of Greenburgh, which has a population of forty thousand, mostly people who commute to New York City. It's only twenty minutes into the city on the express train."

Five minutes later, Erna turned into the parking lot of a six story apartment building. "Here it is," she said. "I'm in the second building."

Her fifth floor apartment appeared to be as refined as Erna herself. After showing me the guest room and facilities, she invited me to the table where grapes and a plate of cookies waited. She poured iced tea, and we sat down to get better acquainted.

"That sure is a beautiful painting," I said, referring to an oil painting near the dining room table. It was a simple but beautiful rendition of orange poppies set into a background of green foliage.

"Oh, thank you," beamed Erna. "I bought that in Denmark in 1961. It was painted by Heir Skow, one of the best known artists in Jutland at the time. He was a good friend of my uncle Thomas; he and Thomas went to art school together. When Thomas found out I was interested in Skow's art, he arranged for us to meet. My mother Christine and I were invited along with Thomas to the Skows for coffee. They live in Bramming. Thomas was an artist, too, you know."

"Perhaps it runs in the family," I said. "Some of my children have artistic talents."

"Tell me again," Erna replied. "How is it that we're related?"

"Well, my father was Hans Mikaelsen, and his parents were Andreas and Maren Michaelsen. And tell me again who your grandparents were."

"My mother's parents were Laurids and Thomasina Michaelsen," Erna replied.

"Okay, I believe Laurids and Andreas were brothers and their father was Michael Thogersen. Of course Laurids and Andreas took the name Michaelsen."

"So my maternal grandfather and your paternal grandfather were brothers," concluded Erna.

"Yes, I believe that's right, which means my father and your mother were cousins and that makes us second cousins. My grandfather Andreas was born in 1833; he was the oldest one in the Thogersen family. When was Laurids born?"

"I think Grandpa Laurids was born in 1845," said Erna.

"He must have been the youngest one in the family," I replied. "But I think our greatest connection is my godmother Else. She is your mother's younger sister. Your mother came with Else to visit us in Ringsted, Iowa, when I was young."

In this fashion Erna and I determined our positions in the Michaelsen family tree as well as our past family connections. With her knowledge of the Laurids Michaelsen family, Erna helped fill in some of the gaps in my genealogy chart. Michael Thogerson, born in 1803, married Anne Andreasdatter, who together raised six children, three of whom had families of their own. Among those three were my grandfather Andreas and Erna's grandfather Laurids. By 1890 Andreas, Laurids, and their sister Maren had produced a total of nineteen children, two of whom were my father Hans and Erna's mother Christine.

I wondered about Erna's work and changed the subject. "Did I understand correctly that you do literacy work?"

"Yes, it has been my entire career. I currently do consulting work for Rochambeau over in White Plains. It is a school for adult continuing education, and I do the entrance testing for the literacy program. I'm currently working with forty-seven students, and I make referrals based on their level of proficiency."

"Is that what you studied in college?"

"Well, partly. I got my degree in education. In fact, I wrote my dissertation on the relationship between parents' expectations and how children learn to read, and I taught college courses on the subject of teaching people to read. Teaching adults to read has become my specialty."

"I wanted to go to college," I said, "but money was really tight, and my father was opposed to it. He didn't even want me to take normal (teacher) training."

"That is so very different from my experience," replied Erna. "According to my parents, education was everything, next to godliness. They insisted on an education for all their children and were willing to pay for it too, and my father was a Lutheran pastor. Could you tell me more about your schooling?"

"We lived in the country, you know, and all of us went to one-room schools through the eighth grade. Only Esther and I went to high school. After high school, I went to a twelve week teacher's training course. I wanted to become a teacher because I admired Lydia so much. She taught high school in Albert Lea, you know, and became the principal and eventually a superintendent. I borrowed the money to go to teacher training. My father didn't want to cosign my loan. He was opposed to any kind of secular college. I also went to Lutheran Bible Institute for half a year in 1948. That was a wonderful experience. But my education isn't much compared to yours."

"You didn't have the opportunities I had," replied Erna.

"Maybe it didn't matter that much because I married a farmer," I said. "Hard work was more important than education. At least that was my father's and my husband's opinion. But I've always tried to impress upon my children the importance of education."

"Education is always important, even if you do not use it in your career, because it enhances your personal development. It allows you to discover your full potential, regardless of your career aspirations."

Erna paused for a moment and then changed the subject, "Would you like to go out for dinner tonight?" she asked. "There's a good Chinese restaurant nearby, and I thought we could go there to eat. It's air conditioned down there, and I think it would be more comfortable to dine out."

"I'll go out for dinner, but I need to lie down for a while before we leave. I've been going all day."

"Okay, you go ahead and lie down, and I'll finish the project I was working on. How about leaving in one hour?"

"Fine with me," I replied. "Thanks for the tea and cookies." I went to the guestroom to lie down and pondered how my life would be different had I been able to go to college. Resting on the foldout bed, my thoughts went back to the farm at Ringsted, memories of school, and my education.

6

Higher Education

Esther graduated from Pleasant View in 1938 and started high school at Ringsted that fall. She thrived there and made lots of friends who liked going to movies, dances and school parties, all sinful activities forbidden by Mama and Papa. We were not even allowed to read magazines or newspapers. Papa thought they were full of sinful images and ideas. Esther resented the strict rules and rebelled at times, but mostly she obeyed and tried to live in harmony with the family. She found solace in her long walks with Fido, who seemed to listen as she poured out her frustrations.

I was more compliant than Esther, although at times I envied those who went to movies and dances. I was not one to test the rules, however, and sublimated my wayward desires into church music and school work. I found great satisfaction in pleasing my teachers, who praised me for my intelligence and hard work. In fifth grade I mastered fractions and became interested in history. I often won the spelling bees at neighboring schools and sang duets with Esther at the singing bees. One year we sang "Marianina" and won the contest.

Not long after Esther graduated from Pleasant View, the appellations we used to address our parents began to change from Mama and Papa to Ma and Pa. One thing that did not change was the amount of work we had to do at home. Esther and I were dedicated helpers on the farm and in the house.

Putting up hay was a chore shared by the whole family. Ma held the reins as the horses pulled the hay wagon around the field. Esther and I jumped around on the hay and packed it down while Pa and Martin pitched it on. The heaping loads of hay were hauled to the barn where the horses were hitched to the hay-lift. This was a long rope that ran through the hayloft. It was attached to a heavy U-shaped metal clamp, which was driven into the loads of hay. As the horses pulled the rope forward, the clamp would lift a large mound of hay upward to the hayloft and then back along the track, which ran just under the peak. A second rope attached to the clamp was used to release the hay. This could be done at any point along the track. Ma drove the horses while Pa and Martin worked in the hayloft, spreading the hay uniformly with pitch forks. Esther and I learned to drive the horses, too, by the time we were thirteen.

When the oats ripened later in the summer, Pa used a horse-drawn binder to cut, bundle, and bind the ripened stems. The bundles were piled in shocks, which stood in rows across the field. Then came the crew of men who traveled farm to farm with a tractor and a big burly threshing machine on wheels. When they arrived, Esther and I helped Ma cook meals to serve the crew. Pa and the boys worked alongside the men, usually eight or ten of them. They loaded up the bundles of oats in the fields and hauled them to the threshing machine, which was powered by the tractor via a long, flat, rubbery belt. The bundles of oats were fed into the threshing machine, which clicked and groaned, separating the oats from the straw and chaff. The oats were funneled into grain sacks. The straw and chaff were blown into a big pile, which Pa later hauled to the barn to be used as bedding for the animals. The sacks of oats were hauled to the granary for storage.

Later in the autumn, when the corn ripened, we all worked together again in the fields. The horses pulled a corn wagon up and down the rows while we husked the ears of corn and tossed them into the wagon. On one side of the wagon box was a three-foot-high bangboard or backstop. A well-aimed toss hit the bangboard so that the ear of corn would land in the wagon. Pa said a good picker could husk a hundred and twenty bushels of corn in a day. Esther and I couldn't pick half that fast, but we enjoyed racing each other to see who could pick the fastest. Because they could pick corn so much faster, Pa and Martin each picked two rows while we each picked one. This continued for weeks until the corn was all picked and stored away in the corn crib.

In the house Esther and I helped Ma wash clothes and dishes. And we kept the house in order too. Ma was a much better cook than a housekeeper, so we became adept at cleaning house and doing laundry. We used starch in the rinse water because there was no permanent press, and we did a lot of ironing. The irons were placed on the stove until hot and then used to press the shirts, pants, dresses, and tablecloths. John mounted a gas engine to drive the agitator on the old wooden washing machine. We still had to turn the wringers manually by way of a hand crank, but the washing was automatic, allowing us to wring out the water and hang clothes on the line while the engine ran the washer. We also learned how to operate Ma's sewing machine and made clothing from cotton flour sacks, which were plentiful and cheap. The creamy white cotton was a godsend when nothing else was affordable.

At Pleasant View, enrollment declined every year. In eighth grade I was one of only four pupils still attending, and the school closed right after my graduation. Someone bought the building, moved it to Ringsted, and converted it to a garage. A few years later Ringsted bought a school bus. It circulated around the countryside and brought the rural kids to school in town, where each class had a teacher and a dozen or more children in the same grade. The discontinuation of country schools was a gradual process that began in the 1930s. At first it affected only those closest to town, but the process accelerated in the 1940s and 1950s. By the late 1960s only a few one-room schools were still in use.

Eighth grade graduation for Emmet County schools was held in Estherville, the county seat. To qualify for graduation or promotion as it was called, the pupils were required to pass a series of tests. Among 225 promoted in 1940, I was one of the top ten honor students. Seated next to me at the ceremony was Donald Henriksen, another honor student, who went to a neighboring school in Denmark Township. I was enraptured by him, but nobody ever knew it, including him, for I never told anyone. After that I began watching the road in front of our house. Whenever I saw Henriksen's car approaching, I raced to the road on my bicycle just to get a glimpse of him. On Saturday nights I went with the neighbors to town, where people loitered on Main Street, which is what people did back then, including the Henriksens. I often spoke to Donald's sister, but around him I was hopelessly tongue-tied.

Higher Education

This fascination with boys had begun the previous summer at my aunt Ingeborg's house. Every summer, Esther and I stayed at Andy and Ingeborg's farm for a week. For some reason, their hired man Norman took an interest in me. During the evenings this jovial teenager, three years my senior, sat talking and laughing with me in the back yard. One day we went to the hay loft, and he started kissing me. I was a little nervous but also thrilled that a boy was taking such an interest in me. When his hand went under my skirt, my wariness turned to alarm, but I did not cry out. Maybe I was afraid someone would discover what was happening. I was horrified by the reaction my parents would have if they knew. The fondling advanced precariously, my head began to swirl, and then I heard Ingeborg hollering for me. It sounded like she was coming toward the barn. Norman tensed and withdrew his hand. I went quickly down the ladder as Ingeborg entered the barn.

"What were you doing up there?" she asked.

"Playing."

"Where is Norman?"

"Um, ah, up there," I stammered.

Ingeborg went to the hayloft door and hollered up, "Norman, come down here!"

He climbed down the ladder sheepishly and stood flushed and embarrassed as Ingeborg rebuked him. Later she told my mother that Norman liked me a little too much and suggested that it was not such a good idea for me to stay there. That was the last time I stayed at Andy and Ingeborg's place other than with my parents on family visits.

The highlight of 1940 was my promotion to high school in Ringsted, where I excelled academically. I loved all the variety in classes and teachers. At Pleasant View I had been all alone in my grade. At Ringsted I was far more challenged by the teachers, subjects, and competition among classmates. Several others in my class were very bright, including Donald Henriksen and Meredee Myers. I was highly motivated and worked hard to stay on top.

Regarding transitions that year, the most confounding one was puberty and my developing interest in boys, which had shifted into overdrive. A more comforting change involved my religion, which gained importance after my confirmation that spring. If one tried to conceive two more conflicting developments, it would be difficult to improve upon this pairing. Ever since the incident with Norman the previous summer, my interest in boys was a palpable distraction, which alternated between guilt and shame and an overwhelming need for sanctification.

That summer, Pa invited the evangelist, Joseph Erickson, and his family to stay at our home for a week while they evangelized in Ringsted. I promptly fell in love with the oldest boy Jay, who was nineteen, but I never said a word about it to him or anyone else. I did, however, become fast friends with his sister Pearl, who was my age.

Pearl Erickson was pretty and petite. When I first lay eyes on her, she had a few faded freckles and two braids that hung nearly to her waist. Brilliant blue eyes and a coy smile gave her a distinctive appearance, and she spoke easily in a very friendly manner. We seemed to be on common ground, and I felt immediately at ease in her presence. The Erickson family was similar to ours in size, age and religious beliefs. My friendship with Pearl developed as we shared our secrets about boys, family, and experiences. However, I never dared to tell her about my infatuation with her brother Jay, whom I adored until he announced his engagement. I didn't even know he had a girlfriend. What a letdown!

As a kind of bulwark against these powerful infatuations, I practiced my religious beliefs. At fourteen I was confirmed a Christian at St. Paul's Lutheran Church. Like a true child of God, I memorized my confirmation vows, attended church every Sunday, sang in the choir, read my Bible, and prayed every day. Pa reinforced these practices with his devotional messages at the breakfast table each day. I hoped that God would forgive my sins and that I would go to heaven.

When Joseph Erickson asked me if I was saved, however, my reply seemed reflexive. "I meant my confirmation vows," I said. But later, I wondered if that answer was sincere; perhaps I lacked real faith. The ecstatic conversion experience claimed by many evangelical Christians was not something I had experienced.

One day the Ericksons took their evangelism to the streets of Ringsted. They were talented musicians and quickly drew a crowd. When

Joseph asked me to witness to the gathering spectators, most of whom I knew, I felt very inadequate. I stepped up to the microphone and recited the words to the song, "I Am Jesus' Little Lamb," which they had just sung and which I knew by heart. I pretended to believe that I was a saved Christian and said I was thankful that I would go to heaven. Afterward I felt like a hypocrite, but I went with the flow and helped them pass out religious tracts on the street. We even went into the tavern and handed each patron a religious tract. These "street meetings" were a tradition for the Ericksons. Each summer they traveled from town to town, carrying their message of faith and Christian love to unbelievers and converting those who wanted salvation.

My inner conflict continued between carnal desires and the need for sanctification and forgiveness. I vacillated erratically between the gravitational pull of the flesh and the Almighty, a conflict that continued throughout my adolescent and young adult years. Ironically, during all the infatuations, I did not go on a single date until I was twenty-one. After the affair with Norman, I no longer trusted myself with boys. Instead, I dedicated myself to helping Ma and Pa at home, cooking, cleaning, and doing field work and chores. I tried to sublimate my sexual energies into school work and church, and I prayed every day for forgiveness.

That summer after the Ericksons left, I went with the Luther League to Bible camp at Lake Okoboji where we shared a cabin and participated in religious activities. One evening during a game of spin the bottle, Milton Madsen, three years older than I, expressed some interest in me. What was probably just a passing fantasy for him became a consuming infatuation for me.

The following school year, while I was still a freshman, Mr. Hamand, the superintendent, drove a carload of students to St. Paul for the Midwest regional music competition and festival. Among several other cars that went along, Milton ended up next to me in the back seat. I was in pure bliss. He never knew I loved him because I never told anyone, but if he glanced my way or said anything to me, I went into a tailspin. After graduating that year, he volunteered for military service, and I rarely saw him after that.

Between house and farm work, school, church, Luther League, and the Inner Mission society, I had little time for dating. On school days Esther and I drove the car to town and delivered our cream to the creamery on the way. At school I was on the student council and served as the librarian. I sang in the glee club and mixed chorus, competed in declamation, and maintained an A average. I was also the class secretary and editor of the school news. In church I sang in the choir with Esther, and I was secretary of the Luther League. Besides that, I took piano and organ lessons from a neighbor lady. Each summer our entire family attended the Deeper Life Conference at Medicine Lake Bible Camp near Minneapolis. It ran a whole week and was always a highlight of my summer.

Martin continued living with us and helping on the farm, but one winter he attended Lutheran Bible Institute (LBI) in Minneapolis. They had a special program whereby farmers could attend during the winter quarter, which many did in hopes of meeting eligible Christian women. For this reason LBI was in good humor also known as "Love Birds Incorporated." True to this moniker, Martin met Pauline Bakken, the girl of his dreams. A few months later he traveled to Mount Carmel Bible Camp, where Pauline worked, and he spent the summer and fall building cabins. He brought her home at Christmas that year to meet the rest of us and announced their engagement.

In 1941 two dramatic events impacted my life, both involving Martin, whom I loved dearly. Of all my family members, he was the one who best understood me. Tall, slender, and very handsome, Martin was kind, good natured, musical, and a lot of fun. At all times he was a wonderful friend and counselor to me.

The first event was Martin's wedding in late May. We drove eight hours to Pauline's home church at Maple Bay in northern Minnesota. After the wedding they spent the summer in Albert Lea where Martin worked for a carpenter. I was delighted when later in the year they moved to Ringsted and rented a house. When Martin didn't have carpentry jobs, he came to the farm to help Pa.

The second event was the Japanese attack on Pearl Harbor, which reverberated through Ringsted for years to come. With draft notices on the way, John enlisted early in the Army Signal Corp and went to North Carolina for training. Martin held off as long as possible because Pauline was pregnant. Baby Marilyn arrived in March, seven months before Martin recieved his draft notice. On an overcast day after Christmas in 1942, Pauline stood with Marilyn in her arms and waved goodbye to Martin as he boarded the bus for boot camp in Kentucky.

Adding to the family upheaval, Esther decided to leave home after graduating from high school earlier that year. With all the young men being drafted, there was a strong demand for women in the labor force. She moved to Minneapolis and went to work for a farm equipment wholesaler.

Within a few short months, I had become the sole helper at home. After Martin's departure, Pauline and baby Marilyn lived alternately with us and Pauline's parents in northern Minnesota. I loved caring for Marilyn, but there was little time for that. Ma and Pa came to rely heavily on me for house work and farm chores. Pauline was of little help in the house. She was frail and often ill, having suffered in her teen years with a severe case of rheumatic fever. Caring for little Marilyn was about all she could manage.

Not long after Martin left, a "roll of honor" billboard went up in Ringsted. A list of names appeared on the billboard to honor the local men serving the country. It was a solemn day when I saw the names of my brothers added to the list. A gold star appeared next to the name of each serviceman who died. By the end of the war, over two hundred names were on the list, eight with gold stars. My one contribution to the war effort took place in school. I volunteered to sell government stamps, which people could trade for rationed goods and war bonds.

As it turned out, Martin was a poor fit for the infantry. He limped through boot camp, longing for his wife and baby. During the long training marches, his arches broke down. He fell behind and spent a night alone in the Kentucky woods. Later he wrote to us and sent us this poem:

One night in a lonely place
I met the master face to face.
I saw him and knew him and blushed to see
that his eyes full of sorrow were fixed on me.

I faltered and fell at his feet to pray,
as my castles melted and vanished away.
My grand schemes vanished and in their place
naught else could I see but the master's face.
I cried aloud "Oh, make me meet
to follow the steps of thy wounded feet."

Much to our surprise, six months after he boarded the bus for Kentucky, Martin came walking up the lane carrying with him a medical discharge. With his broken arches, he could not keep up with the infantry. He received an honorable discharge, and we were overjoyed!

Martin and Pauline moved back to the same rental house in town and kept busy and amused with Marilyn. I often went to their home after school to help Pauline with house chores and to care for Marilyn, with whom I had become very attached. It was also a great comfort for me to be back in Martin's company. He got a job driving the school bus, and during the day he helped Pa on the farm, which took some pressure off me. A few months after his discharge, Martin helped Pa build a new hog house. Although it was only a hog house, it was a masterpiece of workmanship and a reminder to Martin that his calling was in the field of carpentry.

Following extensive training in the states, John was sent to Ireland in 1943 to work on radio communication systems in the Signal Corps. Shortly after D-day, he went to France for the duration of the war. I enjoyed his occasional letters, but most of them went to his girlfriend Luverne, whom he met at Medicine Lake Bible Camp the summer before enlisting.

My social life in Ringsted was mixed. In Luther League and the Inner Mission Society I felt accepted, but in school I was shy and awkward and felt marginalized by my pietistic religious beliefs. I was not allowed to play cards, dance, or go to parties with nonbelievers. Few others in my high school class adhered to this kind of pietism, and they found it difficult to relate to me. It didn't help when in English class I wrote theme papers condemning everything from magazines and movies to dancing and card playing. When I read my papers in class, which was the tradition, my classmates listened in stunned silence. Here is an excerpt from my paper entitled, *Ambition Ruined*:

> *I am old now; my body is full of a disease I got on the dance floor. My life is wasted, and I have accomplished nothing but evil. With remorse and bitter tears, I look back on my youth when I was pure and clean. My ambition is ruined . . .*
> *How can we expect God to have mercy on our nation when even church members go to movies and dances . . .*

In my senior year of high school, I received a five-year diary for Christmas. Beginning on January 1, 1944, I wrote in it nearly every day for the next five years. This was a godsend because I loved writing, and it gave me pause each day to reflect and to record my thoughts and feelings. I found it easier to scribble these down on paper than to discuss them with others. In addition to my diary, I kept regular correspondences with John, Esther, and my friends, Phyllis and Pearl.

Also that January, I applied to Iowa State Teachers College for a twelve week summer session in Estherville, which would qualify me to teach in rural schools. This was a dream I had entertained for years. Pa found out three months later when I asked for his signature on a school loan. He nearly threw a fit!

"No daughter of mine is going to a secular college!" he exclaimed.

"But Pa, it's no different than high school," I replied.

"There is no need for you to attend college. A woman's place is in the home."

Adding her opinion, Ma pleaded, "*Lille* Maaree, we need you at home."

"I don't need to move far from home. There are lots of country schools close by. I could even live at home."

The real problem, it seemed to me, was that my parents were terrified of me leaving home, particularly Ma who still grieved the loss of her close family connections in Denmark. Ma and Pa were much more dependent on me after Esther left home, especially when both John and Martin were gone. When they realized how determined I was, however, and received my assurance that I would not move far from home, their resistance softened. A few days later Pa backed down and agreed to sign the loan. I was thrilled to be going to teachers college, if only for the summer.

As far as I was concerned, high school graduation could have not come soon enough. I was not enjoying school very much, although I worked hard and got good grades. As graduation approached, I began to lighten up and school actually seemed fun. One day the new superintendent, Mr. Marcus, gave me a certificate for being the most outstanding student. I was delighted! At commencement I feigned humility but felt very proud to be valedictorian of the class of 1944. At graduation I looked upon my classmates with affection and realized for the first time how much I would miss them.

Two weeks later, I moved to Estherville, twenty-eight miles from home, where I roomed with five other girls in a boarding house. One of these was Phyllis Peterson, my best friend from Graettinger. All six of us were students at the teachers college. With access to a kitchen in the boarding house, we cooked our own meals and had a blast. It was just a short walk to go swimming in the Des Moines River, which we did often.

My roommates and I crossed a foot bridge over the river and walked several blocks to the college. About one hundred students were enrolled in the summer session. The curriculum included just four courses: teaching methods, home economics, rural school management, and agriculture. There was also an intensive review of all the subjects we had in high school: reading, spelling, manual training (hand writing), civics and government, grammar, music, arithmetic, geography, US history, physiology, and hygiene. To become certified for teaching, one needed to pass examinations in all of these subjects, including the four covered in the summer session.

Everyone who knew me could tell I loved going to college. The summer raced by, and amid all the fun and activity, I kept up with my homework and managed to pass the examinations. To top it off, I landed a teaching job at Rymer School near Huntington in Emmet County. Marie Sorum, the superintendent of Emmet County schools, was sure I would do well and recommended me for the position. She had maintained high hopes ever since my graduation from Pleasant View School. But she and I were about to discover my professional limitations.

The day before school started, I went to Huntington and moved into a room at the director's house. The next day, I strode into Rymer School with nervous anticipation and stumbled badly on my lack of preparation.

Toward nine o'clock my knees began to tremble a bit as my self-confidence slipped away. The next nine days were a nightmare. My first impressions are still with me: eyes peeking around doors, shouting, laughing, whispering, shuffling feet, running noses, unkempt hair, boys with "I do as I please—what do I care" attitudes. My mouth became parched. My mind grew dizzy. The work I had planned for the first day lasted about ten minutes. Hands were up all over the room shaking with impatience. Most were wanting to know, "What can I do now, teacher?" I was desperate. How was I to hold the thirty or more class sessions when the room was pulsating with noisy youngsters, and I, a timid unresourceful teacher, was placed in command? At the end of the first day, I was at wits end. The manuals, units, texts and plans were all in jumbled confusion.

I cannot blame the unruly pupils; this was fairly typical and many were quite intelligent. The failure was mine, as the rigors of schoolhouse management had far exceeded my capabilities. I discovered that I was unprepared and incapable of managing eighteen bright and eager pupils. A country school teacher needed to stay well ahead of the pupils through preparation and organization. Once the school day commenced, lessons proceeded one after another at a steady pace. The teacher had to juggle many activities and keep order and discipline. I was ill prepared for this. Exasperated and nervous in class, I felt panicky after school and could not sleep well at night. After the second day of school, I wrote in my diary, *"Work. Work. Work. I couldn't discipline the children, couldn't eat, and bawled myself to sleep. I'm so nervous, I just don't know what to do."*

After stumbling through nine days of ineffectual teaching on minimal sleep, I resigned in humiliation and skidded into a painful depression. My hopes and dreams were dashed to pieces. I had discovered the essence of emotional equilibrium and what it feels like to lose it. I learned that mental stability is essential for the execution of one's job, no matter how intelligent or well educated one might be. As painful as this failure was, however, it led to something unexpected and something much better.

7

Dinner with Erna

After my nap, I went with Erna to the Chinese restaurant. We ordered entrees and sipped tea while we waited. Pursuing our earlier conversation, Erna inquired, "So, where was it you read about me?"

"When I last traveled to Denmark in eighty-seven, my cousin Alfred, I believe it was Alfred, showed me an old newspaper article about you and your mother visiting Denmark in 1961. I copied the entire article longhand and brought it home with me."

Erna lit up. "Actually the original article was written by Paul Frumpsar, my father's friend, who was a syndicated journalist in Denmark. He wrote it before our trip and published it in twenty-eight newspapers. Upon our arrival, we were contacted at our hotel by a correspondent from *Berlingske Aftenavis*, the main evening newspaper in Copenhagen at the time. Having seen the earlier article, she came to our hotel to interview my mother. The article she wrote might have been the one you read."

"Yes, that's right," I replied. "Actually there were two articles now that you mention it, and I copied both of them."

"It was interesting news over there," continued Erna, "Here was this ninety-year-old woman on only her second trip home. She had emigrated from Denmark in 1889 as a seventeen year-old girl, and she still spoke perfect Danish. That was my second trip to Denmark. We had a wonderful time."

The waiter arrived with mounded plates of rice, sweet and sour chicken, and fried vegetables, more than we could eat. But it was delicious.

"Christine was quite a lady," I said, recalling the articles.

"Yes, she was quite a lady," Erna said. She paused and then changed the subject. "I was wondering what your plans are. Today I am available, but tomorrow and Monday I have other plans, which you knew about, right?"

"Oh, yeah. You told me the first time I called that you were booked on Sunday and Monday. There are two places I was hoping to see in New York: Ellis Island and St. Patrick's Cathedral. I was thinking about going there tomorrow to attend church and see Ellis Island, but I have no plans for Monday."

"If you're interested in museums you could go to the Metropolitan Museum," suggested Erna. "It is one of the finest museums in the world and one of the first stops if you take the express bus."

"I'll think about that," I said.

Over dinner we shared more about our families and history. Erna told me about her father, Christen Christensen. "He came to America in 1891 as a young man," she said, "to attend the Danish Lutheran Seminary in Blair, Nebraska. After graduating, he met and married my mother. My father enjoyed a long career in the ministry both as a pastor and a writer."

"Lydia had one of his books," I said. "I copied part of it because I liked his discourse on Christian doctrine, although he was quite critical of the Grundtvigians."

"Well, the church was divided," replied Erna. "In 1894 about the time my father graduated from seminary, he aligned himself with the Inner Mission Lutherans who were the pietistic 'holy Danes'. They were opposed to the doctrine of N.S.F. Grundtvig. My mother used to tell me about the 'happy Danes', the Grundtvigians. The 'holy Danes' thought they were hopeless sinners."

"I know exactly what you are talking about," I replied. "In fact, we went to the holy-Dane church in Ringsted, and there was a happy-Dane church just outside of town. The happy Danes had square dances at the community hall, and they were allowed to play cards and read secular literature. Grundtvig believed you were a human first and that your spirit needed amusement as well as piety."

"Grundtvig did a lot for the Danish people," Erna added, "at a time when they were very insecure about being Danes. There was a time in

Denmark when the upper class, the nobility, spoke French and everything Danish was a put down. Grundtvig started this whole mentality of being proud of Danish culture and heritage. He started the folk school movement, which gave the average Dane an opportunity to get educated. In fact, my mother went to folk school in Denmark."

"That's interesting. Both of my parents went to folk school, too, before they left Denmark. In fact, I have seen pictures of the folk school my father attended."

"In Denmark there was never a division in the church," continued Erna. "Debate over these issues went on continuously, but the Danish church was always unified. It was only in America the Danish Lutherans split into different synods. In 1894 every church member was required to choose one synod or the other, which often resulted in parishioners leaving their churches to start or join new congregations."

"That's what happened in Ringsted," I said. "Members of St. Ansgar's Lutheran congregation voted and approximately half of them, the pietistic ones, left and started St. Paul's Lutheran Church in town. The two churches were only one mile apart."

After rehashing the happy-Dane, holy-Dane debacle, which had echoed through Danish American family parlors and church halls for decades, Erna changed the subject. "I'm interested in hearing what happened to your teaching career," she said.

"Well, it started badly and ended badly," I replied, "but I enjoyed a couple of good years in between. My teaching career was pretty much over by the time I got married. Country school was a lot of work because you had to teach up to eight grades at a time, and each grade needed separate lessons and tests."

"Have you ever thought of going back to teaching now that your children are grown?" Erna asked.

"Not really, I'm too old now, and I'm quite content to remain a farmer's helpmate. Besides, I'd have to go back to college to get a four year degree."

"Others have done it at your age. What do you have to lose besides a few thousand dollars?"

"Well, I also have plans to research and write the history of my Danish family, and I want to continue the genealogy work. My life is quite full already."

Afterward we drove back to Erna's apartment to retire for the evening. It had been a long day, and I was running out of steam. Getting ready for bed, I reflected on Erna's comments and remembered my school teaching days long ago, which I had rarely thought about in recent years.

8

Giffin School, 1946

It was late on Friday afternoon, the end of my first week at Giffin School. The children had all left for the day. Seated at my desk, I was checking and organizing the assignment sheets for seventeen pupils and reflecting upon the week. A few minutes earlier, the room had been full of noisy exuberant youth. I gazed at the empty desks, imagining possibilities for the future. I reminisced about the past week: the curious and expectant glances on the first day; the enthusiasm of the boys as they caught the balls I batted to them; the beginners who had wandered away from my view into forbidden territory while chasing a butterfly; and the glee with which two boys had herded them back. I felt a twinge of pity for the clumsy, cross-eyed boy. I cringed at the memory of another boy who appeared before my desk with a cut on his brow and blood streaming down his face. I recalled the proud if timid smile which accompanied a bowl of flowers placed on my desk. Suddenly my reverie was interrupted by a hesitant knock at the door. A boyish face appeared.

"Come see my pony, teacher," the boy stammered. As I went out the door, he shouted, "Watch this!" He leapt onto his pony and galloped away in childish delight. A smile lingered long on my face as I watched him disappear down the road. I treasured the moment, glad to be there. Surely this job was the right choice for me.

Giffin School was four miles south of Ringsted, a mile into Palo Alto County. It was only six miles from home, a trip I drove each day in Pa's 1938 Oldsmobile. I had seventeen pupils, nine children in grades one through eight and seven in a primary grade called primer. It was designed to be a kindergarten for the five-year-olds and ran the entire school year. There were only three girls that year, one in first grade and two in primer. School started on August 30. It was my best year as a teacher, the high point of my teaching career. I was twenty years old. It was a lot of work, but they were good kids, mostly, and I grew to love them and the job.

Sturdy and rectangular, Giffin School was a handsome one-room schoolhouse with a hip roof and white clapboard siding. It was nicer and newer than most country schools and actually had indoor toilets. Behind the teacher's desk, a blackboard spanned the entire front wall. A row of windows on the adjacent south wall flooded the room with light. Three rows of desks ran from front to back, facing the teacher. Next to the teacher's desk were several chairs where the pupils sat, one grade at a time, to receive and recite their lessons while the others worked on their assignments.

During the first period we did reading lessons, about ten minutes for each grade. After reading lessons, we had a recess for the pupils to use the toilets or get a drink. Then we did callisthenic exercises for ten minutes, something I had learned at a summer camp that year.

During the second period we did arithmetic and, on alternate days, science. I always began with the primary children. After their lesson, they went to their desks to do seatwork or workbook assignments while the first grade came up for their lessons, then the second grade and so on. In this way the pupils from each grade came forward for their lessons while the others worked at their desks. *Puzzle Pages* was an excellent workbook, which helped to keep them busy. Seatwork, as it was called, involved assignments and exercises I prepared ahead of time for each grade.

At noon we ate lunch and then played games outdoors, or in the basement when the weather was bad. At five minutes before one o'clock, I went to the entry and rang the bell, which was like a church bell only smaller. When all the children were back in their seats, I read from a storybook for fifteen minutes. They loved "Story of a Donkey" and other books I chose, although occasionally some little heads started to nod.

During the third period, I taught history and geography and, on alternate days, hygiene and English. In the fourth period, following afternoon recess, the pupils worked on spelling. I pronounced the words to each class, and afterward they exchanged papers for correction while I spelled the words aloud. Any leftover time was spent honing penmanship skills, and on Friday we did an art project. Music classes were less regular. I preferred to insert music into the schedule when my pupils seemed tired or bored. A phonograph stood in one corner. The room seemed to perk up when I played music, and the children sang along with me.

The school year was divided into two semesters. Each semester was split into three six-week periods. At the end of each six-week period all the pupils were given standardized tests. When pupils failed, as some did, they needed to repeat the test until they passed. I recorded the results of the six-week tests on the report cards and sent them home with the children. It was a lot of work. I prepared the lessons ahead of time each day on four or five subjects for each class. And afterward I corrected the assignments and the tests for each one as well.

I worked hard for my $156 monthly salary, but there was a lot of personal satisfaction, too, because many of the children worked hard and learned on account of my efforts. The job had other benefits as well. I became well known in the community and acquainted with all the parents. I worked with the county superintendent, attended various teaching workshops, and reported to the school director who lived nearby. After directing a successful Christmas program, I received praise and admiration from the parents. Best of all, I felt socially accepted in the community and loved by my pupils. I loved them too and, at times, even found myself imagining they were my own children.

Daily I heard, "Coming out to play, Miss Mikaelsen?" I loved hearing those words and playing ball with the children. During recess and lunch hour, I batted flies and grounders to them in the school yard. They often chose sides and played a game. Usually I was the pitcher. After snowfall we played other games during lunch hour such as "keep-away" or "fox and goose." When the weather was bad, we played games in the basement. These are some of the good memories I have from my second full year as a teacher.

After my disastrous failure at Rymer School, two years earlier, I moved home and tried to recover. I worried about my future, scoured my Bible for comfort, and prayed for strength and forgiveness. Each day I penned grief and shame into my diary, discouraged and depressed, living at home without a direction. Worse yet, I was embarrassed to face my friends and neighbors, ashamed of what they might think of me when they heard about my failure.

Two weeks later I moved to Minneapolis to live with Esther. She helped me get a job downtown at Lindsay Brothers, the farm equipment wholesaler where she worked. I started out as a clerk and a secretary. The work suited me well. I enjoyed the comradeship of my colleagues. Esther and her roommate Lila invited me into their social community. Mostly this was at St. Paul's Lutheran Church, where I joined the choir and had a great time. Better yet, I was far away from the judging eyes back home.

We lived in a boarding house on Park Avenue close to downtown, and I soon became very familiar with Minneapolis. I loved riding the streetcars, which in 1944 went all over the Twin Cities and beyond. I learned to ice skate and enjoyed the skating rinks at Lake Calhoun and Powderhorn Park. In the spring and summer, we went for bike rides around the lakes and picnics and ballgames in the parks. Before long, I all but forgot my bitter failure at Rymer School.

Socially the city was good for me too. On Saturday evenings, every second weekend, we attended the ecumenical "Singspiration" at the Minneapolis Auditorium. Our church choir sang for radio broadcasts. Esther and I sang duets, too, and had several records made. My friends Pearl and Phyllis came to visit me, and I met several new friends and a few interesting young men, but no one ever asked me out.

For ten months, I lived with Esther and worked at Lindsay Brothers, where I was promoted to switchboard operator. I heard through the grapevine that I was among their most valued employees. Financially it was good too. I made enough money to pay off my school loan and actually started a savings account. Every day I recorded my experiences and reflections in my diary, the good and the bad.

Dec 2, Sat: *Don, Janet and I had so much fun typing envelopes today. We laughed all forenoon, Oh, how I love work and Minneapolis! I ate at Powers and shopped all afternoon. Finished Christmas shopping.*

Giffin School, 1946

Spent $35 in all. Wrapped packages. Ate supper in room. Esther and I are alone tonight. Lila is out. I love Esther.

Jan 29, Mon: *Had fun at work. Showed Howard how to run addressograph. I like him. He helped me fill logs to mail. Janet and I ate supper at Forum. Insurance salesman was here tonight and sold a policy to Esther. He stayed a long time. Lila doesn't like me.*

Feb 20, Tues: *This has been such a long and boring day. I have no friends. I always act so dumb. I'm lonesome for some loving. Over to Evelyn's for supper. Had birthday party for Lila. Played games and had big lunch. I feel sad and despondent.*

Feb 26, Mon: *Had a nice time at work today. Helped in mail dept. Been dreaming of Norman today. I wonder if he ever dreams of me. Adeline and I talked of our wedding dreams. Elmer called Lila tonight. I think she acts like a flirt.*

Apr 28, Sat: *I felt silly today at work. Got tired of billing. Ate at Powers. Came home and slept. Feel sinful and wicked. Went to cleaners with clothes. Sailors followed me and everyone whistled. Went to Singspiration with Evelyn and Erma tonight. They announced that Germany surrendered, and I was so happy I could cry, but it turned out to be just a rumor.*

In June, 1945, shortly after V.E. Day, I received a letter from Marie Sorum, my former teaching superintendent. "There's a little school near Graettinger, Iowa, that needs a teacher," she wrote. "I'm sure you will make an excellent teacher if you just give it another chance." She apologized for giving me such a difficult school for my practice teaching and promised to help me get started. She urged me to take the job. My desire to redeem myself and her complimentary remarks clinched the decision to quit my job in Minneapolis and return to Iowa.

This time around, everything went smoothly. I started teaching at Blue Bottom School on the third of September. With only eleven students, the job was much more manageable, and soon I was comfortable in my role as a teacher. The most difficult part for me was the discipline. I might have been overly concerned about whether or not the children liked me, which became a stumbling block in keeping strict order.

One day I caught the older boys smoking behind the schoolhouse. To discipline them, I revoked their recess privileges for one week. After school they retaliated by locking me in the schoolhouse with the padlock that hung on the front door. Delbert, a sixth grader and a model pupil, came to the rescue. He knocked on the window and stammered, "Hand me the key, Miss Mikaelsen. I'll remove the lock."

There was a strict rule against running in the schoolhouse. One day I caught a boy running and told him to stay in his seat during recess. This was the standard punishment. When he tried to leave, I blocked him. Suddenly he leaned over and bit me on the leg.

"Ouch!" I cried. "Why you little . . ." Later I talked to the director. He told me to get tough on these boys and to call him whenever they got out of hand.

The two older boys were particularly mean spirited. One day the older one swore at me. "Yer a jackass," he sneered.

Incensed, I slapped him across the face! "You can apologize right now, or I can call the director!" I retorted.

He stiffened and flushed, "I'm sorry, Miss Mikaelsen," he said. Finally I had his attention, and the others noticed too. After that it was much easier to maintain discipline.

Fortunately, I had the welcome assistance of Mary Ann, an eighth grade girl who was likable, competent, and conscientious. She helped the younger ones and stayed after school each day to help me clean up. Because of her, my job was much easier.

While teaching at Blue Bottom School, I lived at home with my parents. Each day I commuted thirteen miles to and from school in my father's Oldsmobile. When snow or blowing snow left the roads impassable and during severe cold spells, I stayed at the director's house a quarter mile west of the school.

Softball games at Blue Bottom are among my favorite memories. Those kids were really good at softball. We competed with the neighboring schools and usually won.

Giffin School, 1946

Near the end of the school year, I was asked to renew the contract for the following year, but I declined. With country school teachers in short supply, I was hoping there would be a school available closer to home. A few weeks later the opportunity arose at Giffin School. It was a difficult decision because I had come to love many of the children at Blue Bottom, and it had been a great place to do my practice teaching.

An important family event occurred that year too. After completing his military service in France, John went to Denmark to visit our relatives. Then he returned to the states, fetched his fiancée Luverne in Wisconsin, and came home three days before Christmas. We had not seen him in over two years, and it was a wonderful reunion with the entire family home for the holidays. Luverne Wold had corresponded regularly with John the whole time he was gone, and they were eager to get married upon his return. Not only did Lou share his deep religious conviction, she also supported his ambition to become a missionary. At Christmas time, however, she seemed quite preoccupied with planning their January 20 wedding.

In addition to sharing his war stories, John reported the news and detailed descriptions of his trip to Denmark. It had been twenty years since he last saw our grandparents and cousins, so this was a major reunion. With detached curiosity, I listened to the stories about my grandma and grandpa and the many cousins whom I had never met. I found it difficult to share the enthusiasm of those who actually remembered and knew these folks. Perhaps someday I would meet them too, I thought.

Three months later, such an opportunity arose. One of my Danish cousins called from New York to tell us that he and his family would be passing through Omaha on their way to California. I was a little surprised when Pa insisted on driving two hundred miles to Omaha so we could see his nephew Emil for a half hour while the train stopped. Emil and Anna Mikaelsen and their two young children were headed for UC Berkeley. As a young physician, Emil was enrolled to study Chinese for a year before heading to China for missionary work.

We drove six hours to Omaha and went straight to the train depot. Not knowing which one they were on, we checked every westbound train. Late that night after the last train arrived, we went wearily to the Pullman

Hotel and returned the following morning. They didn't arrive till 10:30 that evening. The train had been delayed for 24 hours in Chicago. Nevertheless, I was thrilled when the young Mikaelsen family finally arrived. It was my first introduction to one of my Danish cousins. Conversing easily in Danish, we compressed twenty years of news into a half hour and went on board the train to see their two sleeping children, Thomas and Hanna.

Afterward, we drove all night to get home. Pa and I took turns driving. I slept as much as I could and dreamed about meeting more of my cousins. It was light when we got home. I only had time to change and eat before leaving for Blue Bottom School where I staggered through the day, half exhausted and half energized.

Right after school was out in June, 1946, Emil and Anna returned to Iowa with their children. They took a bus from California during their summer break. Many years later I learned that my father had sent them money to pay their bus fare to Iowa. I was especially impressed with Thomas, their precocious six-year old, who played piano, sang, and entertained us while they stayed at our home. And I loved Hanna, the smiling two-year-old, who followed me around like a puppy. Emil spoke at our church and also at the Inner Mission Fellowship meeting. He came to visit our vacation bible school in town, too, where I taught. Little Thomas was an instant celebrity when he sang in Danish for my class. I was sad to see the Mikaelsens go and hoped I would see them again.

The rest of the summer I helped Ma and Pa on the farm, worked occasionally for the neighbors, and went to summer camps at Mount Carmel and Medicine Lake. And I looked forward to teaching again, which brings me back to Giffin School, where I continued to thrive and loved the children as well as my work.

Miss Oliver—the Palo Alto County superintendent of rural schools—dropped in periodically and gave me helpful ideas and feedback. She always complimented me on my classroom and teaching. Occasionally I went to Emmetsburg where Miss Oliver held teaching workshops. There I met the other rural school teachers from Palo Alto County and obtained needed supplies for school.

Unfortunately, there was no piano in Giffin School. So I decided to buy an accordion with my own money and began using it for music lessons. I played and sang to the children. They sang along and learned many songs.

On January twenty-eighth that year, a snowstorm blew in from Nebraska. I made it to school on the twenty-ninth but only nine were there, and I barely made it home. The next day the storm turned into a blizzard, the worst since 1941. Over the next week and a half, school was open just two days, but attendance was sparse. I made it home February fifth but closed school early on the sixth and could not get home due to drifting snow. I went to stay with Nyles Heggen, the school director, whose family lived just a quarter mile from Giffin School. The next day fierce winds caused whiteout conditions. I tried to call home, but all I could hear was a steady buzz on the telephone lines, rendered useless by the howling winds. I was snowbound four days at the Heggens' house. The weather eventually cleared enough to reopen school on February tenth, but the roads were not plowed until several days later.

Five of the nine older boys at Giffin School were from one family, the Iversons. Russel, the oldest, was very helpful with school chores and seemed to understand my frustrations. He was bigger than I was and a little awkward but a sympathetic listener enshrined with a heart of gold and tender affections. Robert, at thirteen, seemed neglected and timid, but also as good as gold. He had already failed two grades before I discovered he was near-sighted. This put him in the fifth grade along with Melvin, who was sociable and affectionate as well as helpful like Russel. Melvin once told me I was the best teacher they ever had. Roger, in fourth grade, was very withdrawn but worked diligently on his assignments and amused himself. He rarely smiled and never misbehaved. Occasionally I succeeded in provoking his smile, a sight well worth the effort. This often occurred when Roger asked me to play my accordion. He was delighted when I played "Little Red Caboose" and other songs. Derwood, in third grade, was the genius of the family. Unusually alert and talented, he expressed himself beautifully, talking to others as well as to himself. He worked hard, played hard, and was very sweet to everyone.

68

The Iversons were very poor. On Valentine's Day I delivered a crate of oranges to their house. No wonder these boys were in such need of decent clothing—such a pitiful home. I put out the word for clothing donations and gave most of the proceeds to the Iverson boys.

In 1947, Ma and Pa started hunting for a smaller retirement farm back in Minnesota closer to our relatives. Martin and Pauline had moved to Minneapolis in late 1945 so Martin could study carpentry on the GI Bill at Dunwoody Institute. Since I was employed full time as a teacher, Pa was left with no extra help at home. At sixty two, he was no longer able to keep up with the rigors of operating a 120 acre farm. On the first of March, eleven years after moving to Ringsted, we loaded up our belongings and trucked them 110 miles to a new farm seven miles east of Austin near the town of Rose Creek. It was a beautiful eighty acre farm with a two story house.

My parents' move created a dilemma for me. I loved Giffin School and wanted to continue there the following year. On the other hand, I didn't want to be so far away from my family. Staying meant I would need to rent an apartment and get a car. At the time, this held little appeal for me, but my job at Giffin School was about to get even better.

Three other moves occurred that March. First, Nyles Heggen, the school director, moved away. Second, the Boblits moved into the empty Heggen house. I stayed with the Boblits for the final three months of the school year. Third, the Holtorf family moved into the neighborhood. Whereas the Heggens had a five-year-old at Giffin School, the Holtorfs had two older boys, Alvin and Lavern, who sweetened my job considerably. Alvin, in eighth grade, and Lavern, in fifth grade, were two of the most delightful pupils I ever knew. Each morning they greeted me, "Good morning teacher," or "Good morning Miss Mikaelsen." They were consistently thoughtful, helpful and courteous in a very pleasing way. Every day, for example, they carried the drinking water into school without my asking. Better yet, they had an older brother Norman, who was very handsome and friendly. Whenever he drove past the school, he honked and waved. Their father, the new school director, was just as nice as his three boys.

Giffin School, 1946

Torn about the decision to move, I mulled over the pros and cons for the next three months. In the end I decided to move to Rose Creek after the school year ended, a decision I would long regret. Although I rationalized that my parents needed me, I think it was evident that I still needed them. On May 25, my last day full day at Ringsted, I hosted a picnic and a ball game at Giffin School with the children and their families. Afterward, I went to the Vammens for supper, but I wasn't hungry. I left early, went home to the Boblits, and cried myself to sleep. I had grown sentimentally attached to the school, the community, and the children. Apart from the teaching, I was somewhat isolated, and those children were like a family to me.

The day after the picnic, I loaded up my belongings and drove the long road to Rose Creek. Pa had loaned me his car for my last two weeks at Ringsted. I wasted no time in finding a new job and signed a contract two days later for $200 a month at District 121 near the town of Dexter. To get a permit for teaching in Minnesota schools, I needed two six-week courses in Austin at the Mankato State College extension. I enrolled in English composition and physical education for the summer session and received my permit. The rest of the summer I worked at home, helping Ma fix up and paint our new house and helping Pa pick rocks and clean out the farm buildings.

Our farm at Rose Creek was only twenty-five miles from the Erickson's place near Kasson, and Pearl was determined to find me a boyfriend. One Sunday she invited me to a Luther League meeting at South Zumbro Lutheran Church. She wanted me to meet Gordon Gunderson, her neighbor who was a member there. I brought my accordion and played a few numbers. I met Gordon and enjoyed the evening. Afterward Pearl invited Gordon to ride along on the trip to take me home. Pearl rode in front with her fiancé Harold. Gordon and I wedged into the back seat next to another couple. They were more interested in necking than talking. Gordon and I barely spoke ten words. We just sat there, stiff as boards, trying to ignore the two squirming next to us.

Meeting Gordon did not seem important at the time. In fact, I was unmoved. An entry in my diary the next day tells it all: *I was disappointed in Gordon. I didn't fall for him.* I was more attracted to better educated and intellectual men, particularly if they were outgoing or expressed themselves well. Gordon met none of these criteria. He had only an eighth grade education and was painfully shy, although I did notice that he was quite handsome. But I was willing to wait for someone better. A week later, I received a letter from Gordon. I cordially replied a couple weeks later, and that's where it ended, or so it seemed. I saw him at a Luther League rally several weeks later, but he was too bashful even to approach me.

Before the summer was over, I began to prepare myself for District 121, which got off to a bad start. When I submitted an order for books and materials to the school board, I was told to rewrite the order because it was too expensive. It took all afternoon, and I became very discouraged. Unfortunately, the semester did not improve from there. I got the impression the school had been mismanaged, an intuition I had in the first meeting with the school board. Unwittingly, I stepped into a chaotic mess.

On the first day of school twenty-seven children showed up instead of the twenty-one they had advertised. Although surprised, I was not upset by the miscalculation, for I was confident in my ability to manage that many, even if it added appreciably to my work load. Several other issues did bother me, however. The seventh graders weren't able to read the books I ordered. A sixth grade girl was mentally retarded but had been promoted from grade to grade anyway. The second and third graders had not learned to read. The smartest girl in the school and the slowest boy were both in the eighth grade. The lessons were either too slow for her or too fast for him. To make matters worse, several pupils had an "I'll do as I please" attitude.

I slogged through the fall semester, disappointed and lonesome for the children at Giffin School. Contributing to this malaise was my unfamiliarity in the new community, both at work and at home. I had not yet found the security of friends and support that I enjoyed at Ringsted, even after my parents and I joined Zion Lutheran near Dexter, the most evangelical church in the area.

Teaching at District 121 was not a complete disaster either. Among all the problems were a few golden nuggets as well. Whenever a teacher has that many children, there will be a mix of good and bad, and this group was no different. In fact, within that small school, despite the slackers, the misbehavior, and the failures of management, I found the largest group of brilliant pupils I ever knew. Four of them were from the same family. Shirley, the eldest, was the genius in eighth grade and knew more than I did on every subject. Although this caused considerable tension between us, the semester would have been much worse without her assistance. Shirley's younger siblings were every bit as brilliant as she was.

As if to assuage my discontent, Gordon stopped by one Sunday in November and invited me to a Youth for Christ meeting in Austin. With nothing else to do, I accepted and surprised myself by having a good time. For some reason I enjoyed his company. A few weeks earlier, I had seen Gordon at a mission festival in Kasson and noted afterward in my diary, *I like Andy Ness, but I don't like Gordon.* Maybe I shifted because of my unsatisfying work and social life at the time. Maybe I was ambivalent or fickle. The following day I was still thinking about Gordon. Although his intellect and shyness did not appeal to me, he was physically attractive, and I found myself comfortable in his presence.

Fall semester at District 121 was pure drudgery compared to my dream job at Giffin School. I stayed on top of the onerous work load, but it was joyless work. As the semester progressed, I became more discouraged and began to think about quitting. The situation grew worse when Jesse, a new eighth grade pupil, arrived in early December. Jesse broke all the rules and seemed to thrive on disrupting the classroom and annoying me. Worse yet, he was popular with the others and effectively subverted my authority, which made each day a nightmare. His presence in the classroom, my declining spirits, and my brother John's wise counsel all contributed to my decision to resign at the end of the semester. But the Christmas program I had organized and choreographed went ahead as planned. Later I was told it was the best program ever at District 121. However, my decision to leave was firm, and I was relieved to be done.

The time was ripe for a change in course, and opportunity was calling. All three of my siblings had gone to Lutheran Bible Institute in Minneapolis. Now it was my turn. In fact, John and Martin were already registered to attend that winter. With time on my hands and money in the bank, I enrolled at LBI for the winter and spring trimesters. It was the best decision I ever made.

9

St. Patrick's Cathedral

Dawn crept slowly over the Hudson Valley. Gradually I became aware of the sounds outside the open window, mostly birds and early morning traffic on the street below. At 7 a.m. I rolled out of bed and got ready for my Sunday excursion. Before long Erna was up, by the sound of things, and I headed for the kitchen.

"Good morning, Mary. Would you like some coffee?"

"Please."

Erna poured me a cup of coffee as we traded pleasantries. "You have a big day ahead of you," she said. "You mentioned St. Patrick's Cathedral. If you prefer something a little smaller, St. Thomas Episcopal Church is only two blocks away."

"My daughter recommended St. Patrick's Cathedral," I replied, "so I'd like to at least take a look at it. But yes, I might prefer attending a smaller church service. What about you? Aren't you going to a theater?"

"I go with a group of friends several times a year to the Longmore Theater in New Haven. We have a subscription and carpool up there on Sunday several times a year. It's about an hour drive up the interstate but well worth it. The productions often go from there to Broadway, but the price is much lower."

"Isn't Broadway a theater in New York?"

"Yes, but it also refers to a whole class of theaters in the New York Theater District, both on Broadway Avenue and off Broadway. There are over forty theaters in the Theater District. Many of them have over 1000 seats."

"We have a movie theater in Mora."

"I'm not talking about movie theaters. These are all live theater productions like *Phantom of the Opera*, which has been running two years in a row at the Majestic."

"Oh yeah, we have those kind of theaters in the Twin Cities. Gordon and I went to the Chanhassen Dinner Theater with our son to see *Oklahoma*."

"Is that right?" Erna said, flipping through a large phone book. "Excuse me a minute while I call for information." She left the table and returned a few minutes later. "There's a Sunday service at St. Thomas starting at eleven," she said. "Unfortunately Ellis Island is closed for renovation. Tour boats are still running out to Liberty Island and past Ellis Island, however. You can take a cab or any Fifth Avenue bus down to Battery Park to get on the tour boat."

"Well, that should work out really well. Thank you for checking. Do you know how long it takes to get down to St. Patrick's Cathedral from here?"

"About an hour," replied Erna. "The express bus will take you right down Fifth Avenue. St. Patrick's is at Fifty-first Street, and St. Thomas Church is at Fifty-third. I'll walk you to the bus stop. It's only five minutes away."

"I would really appreciate that."

When breakfast was over, Erna cleared the table while I gathered my things. Then we went out the door and walked to the Hartsdale Avenue bus stop. It was a much cooler than the previous day, and the clouds were thickening. A small group of people stood waiting at the bus stop.

When the Westchester-Manhattan Express arrived, I boarded with a half dozen others and took a front seat, next to a younger woman. She smiled amiably and said hello.

"Hi. I'm Mary. Are you from around here?"

"No, not any more. I live in Chicago, but I used to live in New York. I'm just here on business this week. My name is Karen."

"I'm from Minnesota and just came for the week too. It's my first time in New York though." She seemed genuinely interested in me.

The express bus cruised south, stopping once or twice each mile or so to pick up more passengers. Somewhere in Yonkers, it merged onto the Deegan Expressway, which passes through the Bronx, one of the five boroughs that make up New York City and home of the poorest congressional district in the nation. At 138th Street, we crossed over the Harlem River into Manhattan, the most densely populated borough and one of the wealthiest counties in the US. Manhattan is actually an island, twelve miles long and one to two miles wide in the Hudson River. The bus headed south on Fifth Avenue, the central artery bisecting Manhattan.

"This is close to where I lived," said Karen. "It's the best part of town. Actually I lived on the Upper West Side over there on the other side of Central Park. I went to the park almost every day. It's a great place to walk or run. Where are you going today?"

"I'm going to St. Thomas Church this morning. This afternoon I'm going to see the Statue of Liberty and Ellis Island."

"Sounds interesting. If you get a chance, just walk the streets and look around. The city is full of interesting architecture and people. That's the Guggenheim Museum on the left," Karen pointed to an odd-shaped building.

"Looks like a big flower pot," I said.

"Yeah, right. This part of Fifth Avenue is called Museum Mile. There are at least six museums here. If you have any extra time I would recommend the Metropolitan Museum of Art. You could spend a whole day in there and you wouldn't see it all."

"My cousin recommended the Metropolitan too."

"This used to be called Millionaire's Row. That's why there are so many museums here now. Some rich people built museums and donated their art collections. The neighborhood just beyond is called the Upper East Side. It's one of the wealthiest neighborhoods in the country, home to people like the Roosevelts, Kennedys, and Rockefellers." Pointing ahead she said, "That's the Metropolitan Museum."

I studied the massive building with the ornate façade. "No wonder it takes all day to see it. It must be three blocks long. Have you ever been to St. Patrick's Cathedral?"

"I used to go there once in a while just to sit and observe," replied Karen, "but that was years ago. It's a good idea to go to St. Thomas for

Sunday service. St. Patrick's can be a little intimidating. You'll see what I mean."

Like a personal tour guide, Karen explained all sorts of interesting things about the city. South of Central Park we disappeared into a forest of skyscrapers. At Fifty-second Street, I pulled the cord, and the bus stopped at the curb across from St. Patrick's Cathedral. "Goodbye, Karen." I said. "It was really nice to meet you."

"You have a great day, and good luck."

I stepped onto the sidewalk, and the bus pulled away. Across the street stood St. Patrick's, the largest Catholic cathedral in North America, its twin gothic spires soaring 330 feet overhead toward a backdrop of low clouds. Built in the style of Europe's great medieval cathedrals, St. Patrick's opened in 1879 in honor of the patron saint of Ireland, reflective of the large Irish American community in New York City. I crossed Fifth Avenue and found my way to the front steps. The massive bronze double doors— eighteen feet high and weighing twenty thousand pounds each—stood wide open.

Entering the cathedral, I stopped, and gazed at the spectacle before me, four hundred feet to the far end and a hundred and fifty feet to the vaulted ceiling above. The rows of pews stretching out in front of me could seat 2400 people, although they seemed practically empty at the time. However, lots of visitors were moving about the sanctuary, gazing upward and viewing the side chapels dedicated to various saints. I strolled over to the receptionist sitting at a table nearby. "Could you please direct me to the ladies room?" I inquired.

"I'm sorry we have no public facilities available here," the woman replied. "You might try across the street."

Having consumed a cup of coffee and a glass of juice earlier, I was disappointed that a church would not have a ladies room available. So I went out the door, crossed the street, and headed north. It was barely half past ten when I entered St. Thomas Episcopal Church, a very large church by rural Minnesota standards but almost small compared to St. Patrick's Cathedral. The narthex was nearly empty as I crossed the marble floor. At the door to the sanctuary, a man stood grinning and handed me a bulletin.

"You are quite early," he said, "but please make yourself comfortable. The organ prelude will begin soon."

"Thank you," I replied. "Is there a ladies room?"

"Right behind you and to the left, Ma'am."

I thanked the man again, used the toilet, and found my way back to the sanctuary. Proceeding up the left aisle, I took a seat in the center row of pews. St. Thomas Church, with its stone pillars and exquisite carvings, reminded me of the large churches I visited in Minneapolis years ago. During my second sojourn in Minneapolis, I attended Lutheran Bible Institute. These are some of my best memories. I pictured the brick building on Portland Avenue and 17th Street, where I enjoyed five precious months.

10

LBI and the Men of My Dreams

LBI was a mountaintop experience. On January 3, 1948, I moved to Martin and Pauline's house in South Minneapolis, just seven blocks from Minnehaha Falls. Lutheran Bible Institute was five miles away on Portland Avenue. My attitude improved overnight along with my spirits. I went to three classes a day, five days a week. The twelve courses on my schedule were general epistles, bible antiquities, bible doctrine, catechism, Kings, Galatians, mission survey, how to teach, personal work, hymnology, book synopsis, and speech. Outside of class, I spent most of my time studying in the library or playing the piano or playing games in the recreation room.

Among 350 students enrolled that year, I was part of the winter cohort, the students who came just for the winter. Marie Tweet and Norma Lein, whom I knew from church camp, were also there that year. I felt comfortable from the start and made many new friends, including some interesting young men. Farmers from all over the Midwest were a major component of the winter cohort, and I enjoyed getting to know them.

Soon I found myself a part of an expanding social group. Not since church camp had I experienced so much fun. My friends often gathered in the rec. room to sing along while I played the piano. I felt liked and accepted, surrounded by other evangelical Christians comfortable with the degree of piety to which I was accustomed.

One day during my first week, while I studied at the library, a handsome fellow came and sat down at my table.

"Hi. I'm Clifton," he said, reaching out to shake my hand.

"Hello. I'm Mary." I was thrilled that he was interested.

"Is this your first quarter?"

"Just started Monday. And you?" My heart quickened.

"I started Monday too. Just for the winter quarter," he answered, smiling warmly.

I smiled back. "I saw you in my Bible doctrine class," I said. "What other classes do you have?"

He listed a half dozen classes but none that I was in. This was unfamiliar territory for me, this casual conversation with a good looking stranger. I felt a little nervous and went back to reading my assignment. He opened a book, too.

Later in the cafeteria, Clifton followed me in the supper line. He was outgoing and affable and always knew what to say. I answered his questions easily enough, but then I felt tongue-tied. I couldn't think of anything to say or to ask in return, something I detested about myself. When I got my food, I headed straight for the table where my friends were sitting and then regretted that I had not waited for Clifton. Maybe he wanted to sit with me. I lacked experience around men and did not know how to respond when they showed interest.

The next Monday, Clifton followed me again in the supper line. I was almost surprised that he remembered my name, and I felt honored when he introduced me to some other young men. My fantasies of Clifton and the hope I had built over the weekend conspired with this new show of interest and overwhelmed me. I was smitten and fell head over heels in love with him. Falling too quickly in love was a troubling pattern, which had afflicted me ever since my affair with Norman years earlier.

On Tuesday, riding together in the car, I fantasized that my brother Martin was Clifton. The fantasy worked like a drug. On Wednesday, I saw Clifton in the library, and he flashed me the sweetest smile. Wow, he electrified me! Suddenly, however, I noticed he was talking to another girl and smiling at her. I felt jealous and miserable and began to wonder if he treated every girl that way. Confused and shaken, I prayed for release from my obsession, that I would be able to accept whatever was in store. On Thursday Clifton came to the student lounge and sang along with the group, while I played the piano. He looked at me in such a friendly loving way. My hopes revived. On Friday he sat by me again in the library. On Saturday, he followed me again in the supper line, and I introduced him to my friend. Soon he was engrossed in conversation with her. It was almost like I wasn't there. Later he sat with her at the movie.

I began to recognize the folly of this wayward infatuation, feeling whiplashed by Clifton's whims and my own emotional gyrations. Without discussing with Clifton the possibility of a relationship or even a date, I was already emotionally attached to him and filled with expectations. This was so foolish. From then on, I tried to stay detached and diverted my affections elsewhere. Marie and Norma were fun, and I loved spending time with them. I began to meet lots of other guys too, like Sophus, Silas, Melvin, and Thor, Leland, Lloyd, Obert, and Duane. As my social group expanded, I had more and more fun. We sang in the lounge, played games, teased and laughed, and also studied together. Thor and Obert offered to give me a ride home and a few days later, Bonner offered too. One evening four different guys offered to give me a ride home. Anna and Helen teased me relentlessly.

Because Clifton was also a part of my social group, I began to see him in a different light. When I observed him interacting with the others, I realized that he was self-centered, and I did not find him so attractive. Soon he became just a friend like all the others. I began to feel more relaxed around the men, and I found myself interested in knowing all of them. Each one had qualities I liked. It was just a matter of time, however, before one of them would ask me for a date. I hoped it would be Melvin or Leland, whom I liked the best.

The request came not from Melvin or Leland but from Obert, a farmer from Clarkfield who was twice my age. It was near the end of winter quarter, and he would soon be returning to the farm. Although a good-looking man, he was not even close to my heart's desire. But his offer to take me for a ride in his airplane was too good to refuse. Besides, I did not know how to politely say no, especially after I had accepted so many rides and gifts from him already. So I accepted. He picked me up at LBI on a Sunday afternoon. I was embarrassed about it, so I had kept it a secret and did not tell my family and friends. After the airplane ride, we went for a drive in the country. On a deserted road he pulled to the side and parked the car.

Turning to me, he said in his most sincere voice, "I have become very attached to you, Mary. I know you're concerned about my age, but I can assure you, I am capable of treating you as if I were 15 years younger." Of course these were things I already knew, but then he added this plea, "Will you come with me to Clarkfield and be mine?"

I should have seen this coming, but I was caught off guard. Obert seemed infatuated with me. I recognized the behavior. But this sounded like a marriage proposal. Considering all his gifts and favors, I felt pressured to comply. I gathered my courage and told him honestly, "I don't love you, Obert. I think of you as a father, not a lover. I'm sorry if I led you to believe that I am interested in more than a friendship. Please accept my apologies. And I still want you as a friend."

I thought this would put an end to his displays of affection and generous gift giving. Instead Obert turned up the heat. The next day, his last full day in town, he loaned me his car for my move to the dorm. Later he came to the library where I was studying and gave me another gift. It was a book. Then he walked me to the dormitory and gave me a box of chocolate-covered cherries. The following day, he asked me to go for a ride with him. I accepted but not without considerable anxiety. I had not yet learned when to say no, or to set boundaries. The next day after school, Obert met me at the dorm and walked me to his car.

"Where would you like to go?" he asked.

"Anywhere. You're driving, where do you want to go?"

"I wanna take you shopping," he said, handing me the keys. "It will be the highlight of your semester."

"Okay Obert, you asked for it." I had always liked driving in the city, and by then I knew my way around, which he apparently understood. I started the car, zoomed off down Portland Avenue and turned right on Franklin. I crossed Lyndale and Hennepin and headed west to Lake of the Isles. The lakes and parkways were my favorite part of town. Obert smiled as I turned onto Lake of the Isles Parkway. I drove around the lake, crossed Lake Street, and circled Lake Calhoun before heading to Penney's downtown.

I needed new shoes. If he wanted to take me shopping, at least it would be for something useful. That was the last thing Obert did before he left town. He bought me shoes. It was the last time I ever saw him, too, although he continued to send me gifts and letters for months. But I had told Obert the truth and eventually he figured it out. I had no interest in marrying him and my love could not be purchased.

Spring term at LBI wasn't as much fun as winter term. The farmers and other winter cohorts had all gone home. Melvin, whom I admired dearly, was still there, but he never asked me out. Later I learned he was dating another girl. What a letdown!

At school I did well academically and continued to enjoy my studies during the spring, particularly the course in vacation bible school (VBS). This was a subject I loved and could put to practical use; in fact, I signed up for two summer jobs to teach VBS, at Peterson and at Carver. I also committed to another teaching job that would begin in August at Toeterville, Iowa, fifteen miles south of my parent's farm. In the meantime, I took a part-time clerical job at Asbury Hospital. It was only three hours a day, but I enjoyed the work and needed the income.

The major event of the spring was the upcoming wedding. Esther had met and fallen in love with Harold Lundberg the previous summer. A brother of Esther's friend at work, Harold was a charming fellow and a gifted singer from a good Christian family in St. Paul. He had moved to Arizona several years earlier for his arthritis but returned each year to Minnesota for his summer vacation. The wedding was scheduled for May 30. All during that spring, we enjoyed the anticipation and preparations.

On May 20 I took my final exams at LBI and prepared to leave. I picked up my last check at Asbury, said goodbye to all my friends, and got a ride to the train depot. Passenger trains were still running to Albert Lea and Austin from Minneapolis. The ride home provided me a welcome respite from the incessant activities on both ends. Gazing wistfully out at the budding trees and newly planted fields, I thanked God and yielded to the closing of a wonderful chapter in my life.

Our home was bustling with activity. Harold had arrived from Arizona. Esther had moved home and was getting ready for the wedding. Mom was busy cooking and planting her garden, and Dad was busy with spring planting. I went to work immediately, washing and waxing the floors, helping Dad in the field, cooking and cleaning. In the midst of it all, I repacked my bags for the move to Peterson and began preparing for vacation Bible school the following week.

Esther was glowing conspicuously, clearly in love and happy with Harold. Their bliss was palpable. I was pleased and amused, yet I felt a little envious, still alone with no boyfriend. The grand displays of affection between Esther and Harold were the elixir I craved for myself. Their happiness and all the excitement about the wedding only added to this longing.

The wedding took place on a Sunday afternoon a few miles south of home near the Iowa border. Six Mile Grove Lutheran Church was not our home church, but it was Andy and Ingeborg's church, and it was the church Esther liked. I was proud to be her bridesmaid, to stand by Esther at the altar and walk down the aisle. She was beaming and beautiful; Harold was handsome and happy in front of Pastor Torvic and a small crowd of family and friends. After a rousing reception replete with the usual lunch food delicacies, frosted wedding cake, and coffee by the gallon, the newly-weds drove off in Dad's Oldsmobile to begin their honeymoon.

Early the next morning, Martin and Dad drove me to the Boyum farm near the town of Peterson. The VBS placement service at LBI had assigned me to a three week vacation Bible school at Arendahl and North Prairie Lutheran churches. Upon our arrival at the Boyum farm, I was thrilled to see the beautiful farm home where I would stay. But I was even more impressed with the host family who lived there.

Andrew and Ida Boyum had four children: Imogene, thirteen; Andrew, fifteen; Goodwin, seventeen; and Kenley, twenty five. Kenley made the biggest impression on me. A finer figure of a young man would be difficult to conceive. He was tall, lean, and handsome with a warm personality. His sharp wit and intellect complemented his pleasing appearance.

Dad and Martin drove away as the kids helped me carry my things to the house. When I was ready, Kenley drove Imogene and me a mile or so down the gravel road to Grover School where the VBS classes were to be held.

"Been doing this kind of work long?" Kenley asked.

"I taught vacation Bible school in Iowa a couple years ago, and I just finished the course at LBI, so I have lots of good ideas."

"Well I'm sure you'll be a great teacher," said Kenley. "Come on, I'll show you the school." We stepped from the car and walked over to the red brick school house. "I went to school here for eight years," he said. "Imogene went here, too, until they closed it four years ago. Now everyone around here rides the bus to Peterson."

"I liked it here," said Imogene, "but the school in Peterson is more fun."

"I taught three years at schools like this," I said.

Kenley unlocked the door and entered with Imogene close behind. Inside it was a typical country school. I liked it immediately and went to deposit my things on the teacher's desk. "Did you go to high school, too?" I asked Kenley.

"I graduated from Lanesboro in forty-one," he said. "And you?"

"Ringsted, Iowa. I grew up there and graduated from high school in forty-four." Laying down my load of materials I said, "The children are due in a half hour. I better get started."

"Okay, I'll be back at half past four," Kenley said.

I watched him go out the door. Then I shifted into high gear and organized my materials. Before long, the children began to arrive. All fifteen of them came. These were the best behaved group of kids I ever knew. The first day went better than I could have imagined. The children were attentive, respectful, and interested in everything. Imogene played her flute, I played my accordion, and the children all sang along.

I was especially pleased with the flannel-graph, which I had learned about at LBI. I constructed it myself. Cutting the silhouettes out of colorful sheets of felt, I created the images of all my favorite Bible characters and animals. When placed on the flannel board they held fast to the board but peeled off easily. Placed in groupings or one at a time on the flannel board, the characters depicted the scenes of each story as I told it. This was a hit with the children. They gazed with rapt attention at the colorful scenes I assembled before them. My favorite, and theirs too, was the story of Esther.

School was over at four o'clock, which gave me time to clean up and organize before Kenley came to get the two of us. Imogene was a cheerful and helpful assistant as well as a great pupil. It was nice to have her there for closing, to help me clean up.

Evenings at the Boyum farm were even better than school. I felt like one of the family and went along with them to various activities such as 4H with the kids. When they discovered I spoke Danish, Andrew and Ida, also children of immigrants, began speaking to me in Norwegian, which I understood almost as well as Danish.

Each morning Kenley brought Imogene and me to school and came back to get us in the afternoon. Whenever I got close to Kenley, I felt butterflies and a rush of euphoria. On Sunday he sat by me in church, and then he took me on a tour of the Harmony Cave. In the evening we went to supper and a concert at church. By the end of the day I was fighting off a storm of fantasies. The urge to dream about a future with Kenley was irresistible.

The days raced by. I felt high, like I was floating in the clouds. Each week I stayed with a different family but continued to see the Boyums, including Kenley, almost daily. Midway through the second week, Esther and Harold stopped by the school on the way back from their honeymoon. I closed school early and rode with them to visit the Boyums, who welcomed us and invited us in for lunch. Kenley was there too, which made it that much more enjoyable. I felt sad to see Esther and Harold leave. They were going to Arizona to live, and I would not see them for a very long time.

By the end of the second week, I was seriously smitten. On June 12, this is what I wrote in my diary: *I can't get over how wonderful Kenley is. I can hardly eat when I think of him. Oh, if he would only love me.*

The next day was Sunday. At Luther League I gave a talk on "yielding ourselves as instruments of God." Kenley was there, but we did not speak to each other. Later I wrote: *I feel terribly lonely. Can't get to sleep because of Kenley.*

In retrospect it seems silly that I allowed myself to get so emotionally involved with someone who had made little indication that he was romantically interested in me. But somewhere within me there was a palpable force beyond my control. I tried often to turn the matter over to God. *Not my will but Thine be done,* I prayed. The prayers seemed to have little effect on the infatuation.

During the third week I stayed with the Aarsvold family. Mrs. Aarsvold poured some cold water on the flames. "I'm pretty sure Kenley has a girlfriend already," she said. It stung, but finally I was able to rein it in a little.

On Wednesday, however, I played the pipe organ for the church program. Kenley came to my display table afterward and complimented me. I was thrilled.

Bible school ended well with all the parents attending on the third Friday. I gave a farewell speech, handed out report cards, and received my paycheck. The Paulson kids cried when it was time for me to leave. Mom and Dad came at closing time, and I was back home at Rose Creek for the weekend.

On Sunday I took the train to Minneapolis and spent the night at Martin's. Early the next morning he drove me to West Union Church near Carver, where I started a two week session of Bible school. I stayed at the parsonage with Pastor Burman's family and taught fifteen children at the community hall near the church. This was another wonderful experience. My flannelgraph and music were a hit, the children loved me and I loved them. And the parsonage was a comfortable place to stay. The church had a pipe organ too. Juanita, the organist, told me I could use it whenever I pleased. I practiced on it every chance I got. Toward the end of the session, I directed my class in presenting a musical program at the church. The children were splendid, and I received many compliments on what we had accomplished. I was on top of the world.

As well as everything went, however, the highlight of the two week session was a letter that arrived on Wednesday during the second week. Kenley wrote to tell me he was coming to visit me the following Sunday at Rose Creek. I wrote back right away. The rest of the week, I could barely conceal my elation. Martin, Pauline, and Marilyn came on the last day and drove me home to Rose Creek where they spent the Fourth of July weekend. My energy was boundless as I set to work cleaning the house.

Later I rhapsodized in my diary: *I love everyone and everything seems so rosy. Oh, what happiness and joy is mine. God bless tomorrow.* The significance of Kenley's letter was monumental to me. His desire to visit me meant two things: it was proof that he was available, and it was positive evidence of his interest in me.

Sunday turned out to be a mixed bag. Kenley arrived two hours late, long after I had given up hope that he was coming. We went for a drive to Austin and Rose Creek where we walked and took pictures of each other. Then we got home in time to have supper with my family, which wasn't such a good idea. Dad started questioning Kenley about his religious beliefs. "What role does Christ play in your personal life?" he asked.

"I go to church with my family almost every Sunday." Kenley replied.

Kenley's answer was a red flag. Dad frowned and pursed his lips. He gave Kenley that stern preacher look, and said, "One is not saved by good works or going to church; one is saved only through belief in Jesus Christ and the acceptance of His teachings as the Word of God."

Kenley stayed calm and replied, "Yes sir." Though he was raised in a good Christian family, he was not a true believer in our born-again evangelical style.

Fidgeting, Martin went to the rescue. "What are your plans for the future?" he asked Kenley.

"Just helping my father on the farm in the near term, but I'm planning to enroll in agriculture school at the University of Minnesota next year."

I was furious at Dad's pontification and relieved by the change in subject, but deep down I felt disconcerted with Kenley's answer and his apparent lack of conformity to our way of believing. The discomfort, however, did not dampen my love for him. I believed he would see the light and be saved by Christ.

Later as he prepared to leave, Kenley seemed disturbed and ambivalent.

"When will I see you again?" I asked.

"I'm not sure if I should come back."

"Why not?"

"It doesn't seem like I fit in here very well."

"Don't worry about Dad. He preaches to everyone like that. Please come back. I'll be praying for you."

The next two weeks I dove into summer activities. Mom and Dad bought their first refrigerator, and I started making refrigerator desserts. I went to Albert Lea to help cousin Lydia care for her baby and clean house. And I dreamed about Kenley and all the possibilities. In my diary, I wrote, *Oh how empty I feel. I'm so desperate for love and a Christian companion.*

This feeling of urgency over finding a husband intensified upon the arrival of news that both Pearl and Phyllis were engaged, not to mention the upcoming wedding of Norma Lein, my friend from LBI. I prayed daily for Kenley. I prayed for his soul, that he would accept Christ into his heart and become a saved Christian.

Back home I was elated to find a letter from Kenley. He was coming to see me again. I could hardly eat or sleep, waiting for Sunday to arrive. This time things went much better. He arrived on time and took me for a drive to Albert Lea where we toured around the lakes and stopped to eat at a restaurant. Later we attended a service at the Baptist church, and I felt pure bliss sitting by him. To sum it up later in my diary, I wrote, *This was the most wonderful day of my life so far.*

We continued seeing each other over the next several months. And I continued hoping and praying. Diary, July 20: *I dream and build air castles in my future. Oh, that I might be found worthy to be a wife and a mother, and I sure could go for Kenley as father, but oh, I don't dare dream or build my castles too high or it will be an awful let down.*

July 23: *I'm just so happy. I cannot contain myself for joy. I have truly entered the promised land of God.*

I should have seen the warning signals. At my invitation and urging, Kenley came to Medicine Lake Bible Camp for the first time that summer with a group from Peterson. On Saturday Kenley and I went to services together and walked on the beach, holding hands. On Sunday, however, I was anxious. Diary, July 25: *On pins and needles all morning because Kenley seems ashamed to be with me and introduces me to no one . . . He is burdened by sin. Set him free, oh Lord.* He drove me home to Rose Creek later that day, however, and I was in pure bliss.

At home I busied myself helping Mom and Dad and caring for my nieces, Judy and Ruthie. Diary, July 28: *I wrote a poem prayer for Kenley. He really could be the man I've been looking for.*

July 29: *My cup is full and running over. I have such wonderful memories stored up in my mind to dwell upon.*

July 30: *I got a letter from Kenly and went to bed with the letter.*

August 3: *I think so much of Kenley. I wonder if he thinks of me as I think of him. Oh, how I pray that he will become a new creature in Christ.* On August 8 the Kasson group, including Gordon, came to Zion Lutheran for a fellowship meeting. Diary: *Gordon didn't even talk to me. He's too bashful.*

My true heart's desire continued. Diary, August 11: *. . . letter from Kenley. What a time. I felt like floating on the clouds. Sat by a tree and read the letter. I wrote one to him right away.* On August 15 Kenley took me to the fair in Austin. We looked at machinery, walked through the 4H building and the midway, and had our pictures taken. Diary: *I could sit by Kenley's side forever.*

August 16: *I could hardly sleep tonight for thinking about dear Kenley.*

August 18: *Can't take my eyes off the picture of me and Kenley. I can't get over the wonder of it. How could he ever want a picture with me?*

August 26: *I'm so lonely for Kenley, oh so lonesome. I wonder if I'm in love?*

August 27: *Dad said I should quit Kenley since he doesn't seem to be coming through for Christ, but I can't because I love him so. Jesus, save him.*

August 31 was the first day of school at Toeterville. I went early to get organized before my pupils arrived. All eleven children came and everything went as planned. My hunch that day proved correct: these were some of the best children I ever taught. After school I moved my things into a boarding room in town at the home of Mrs. Langrock, an elderly woman. This was to be my home away from home on Monday through Friday.

With a delightful group of bright, cooperative children, the teaching job went exceedingly well. Despite this success, I was preoccupied with a constant anxiety about losing Kenley. As autumn approached, that anxiety began to overshadow everything else.

By September 12 it had been nearly a month since I last saw Kenley, and he had not answered my last letter. The shift in his behavior was troubling, but I was unable to accept that my relationship with him was slipping away. I was crushed when no letter came on Monday. Finally a letter came on Tuesday, and I was elated to learn that he would be coming to see me that Sunday. He did not mention receiving my letter, so I assumed he had not gotten it. Once again I was floating on cloud nine and dreaming of Kenley. Diary, September 15: *I am so tired today because I didn't sleep much last night for excitement over Sunday's date, but I'm so happy he's coming.*

The excitement was short-lived. On Sunday I waited all day, but Kenley never came. That night I cried myself to sleep. On Tuesday I received a letter from him, which included some feeble excuse. He promised to come instead the following Sunday. I was crestfallen in school that week, and the next Sunday, Kenley failed to show up again.

The writing was on the wall regarding Kenley's dwindling interest, but I had little capacity for letting go of love or grieving his loss. I could not deal with the ending when it was staring me in the face. I had become infatuated with Kenley. My perception of his love and the fantasies I cultivated were the source of all my energy and hope. When he seemed interested in me, I was on cloud nine, everything looked rosy, and I could accomplish an amazing amount of work. Much as I believed that my faith in God was strong, that Jesus would guide me through the gauntlet of life and loss, and that prayer would protect me from harm, I had become completely dependent on the affections of an undependable, distant boyfriend.

Kenley finally came to see me on Sunday, October 3. He came late, and I was irritated when he arrived. Nevertheless, we drove off to the Youth-for-Christ meeting in Austin and then went parking on the way home. Necking with Kenley was a sublime pleasure, but afterward I still felt troubled. On one hand, I was in love and extremely attracted to him;

on the other hand, I was hurt and anxious about his continuing neglect. He seemed unconcerned and very amorous.

Two weeks later Kenley came back on a Sunday afternoon. I enjoyed his company, and as usual I was struck by his charm and good looks. As if to reassure me he said, "I know your dad doubts it, but I am a Christian."

He was not very convincing, but I felt encouraged. "Don't pay any attention to my dad," I replied. "What's in your heart is what matters."

That was the last time I saw Kenley. Our pattern was to send each other a letter after each visit. I sent him a letter as usual, dreaming of him and hoping he would commit to me, but no answer came that week. In the weeks that followed, my hope turned to fear and despair.

Diary, October 22: *No letter from Kenley this week. Why? Oh dear, oh dear.*

November 1: *No letter. I can't understand why I don't hear. Oh, why did I say what I did? Why did I invite him in? Why, oh why?*

November 3: *No letter. I about bawl my eyes out every night. My heart aches.*

November 8: *Oh, how I wait for a letter, but it doesn't come. What if I never hear? Why, oh why?* This was the last entry I made in the diary, which I had kept faithfully for almost five years.

All through November and into December, teaching was automatic. Though I did my job, I lost interest in everything but the mailbox. I didn't enjoy singing in the County Chorus, and I wasn't eager for Christmas to come. I cried myself to sleep, when I could sleep, and I began vomiting every morning. When Kenley's letter finally arrived, it was to say he would not be coming to see me again. Two days before my school Christmas program was to be held in the village hall, I told my director I was having a nervous breakdown.

"Maybe you should talk to the doctor," she replied.

I went to see the doctor, and he agreed about the nervous breakdown. And he suggested I quit teaching. Based on his recommendation and my confusion after weeks without adequate sleep, I submitted my resignation. However, there was no relief in this decision because it involved the loss of my livelihood and purpose. Teaching had become part of my identity and part of the foundation of my self-worth. With the rejection letter from Kenley and the sudden ending of my job, my reason for living and purpose in life seemed to be over.

Had I fallen ill with almost any severe physical illness or received a severe injury such as what one might sustain in a car accident, the outcome likely would have been very different. A substitute would have been found to cover during my absence, and upon recuperation, I would have been welcomed back to the school. I was always well liked by the parents and the communities in which I taught, and that was true in Toeterville too. It seems strange in retrospect that I resigned so quickly. I could have refused the doctor's advice and made arrangements with the school board to take some time off.

"If only I hadn't quit," I said over and over to Mother. "What is a nervous breakdown anyway? Nerves don't break down. You can't lose your mind unless you cut your head off! Why is everyone so afraid I'm going crazy? Why did I quit? God must hate me. Everyone irritates me. Oh, if only I hadn't quit."

I thought erroneously that I had grieved the Holy Spirit and that God had turned against me. Isaiah 63:10 states, *But they rebelled and grieved His Holy Spirit, therefore He turned to be their enemy.* Among all my self-aspersions and twisted thinking, this one was perhaps the most damaging.

Gordon heard I was no longer dating Kenley and came to see me at Christmas. I stayed in my room and refused to see him. He visited with my parents and left me a gift. Later I opened it and found a nice bracelet. Pauline, who was staying for Christmas, asked me, "Do you love Gordon?"

"I don't know."

"You shouldn't keep the bracelet if you don't love him," she said.

I did not reply.

One day Eugene Anderson stopped by to ask if I would go out with him. He was a nice looking young man from a well-known local family. I knew him from the youth fellowship meetings in Lyle, where he had shown an interest in me during that summer and fall. Under ordinary circumstances, I would have been very interested in him. As it was, I told him I wasn't feeling well and went back to my room.

All the spiritual conversations of my family drifted up to me. I felt worse and worse. Believing I had sinned the Holy Spirit away from me, there was nothing left for me but darkness and hell. It seemed as though I might as well go to hell right then rather than later because, as far as I comprehended, I was already there.

After Christmas I descended into such a dreadful depression. And that's when I began contemplating suicide. Mother became very alarmed. She persuaded Dad to call a Christian psychiatrist in Minneapolis, who was recommended by a friend. Dad took me up there to see him. At the end of the session, the psychiatrist said, "You will recover in time. A vacation or a month in a hospital might do you some good."

We chose a trip to Arizona. My cousin drove the three of us— Mom, Dad and me—to the train depot. I was the unhappiest person ever to go on a trip, I'm sure. Mostly I thought about leaping from the train onto the tracks. It would be an easy end to my misery, and then I wouldn't be so much bother to everyone else. How I made it to Arizona, I will never know.

At the sight of my sister, I actually smiled. Esther took us to her little house in Glendale. I envied her life and happiness with Harold. However, I spent a lot of time in the bathroom trying to get up the courage to cut my wrist with a razor blade. One day I walked downtown to the library and did not return as my parents anticipated. When they found me, I was standing lost and alone in the park.

Not knowing what else to do or how to help, my parents took me to Orange Road Sanitarium in Phoenix. The doctor told them not to come back for two weeks because I would lose my memory from the electro-shock treatments. It was their policy not to allow any visitors during that time.

I welcomed the supervision and felt relieved to get away from my family. When it was time for my shock treatment, I was asked to lie down on a padded platform. There seemed to be a rubber sheet over it. I was told to put my hands at my side. Three aides stood on either side of me. They looked at me with friendly eyes. The doctor, confident and assuring, smiled and said, "We're going to give you a slight shock. The aides will hold on to you so no harm will come."

I went happily into oblivion. When I awoke, I was lying in my bed with no memory of the procedure. After two weeks of electroshock therapy, being a resident in this family-type home, helping with dishes, working in the hobby shop, playing croquet on the lawn, and getting to know the other residents, I felt like a new person. When my parents came to visit, I smiled broadly. We went sightseeing with Esther and Harold in the hills around Phoenix, but I was glad to get back to the sanitarium, to the people who understood and accepted me.

During my stay at Orange Road, Gordon wrote me an encouraging letter, which I answered readily. And soon I was looking forward to going home to Minnesota, to begin dating the man who had been of so little interest to me in the past. The doctor advised me to forget about teaching. He seemed to think farming with my parents was a good idea. Upon our return to Rose Creek, my prospects seemed limited. I spent my time planting potatoes, raising chickens, helping with field work, and writing letters to Gordon. And gradually I began to enjoy life again.

11

St. Thomas Church

Compared to churches I saw in Minneapolis, St. Thomas is a very large church. It is capable of seating 1700 at full capacity. At that moment only a few hundred worshipers were present, with more drifting slowly in. From my center pew, I enjoyed the glorious organ prelude and studied the magnificent reredos, forty feet wide and eighty feet high, mounted on the front wall behind the altar. It is thought to be the largest reredos in the world, carved from Dunville limestone quarried in western Wisconsin. It features the life-size sculptures of many Christian leaders and biblical characters including Christ himself in the center with the Blessed Virgin Mary and St. John the Disciple.

Behind me, high on the rear wall, was a magnificent rose window, twenty-five feet in diameter. The intricate stained glass mosaic was glowing red and blue with stunning depth and brilliance. Mounted beneath the rose window was a giant organ of spectacular beauty and quality. Silver and gold pipes stood vertically in a forty-foot-high golden oak frame, bracketed by cobalt blue shutters spreading like wings on both sides. Emanating forth was the most exquisite organ music I ever heard, reverberating through the church and sending chills down my spine. This was way better than I imagined.

The organ prelude was followed by a hymn, after which the Reverend Howard Stringfellow made his opening remarks. He declared absolution and remission of sins and then continued with the *venite,* the Psalms, the first lesson, the first canticle, the second lesson, the second canticle, and the *benedictus*. During the prayers of intercession, I remembered Gordon and each one of my children, especially Eunice, whom I hoped would someday sing her beautiful songs in a church such as this.

I did not mind that this was an Episcopal church, far from my theological roots. Over the years, I had learned to appreciate the other Christian denominations. Although I recognized the differences, I saw the value and purpose in other theological perspectives, even when I did not necessarily agree with them. While not entirely familiar with the history of the Episcopal Church, I understood it had originated from the Anglican Church, the Church of England.

Later I learned the Anglican Church split away from the Catholic Church during the Reformation, like other protestant denominations. However, the Anglicans retained many of the Catholic traditions, and for that reason, became known as the *via media*, or middle way, between the Roman Catholic Church and other protestant denominations. After the Revolutionary War, the Anglican Church in America adopted the Episcopal name, which signifies its retention of bishops.

My theological roots are a far different story. I was a product of my parents' Inner Mission Lutheran theology, an artifact of the Great Awakening, a religious movement that swept across Northern Europe and North America in the eighteenth and nineteenth centuries. Here the ultimate authority was the Holy Scripture, believed to be the actual word of God, to be interpreted literally and given precedence over all other religious texts and truths. The Lutheran Church in Ringsted, where I was confirmed, was founded by Inner Mission Danes.

During my lifetime, I shifted from the pietistic Inner Mission tradition toward a more ecumenical theology, and it was that transformation which enabled me to become fully engaged in the worship experience at St. Thomas Church. Indeed, that service enabled me to worship God more fully than ever before.

Upon the invitation to kneel, however, I remained seated according to my Lutheran tradition. In the silence that followed, I confessed my sins and humbly besought God's forgiveness and mercy. I joined in reciting the general confession: *Almighty and most merciful Father, we have erred and strayed from thy ways like lost sheep . . .*

How true this was for me during the dark days surrounding my first nervous breakdown. What folly, pinning my hopes on an unattainable boyfriend. In some ways, too, my pietistic beliefs may actually have contributed to my breakdown. Instead of trusting in God to forgive me, I believed that He had turned against me because I had sinned, which only compounded my despair.

At the time, I was a relative newcomer to the Rose Creek area. My main social support came from family members. After moving to Toeterville, a very small town with little social life, my isolation only intensified. Worse yet, I also suffered from a lack of wise counsel from professionals and mentors, who might have helped me before my condition got out of hand.

In retrospect, however, I see a silver lining in my painful breakdown because of two eventual outcomes. First was my conversion to a more lenient theology. Second was my marriage to Gordon, the shy farmer from Kasson, who eased into the void left by Kenley Boyum. Our marriage produced eleven beautiful children and a lifetime of memories.

12

Marriage and Family, 1949-1958

Gordon earned his place in my heart. The letters he sent me in Arizona helped soothe the pain of Kenley's rejection. I began to view Gordon differently, choosing to focus on his strengths rather than his shortcomings. He was a good Christian man. He was steady, hardworking, and very dependable.

Beginning with spring thaw, through the end of fall harvest, Gordon was up at five a.m. each day. He worked all day till after sundown, except, of course, on Sunday. At age twenty-seven he still lived with his parents, Ole and Lily Gunderson. He worked Ole's eighty acre farm in addition to the eighty acres he rented. It had been Gordon's childhood dream to become a farmer. He had minimal skill and little interest in the carpentry trade of his father. After graduating from the eighth grade, Gordon followed his dream and went to work for a neighboring farmer to learn the business of farming.

Lean, five-foot-nine, and good looking, Gordon had a dark complexion and nearly black hair. Shyness was his most noticeable character trait around others. Social skills were not well modeled by his reserved and stoical father. On the farm, however, his penchant for hard work was Gordon's distinguishing attribute, a quality well modeled by Ole and a necessary asset in successful farming. Despite his limited education, Gordon had a gift for numbers, which he often used in his farming business, computing arithmetic complexities in his head with ease.

To fully understand Gordon, it is helpful to know a little history regarding his parents. Ole moved with Lily to Minnesota from Alberta in 1924 when Gordon was two years old. They settled near Kasson on the

Gunderson family farm, where Ole had grown up and lived before moving to Canada in 1912. Ole was a gifted carpenter much like his Norwegian immigrant father Knud. While homesteading in Alberta, Ole raised horses on his land and practiced his trade, building barns and houses for other prairie settlers. In his spare time he enjoyed dancing at the town hall, where he met Lily Davie, a lovely Scotch-Irish farm girl fifteen years his junior. The two became somewhat of a local sensation on the dance floor. Eventually, Lily became pregnant out of wedlock and a December wedding was planned. Ole and Lily were married in Edmonton four months before Gordon arrived.

After sowing his wild oats on the plains of Alberta, Ole returned to Minnesota with his young family to care for his aging uncle Jorgen and to claim his inheritance, the eighty acre farm. Not long after returning to Kasson, Lily became pregnant again and in 1925 gave birth to Lorraine, which completed the family Ole and Lily would raise in this staunch Norwegian Lutheran community. The Gunderson farm was six miles southeast of Kasson in the Zumbro River drainage west of Rochester.

The social hub of this rural community is South Zumbro Lutheran Church, named after the river a mile or two south. This church was part of the Hauge Lutheran Synod, the Norwegian counterpart of the Inner Mission movement in America. Ole Bergh, the first pastor at South Zumbro, was actually a disciple of Hans Hauge, the founder of the pietistic Hauge Movement in Norway. In 1885, the year before Ole Bergh retired, Knud and Martha Gunderson left Norway to settle on a farm near South Zumbro. Their son Ole was born in 1887. Throughout Ole's childhood, Bergh continued preaching occasionally at South Zumbro.

The Christian zeal Bergh brought to the South Zumbro community, which failed to captivate Ole in his youth, was the pietistic crucible into which he returned to raise his family. Like Ole, Gordon was at first unmoved by the pietism and lived, in his words, a somewhat ungodly existence, which included occasional visits to the tavern. At the age of twenty, however, Gordon experienced a powerful and blissful conversion.Where Ole Gunderson remained a willing observer, Gordon became a devout born-again Christian and a stalwart believer in the Inner Mission theology brought to South Zumbro by Ole Bergh.

Marriage and Family, 1949–1958

When Pearl introduced me to Gordon, I was unimpressed but not altogether disinterested. He was as good looking as Kenley Boyum but painfully bashful and ill-at-ease around women. For some reason, I always felt more drawn to sociable and outgoing men, especially the better educated ones. Even though he was a devout Lutheran active in my Christian youth community, Gordon did not originally strike me as one who would be more than just a friend. Maybe I mistook his shyness for lack of depth. Perhaps his social awkwardness repelled me.

After the nervous breakdown, however, my attitude toward Gordon began to change. I was grateful for the gifts and letters he sent me while I was ill. It never seemed to bother him that I had been mentally incapacitated. Actually he seemed even more interested in me. In one of his letters Gordon suggested I read the book *My Nervous Breakdown*, by Reverend Anton Cedarholm. Gordon had read the book and seemed to understand my experience of anxiety and depression. "A nervous breakdown is not insanity," he assured me. Upon my return from Arizona, I was looking forward to seeing Gordon and getting to know him better.

Beyond Gordon, my options seemed limited. The doctor had discouraged my return to teaching, as if teaching had anything to do with my breakdown. My self-esteem and social cachet had dropped to an all-time low. With little hope for rebuilding my career, social standing, and shattered self-image, I felt there was no alternative but to work at home and welcome Gordon's pursuit. So I began to do the things I knew well: farm work, house work, and letters to Gordon. At first I was noncommittal and cautious because I still carried a small flame for Kenley. His church pastor contacted me to ask if I would teach vacation Bible school again. My parents, however, were opposed to any activity that would bring me back into contact with Kenley.

In friendly letters to Gordon, I had reported the details of my treatment and the progress of my condition, replete with the bitterness of my self-contempt. I continued to warn him about my darker side which, if he ever saw it, would send him running. For instance on April 4th I wrote, *I shouldn't judge by outward appearances, at least I hope no one judges me that way, for they would come to a horrible conclusion. Much worse though if they saw the inside! I am glad no one can!* On April 25 I wrote,

100

I got the impression that perhaps you have a better opinion of me than you should have. I'm afraid when you really get to know me, if you ever do, you will be greatly disappointed.

Gordon kindly brushed these self-aspersions aside with complimentary rebuttals and reassurances. From the time we met, so he claimed, he had known I was meant for him. No warning or bitter failure on my part could discourage him.

We began seeing each other shortly after my return from Arizona. Soon I was writing him wordy epistles on everything from theology to housework. Gradually these evolved into long rhapsodic love letters, and sometime in May my closings shifted from "sincerely" to "lovingly."The man who previously held so little appeal for me had become my mortal savior and soul mate.

During the seven month period from March to October, we sent each other seventy letters. Gordon's letters were usually brief, rarely more than one page; mine averaged over six pages each. Expressing his recognition of this, Gordon lamented on May 26, *Oh, I wish I could write about 3 times as much in about 1/3 the time. I wish too that I had been more studious in English and grammar.*

Other than seeing Gordon, the summer of 1949 held little excitement for me. Mostly I stayed close to home and helped my parents on the farm. Among other things, I grew and harvested 1000 pounds of potatoes on a half-acre plot, and I raised 200 leghorns (chickens) for market. Gordon came to visit me every Sunday afternoon, and I looked forward to his visits. On June 12 he proposed, and I readily accepted. The next morning, however, I felt troubled. My Dad noticed I was preoccupied. "What's on your mind, Mary?" he asked.

"Gordon asked me to marry him last night, and now I feel confused."

"Mary, this is wonderful. What are you confused about?"

"I accepted his proposal, but today I am filled with doubts. Maybe I answered too soon. Maybe I don't love him well enough yet."

Dad, who was practically in love with Gordon himself, said, "Even the best lovers have doubts. You must pray and seek God's will. If He doesn't want you to marry Gordon, He will fill you with disturbances and you will know it is not meant to be."

"But, Dad, are my doubts not disturbances?"

"I can only advise you to pray about it and give it more time. If you are disturbed about marrying him, it will become clear."

I took Dad's advice, praying and mulling it over. By the next day, I felt more confident about my decision, convinced that Gordon was the right one for me. From beneath the doubt and fear arose an irrepressible certainty, welling up in my heart, and before the week was over Gordon gave me a diamond ring. Full of anticipation, I never seriously looked back after that. The rest of the summer and into the fall, I was deeply happy and busy planning the wedding and accumulating the necessities of independent living.

Gordon and I were married on October 16, 1949. The wedding was at Zion Lutheran Church, three miles north of Dexter, my home church for the previous two years. Gordon's sister Lorraine was maid of honor; my friend Phyllis was the bridesmaid; Lorraine's husband Wallace was best man; Martin was the groomsman. John and Lou had already gone to the mission field in Bolivia and were not present at the wedding. Before leaving in August, they sold us their trailer house, which became our first home after a four day honeymoon to the North Shore of Lake Superior.

We parked the trailer house in the yard behind Ole and Lily's farmhouse. Heated by kerosene, it was about twenty feet long, eight feet wide, and looked like an oversized silver toaster. As small and humble as it was, it was just what we needed, a cozy love nest during our first year of marriage. I helped Gordon with farm chores during the day. We cuddled happily together at night. If I could no longer have a school full of pupils, then I was determined to have a house full of children, and toward that end Gordon was completely agreeable. I was pregnant by the end of the first month.

Our first year together was highlighted by the birth of Elaine Esther in August. She was a beautiful baby, if a little temperamental. Along with the joy of motherhood came a host of related issues. In caring for her, I discovered the clash of parenting styles between Gordon and me. In general he was loving toward Elaine. Raised by strict disciplinarians, however,

Gordon disciplined his own child with similar severity. I was horrified when he carried Elaine, nine months old, out of church and spanked her for fussing. My inclination was to cuddle, comfort, and breast feed my baby when she fussed. Instead, I was told to put her on a strict four hour feeding schedule and to let her cry at night. Owing to Dr. Spock, this was the prevailing wisdom on infant care. Gordon warned, "Holding and comforting Elaine when she cries will only encourage the bad behavior and spoil her." Despite the painful learning curve and difficult adjustments in the marital relationship, I enjoyed my beautiful baby Elaine.

In addition to our difference in parenting style, I discovered other differences as well, which I suppose is common for newlyweds. Though we were both frugal, Gordon had control of the purse strings, and his priorities differed from mine. If I was frugal in regard to home improvements, he was parsimonious. Gordon took frugality to a whole new level, particularly when it involved expenditures for the house and home, just like my father during the Depression.

One year after our wedding, we bought the old Boyum place two miles away. With eighty-five acres, it had a large four-bedroom, two-story house with a walkout basement. There had been a fire in the basement, and the house had not been used in four years. We worked like galley slaves, cleaning up the smoke damage and making the house livable again. I often wondered if the hard labor, working on that house in grimy conditions, contributed to the miscarriage I had six months after Elaine was born.

On our east property line was a small creek, which cut a narrow winding trench through a small valley. The buildings were set into the side of the valley and surrounded by big oak trees, which gave the place charm and beauty. The modest barn was well sized for the dairy herd Gordon was raising. The amenities, however, were more than offset by several drawbacks: no electrical service, no corn crib, and no plumbing in the house. To make matters worse, the driveway was a mere wagon trail, which followed the creek a quarter mile out to the nearest road. Adding a serviceable driveway was a top priority.

That this was a fixer-upper might have been an understatement. Yet the land was affordable, fertile, and picturesque. We plowed a garden plot close to the house, and I was able to grow and preserve much of our food. To keep up with the heavy work load, Gordon toiled from dawn to dusk, making improvements, building up his dairy herd, and raising crops. He got help from both his father and mine to construct a new driveway, a bridge, and a corncrib. We spent $500 putting in electrical service but went without plumbing in the house. The only well was down by the barn and water had to be carried in pails uphill to the house.

My parents loved visiting us and spending time with Elaine. But it was a long drive from their house, which limited the frequency of their visits. I think they were lonesome at home. The year after Elaine was born, they sold their place at Rose Creek and moved to a small farm near Kasson. After that they came to visit more often.

Between caring for Elaine and working on the house and garden, I had little time for helping Gordon in the field. With the ceaseless work, it seemed the romance had gone out of our marriage. The courtship and honeymoon were a distant memory. Nevertheless, it was not long before I became pregnant again, and in July of 1952, David Mark was born. The necessity of caring for two children kept me even more confined to the house and yard while Gordon, without my help, was more confined to the barn and fields. He often went to his parents' house and sometimes took Elaine, who loved her grandma Lily. Evidently, Lily used these opportunities to advise Gordon on matters of housekeeping and child care. I recognized her influence in the suggestions he made like spanking the children and yelling "No! No!" to keep them away from things they weren't supposed to touch.

I worked as hard as Gordon and had nearly as much experience in farming, yet I was not treated as an equal partner in our farming business. Lorraine did our accounting and taxes, and it seemed like she and Lily had more influence on the strategic decisions than I did. One day Gordon told me Lily had opposed our marriage because I had a nervous breakdown. This really hurt. To make matters worse, I felt relegated to the position of servant and housekeeper while my ideas on everything else were ignored if not ridiculed. Feeling outmaneuvered and powerless, I stuffed my anger and began to withdraw from Gordon. I tried to sublimate the resentment into my work. And here is where the story takes a nasty turn as fate was about to deliver an unexpected blow.

In September 1952 my world was shaken by the sudden illness and death of my brother Martin. The polio epidemic, which plagued the nation for a whole decade, was reaching its terrible climax in Minnesota. It came to take one of our own, two full years before Dr. Salk developed the polio vaccine. Martin had held a sick child at church and fell ill a few days later. He entered the hospital with the diagnosis of polio and died four days later. I was stunned. Gordon and I had just been up to visit Martin and Pauline in Minneapolis two weeks earlier. Their two year old boy Nathan was the same age as Elaine, and we enjoyed watching them play together.

No other person was as dear to me as Martin. He was my only sibling left in Minnesota, and above all others, he was the most supportive of me and understood me the best. Grief stricken, I began a downward spiral after the funeral. Gordon tried to console me, but I was still angry at him over his earlier transgressions. Tormented by a persistent anxiety, I was inconsolable and unable to sleep, which resulted in my second nervous breakdown. One day I completely fell apart. Gordon shook me and pleaded, "Mary, get a hold of yourself."

When I stopped speaking to him, he called my parents over in alarm. I overheard my dad telling Gordon, "She's just like her mother."

"I want a divorce," I scowled.

"But Mary," my mother reasoned, "Gordon is such a good man."

My anger toward Gordon had built to an intolerable level. It fused with my grief, and I had no ability to articulate it. I stonewalled, and of course, Gordon was not even aware of what it was about. Simply put, I did not know how to express my indignation. Each day I withdrew, more resentment was added to my load of bitterness. I became exhausted and confused without sleep. At wits end, Gordon took me St. Mary's Hospital in Rochester. When he returned to visit the following day, I refused to acknowledge him and acted like he wasn't there.

Later I called Gordon at home and asked him to take me to Glenwood Hills Sanitarium in Minneapolis where a friend of mine had gone for help. He agreed and took me there a few days later at no small sacrifice. To pay for my three week stay, Gordon sold his tractor and the corn picker. His parents and mine became temporary caretakers for little David and Elaine.

At Glenwood Hills I was treated with insulin shock therapy, one of the popular treatments for mental illness at the time. This was before the discovery of a statistically significant mortality rate associated with repeated insulin shock and mental recovery rates no better than those who had no treatment at all. Like the doctor, I was oblivious to this reality. I only knew that I was seriously ill and did not want to go home. The insulin treatments were similar to the electric shock (ECT) in one sense: I was put on a padded platform with side rails. Several attendants in white lab coats stood on each side of me as the doctor injected me with insulin. Gradually I went to sleep, or lost consciousness, and then into a coma for one hour. An injection of glucose was administered to restore me to consciousness. This was repeated each day for two weeks.

The true healing force at Glenwood Hills came with my ability to sleep. Sedated, I went to sleep easily, which could have been achieved at home, of course, with the same prescription of sleep medication. Another outcome of the hospitalization came as a result of Gordon's reaction when I began to communicate. He was surprised to find that I felt mistreated by him. Because I was unable to communicate my grievances when they occurred, he had not known I felt this way.

With my disillusionment sufficiently in the open, Gordon bent over backward to regain my esteem. I wrote him a few encouraging letters when my equilibrium returned. He came to visit me on the weekend and wrote back every other day to report his daily activities with David and Elaine. Before long I was ready to go home and resume my household and parenting responsibilities. I accepted my lot in life and resolved to adapt myself to Gordon, to forget my romantic illusions, and to find joy and meaning in life through my children, home, and music. And Gordon tried to be more sensitive to my needs and feelings.

After their move to Kasson, my parents lived just six miles away, and they often came over to see us. How I loved to see them drive in. Better yet, they offered to care for David and Elaine while I went off to play my accordion in a local string band.

Elaine and I continued to develop a close relationship. She was perceptive and very bright; she talked constantly and became a great companion and a reliable helper. She entertained David by the hour and reported his every move, and she asked a million questions. My communication with Elaine was exceptional, but I still withheld my views from Gordon because I felt they were not given due consideration. I detested his superior attitude and his cynical responses. The concern he showed during my recovery gradually faded. Adding insult to injury, I overheard disparaging comments from his family regarding my nervous breakdown.

Maybe it was something I gained at Glenwood Hills that helped me live with the discord. Maybe it was the closer proximity to my parents, or the new kitchen flooring Gordon installed, or the new kitchen stove he bought. Whatever the reason, I was able to lighten up and stay committed to Gordon, and before long I was pregnant again. Ernest Michael was born in December of 1953. He was a big beautiful baby with a wonderful sweet smile. In nursing him I found an excuse to sit and rest. I loved all three of my children and was very proud of them. Gordon and my parents loved the children too. Unfortunately, fate was about to deliver another blow.

One day my mother called in a fright. "There's something wrong with Dad. Come over quickly!" she cried.

We jumped in the car and rushed over to find Dad moaning in pain. He became delirious and started vomiting. We called an ambulance, and he was taken to St. Mary's Hospital in Rochester where he lay in critical condition for several days. Gradually he stabilized and regained strength, but the stroke had paralyzed his right side, and he was unable to speak. After eleven days in the hospital, we brought him to our home where we had prepared a small apartment for him and my mother. Gordon graciously accepted the responsibility of helping me care for my parents in our home. What else could we do? There seemed to be no other choice. But we had no idea how much work it would be.

The worst problem was the lack of plumbing. To avoid cold trips to the outhouse, we used a so-called chemical toilet in the back porch. With my parents in the house and three children, Gordon had to carry out the toilet "pail" every day. Several more times each day he carried in pails of water from the well down by the barn. Because of the money we had already spent on improvements, we could not afford to add plumbing. Moreover, we had not made a taxable profit in five years, despite all of our hard work. We earned enough money to pay the bills and the interest on the farm loan but not enough to make any payment on the principle. Therefore, our lender began applying pressure on Gordon to pay up on the principal as specified in the promissory note.

For a year and a half longer we toiled to keep up our farm payment and care for my parents. My dad began moving about on crutches and regained his speech. I became pregnant again and gave birth to Margaret Ann in February of 1955. Thanks to Mother's help in caring for Margaret, I was able to carry on with the cleaning, gardening, canning, and baking. However, Gordon became increasingly discouraged with the situation. He could not see that the farm, with only 70 acres of tillable land, would ever produce enough profit for us to get ahead. Frankly, too, I think Gordon was tired of dealing with my parents who had become much too intrusive for him, and he began to think about moving. One day Pauline's nephew Lloyd stopped by and told us about some attractive farming opportunities in northwestern Minnesota, Lloyd's neck of the woods. He was on his way home to visit his parents and invited us to come along with him and check out the possibilities.

There comes a time for risky choices in every man's life; some are successful, and some meet with failure, sometimes costly failure. Maybe it was Gordon's time, for I had learned to keep my opinions to myself and let Gordon make the important decisions. I was willing to support whatever he wanted to do. We called it a vacation and asked my parents to care for the three older ones while Gordon, baby Margaret, and I headed north with Lloyd. I mainly wanted to visit Pearl and her husband Harold, who was interning as a Lutheran pastor near Thief River Falls. As fate would have it, we found a nice farm for rent eight miles east of town. It was 240 acres of level ground, nearly all tillable. Gordon seized the moment and made the decision to move.

At home the decision was met with shock and disbelief. My parents felt they were being abandoned. Gordon's parents and sister felt it would be a costly mistake, but Gordon was undeterred. He had had enough. He listed our farm for sale in the fall of 1955 and sold it back to the previous owner for a tidy profit. Around that time, we also discovered I was pregnant again.

We convinced my anxious and disgruntled parents to move to Arizona where they could live by Esther and Harold, who owned a rental house next door. Even though Hans and Anna had hoped to retire in Arizona one day, they were hurt and filled with anxiety about the turn of events. After a farewell party at church, we drove them to Owatonna and put them on the train, crutches and all. Mother clung to little Ernie and Margaret, for they had become very attached. Gordon crated and shipped some of their belongings, too, which they needed for their little house in Glendale. It was a pitiful sight as the train rolled slowly away with my bewildered parents waving goodbye.

The rest of their things along with many of ours were sold at the farm auction. In early April, we loaded our remaining possessions into a truck and drove four hundred miles with our children to Thief River Falls. When we left Kasson, farmers were already in the fields planting their grain crops. Upon our arrival in northwestern Minnesota, we were surprised and disillusioned to find the fields still frozen under a sheet of ice. The previous tenants had not yet moved because of flooding, so we spent our first days at Pearl and Harold's house until our farm was vacated. The buildings were left in a terrible mess. We spent weeks cleaning out the house and barn. Gordon bought more cattle, some hay, and machinery and set up his repair shop while he waited for the fields to dry. He planted the grain crops eventually but not before swarms of mosquitoes arrived. The pesky bugs plagued us all summer. But they didn't dampen the highlight, which was the birth of Kenneth Gordon in August of 1956.

Determined to make a success of the new venture, we worked hard and made significant progress that summer. I fixed up the house, planted a garden, kept the lawn mowed, and did my usual canning. The children played in the yard and entertained themselves. It would be ten more years before we could afford a television set.

We realized the oat crop would be a failure when it rained for three weeks just after swathing. The oats mostly rotted in the field, and the flax wasn't much better. Our crop failure was mitigated by the fact that the rent was based on a one third share of the crop. At least we did not have to pay full rent on top of the crop loss. Fortunately, the cows began calving in the fall, and the monthly milk check helped pay the bills.

To make a long story short, things went from bad to worse that winter. We weren't entirely prepared for the cold temperatures which arrived in November. The neighbors up there barely winced at thirty below zero, which was the temperature on the night of the children's Christmas program at Elaine's school. The program was well attended in spite of the cold.

In January it got even colder. When the well froze, we were unable to get water for our cattle. The landlord told us it was our problem to fix. Gordon tried in vain to get the well thawed and the pump working but to no avail. On a cold day in January, he gave up the struggle and called a cattle buyer. Our cows were shipped the next day.

In the dead of winter, with money in the bank and no livestock or field work, we decided to take a vacation. It seemed like a perfect time to visit my parents in Arizona. We drove to Owatonna and got on the same train my parents took a year earlier. In a state of utter defeat we headed for warmth and a family reunion, just the tonic we needed. The trip was a great adventure. The children loved riding the train. Just six months old, Kenny was still nursing, but easy to manage.

It was a wonderful reunion when Esther met us at the train depot. My parents were overjoyed to see us. They had survived the move to Arizona and were enjoying their little house in Glendale, a suburb of Phoenix. Esther and Harold, who lived next door, welcomed us into their home. Their boys Jonathan and Danny were the same ages as David and Elaine, and their baby Bruce was four months old. We crowded into the two homes and spent ten glorious days in the warmth and sun. Harold took us sightseeing at Mingus Mountain and the Painted Desert, and one day he let us use his car for a drive to South Mountain. All too soon our vacation was over. It was a long lonely trip back to Minnesota.

"Winter should be about over when we get back," Gordon predicted.

It was still twenty below zero and the heating oil had jelled. The house was so cold the potatoes had frozen in the basement. Gordon's determination to succeed in Thief River was gone. He drove to Kasson for his uncle Gunder's funeral and came back Easter Sunday with good news. "I found a construction job in Kasson," he reported.

We hired an auctioneer, sold our machinery, and moved back to Kasson in the spring of 1957. There we rented a farm house not far from the old Boyum place. The house, which had been freshly papered and repainted, was also owned by a Boyum family. We called it the new Boyum place.

It was a transitional move. We lived on the new Boyum place for just one year. Gordon had spent most of the $7000 he had taken to Thief River, and now he was willing to labor ten hours a day on a construction job to save for another down payment. Employed by the McFadden Construction Company, Gordon was put to work on a new school building in West Concord. He did not enjoy the work, but we sorely needed the money. The hardest part for Gordon was comparing himself to his peers, who by then had become well established and quite successful on their farms. He was reminded of this every time we drove through our old neighborhood. Decades would pass before Gordon forgave himself for leaving the old Boyum farm. As for me, I settled into the rental house, cared for the children, planted a big garden, and did all the usual canning.

Meanwhile our family kept growing. Carol JoAnn was born in August, 1957. Kenny was only one year old when Carol was born so he was not the baby very long. He slept in his brown crib by the kitchen stove. Carol's little white crib was in the downstairs bedroom. Margaret and Elaine slept upstairs in the little bedroom. David and Ernie shared the big bedroom upstairs with Gordon and me. I could usually hear when a baby cried downstairs. When I went down in the morning, Kenny was jumping up and down in his crib all happy and excited to see me. I changed his diaper, put him in the high-chair, and then tended to Carol.

Things went well until one day Kenny fell out of the high chair and broke his leg. He wore a cast for six weeks. A few weeks later, Margaret fell off the teeter totter and broke her arm. That November my father had another stroke in Arizona. He lay in critical condition for eleven days in the hospital. The day he died, Pastor Stensland came by to tell us the news. I could only imagine what the funeral was like. How scared and lonely my mother must have been.

That Christmas we celebrated by ourselves, but the following day Anders and Ingeborg drove in with toys for each of the children. I think people felt sorry for us and took pity. One Sunday, Pastor Stensland preached a sermon about a poor family that thrived despite the lack of money. He summed it up like this: "When God's love is alive in the family and the surrounding community, poverty need not be pitiful." Deep down I knew he was talking about us. He must have heard the talk about our financial woes.

One thing Gordon and I had appreciated about living up north was our feeling of independence, both in the community and among our extended family. Back in Kasson we felt judged about our lack of financial success and birth control. For this reason we were inclined to head north again when it came time to find a new farm. Moreover, we had discovered land was less expensive farther north. In the spring of 1958 Gordon found a one hundred acre farm available for $10,000 near Rush City in east central Minnesota. Two years earlier we had sold the eighty-five acre Boyum place for $10,500, so the Rush City farm seemed like a reasonable bargain. Better yet, Gordon found a job at the state hospital in Cambridge, twelve miles away, which would provide us with income until we could get better established in farming. For the third time in as many years we packed up all our belongings to move across the state.

A silver lining to our failure at Thief River was the serendipitous discovery that our marital relationship was more cohesive and satisfying without frequent involvement of our well-meaning in-laws. Looking forward to a new beginning, we departed with our children and belongings for the little farm near Rush Lake, our home and subsistence for the next sixteen years.

13

Bread and Wine

Howard Stringfellow, tall and youthful looking, stepped into the carved oak pulpit elevated on a marble pedestal. That day the reverend was preaching on Paul's letter to the Romans. He began in a somber tone:

> Life on this earth is filled with challenges. One challenge that we all are familiar with is that of learning how to accept that every aspect of life is a mixture of good and evil, of pure and impure. Take for example the natural seasons of the earth—winter, spring, summer, fall—and the beauty, comfort and gifts for life which each brings. Yet, within the earth and within the same seasons are forces which may wreak such havoc, destruction and death as to eliminate entire populations or affect their lives for generations.
>
> Take human institutions, for another example, be they commercial, religious, public or private. Generally, they have been created for the protection and common good of society. Yet, because of the mixed motives of the people involved, these very institutions often become the source of much human degradation, suffering and death.
>
> Actually, we don't have to go outside of ourselves to find an example. Our own purest motives get contaminated by motives that are not so pure, and we experience the conflict between good and evil in our personal actions in relation to self and others. As St. Paul puts it in the letter to the Romans, ". . . when I want to do what is good, evil lies close at hand . . ."

Reverend Stringfellow was not like the strict Bible preacher to whom I was accustomed, but I could relate to this mix of good and evil, pure and impure. I recalled several times, for example, when our crops were ruined by hail or early frost or stunted by drought, yet often we were blessed with bumper crops. Indeed, Gordon and I had enjoyed many blessings and endured many hardships. We lived hand-to-mouth the first ten years of our marriage, suffering through several moves and setbacks, like echoes from the past.

The reverend finished his sermon and stepped from the pulpit. The choir rose to sing an offertory anthem while the offering plates were passed and carried to the altar. I remained seated during the celebration of the Eucharist. In my Missouri Synod Lutheran tradition, only confirmed members of the church are welcome to partake of the bread and wine, and I was not familiar with the Episcopal tradition.

Placing his hands over the bread and wine, the reverend recited from Matthew, Chapter 26:

> For in the night in which he was betrayed, he took the bread. And when he had given thanks, he broke it and gave it to his disciples, saying, 'Take, eat, this is my body, which is given for you. Do this in remembrance of me.' Likewise, after supper, he took the cup, and when he had given thanks, he gave it to them, saying, 'Drink this all of you, for this is my blood of the new covenant, which is shed for you . . .'"

My Lutheran forefathers rejected the Catholic doctrine of transubstantiation, but I had no idea where the Episcopalians stood on this issue. The notion that bread and wine are miraculously converted in substance to the actual body and blood of Christ is not my belief, even if Reverend Stringfellow's words—taken verbatim from Matthew—might suggest this is true.

Accustomed to controversies in biblical interpretation, however, I am not one to argue over these details. Yet, I am solidly committed to the basic tenets of Christianity and believe wholeheartedly that Jesus was both Son of God and son of man. I believe that God in heaven was the Father of Jesus, and the Virgin Mary was impregnated by His Holy Spirit. I believe that Jesus suffered and died on the cross to save the rest of us from eternal damnation and that his crucifixion by the Roman authorities was God's divine plan for our redemption and salvation. In addition to Jesus the Christ, I believe that God is also manifest in the Holy Spirit, which lives and moves in us and among us. This trinity of God the Father, Jesus Christ the Son of God, and the Holy Spirit is the essence and centerpiece of my theology. My steadfast faith in God is the foundation of my existence.

The congregants moved into the aisles and went slowly forward to receive the sacrament of Holy Communion. Reverend Stringfellow gave each one a small wafer of bread and a sip of wine. "The body of Christ given for you. The blood of Christ shed for you," he proclaimed.

I sat quietly enjoying the glorious choral anthems by the St. Thomas choir, which accompanied the celebration of the Eucharist. Ever since my childhood, especially since my confirmation, I have believed the sacraments of Holy Communion and baptism, along with prayer and the Holy Scriptures, are the primary means of receiving God's grace. Indeed, it was through the strict observance of these beliefs that I managed to cope with the stress and losses in my life.

In the presence of God, that day, I remembered these losses and prayed for God's mercy on my loved ones who had long since departed. I especially remembered Elaine, who seemed both blessed and cursed and who died so young and left me with so much heartache. I visualized our farm near Rush City where Elaine flourished briefly and then floundered during her short and troubled life.

14

Blessed and Cursed, 1958-1973

Nestled among rolling hills and eskers west of Rush City, between the east and west lobes of the largest lake in Chisago County, lay the one hundred acre farm that was our destination. Rush Lake as well as the nearby town took their names from the bulrush, or cattail, which grows in profusion along the edges of the lake and its outlet.

On the first of June, 1958, the truck that held all of our possessions rumbled behind us. We drove slowly up the gravel "point" road, which bisects the broad peninsula between East and West Rush Lake. Turning east we followed a dirt road downhill past two small ponds, then uphill to the sandy driveway which led to our new home. It was a white two-story farmhouse huddled among mature trees and a weathered collection of red farm buildings. To the east and south lay an expanse of sandy loam fields. To the west stood a dense woodlot of old-growth white pines, maples, oaks and elms. It was a slice of paradise amid a semi-wilderness of pothole lakes and forested hills.

Our move had been delayed so that Elaine could finish her second year of school at Kasson. Gordon had already gone to start his job at Cambridge State Hospital a week earlier. With a full time job, he would not be able to manage crops and a dairy herd until the boys were old enough to help. We opted to put our land in the "soil-bank," a federal program that paid farmers to idle their land for five years. This allowed us to buy machinery as we could afford it and gradually build up our dairy herd. Gordon had only to mow the fields each year before the weeds went to seed. By this time we were well aware of the Herculean effort required to get a farm up and running and well aware of the risks. Far from the helping

116

hands of our relatives, we started anew without the substantial bankroll we had at Thief River. It would be several years before the older boys were big enough to help with the farm work.

I liked our new home and went right to work. Gordon had budgeted $100 to buy paint, wallpaper and supplies to fix up the house. Each day I put Margaret in the playpen, Kenny in the stroller, Carol in the jumper, and then rolled up my sleeves and went to work. Elaine served reliably as my baby sitter. David and Ernie took turns pushing the old rotary mower around the yard to keep the grass cut, and they helped their father cut and stack firewood for the winter. Indoors we had only the old chemical toilet, which Gordon emptied each day in the outhouse behind the garage.

Before long we were established in our new home and the neighborhood, and Gordon kept bringing home the paychecks. Elaine started third grade that fall in Rush City, and David started first grade. We attended First Lutheran Church, also in Rush City, and enrolled our children in the Sunday school there. Besides Sunday school, I gave them religious instruction at home, using my flannel board to illustrate the Bible stories.

One Sunday, as we got ready to leave for First Lutheran, a seven-mile drive, we could hear the church bell ringing at Calvary Lutheran a couple miles southwest of our farm. "We should go there sometime," said Gordon. "It's so much closer."

"I'm for that," I replied, "some of our neighbors go there too." After attending church in Rush City for two years, we transferred our membership to Calvary Lutheran, the country church near the village of Rush Point, where we stayed for many years.

Barely more than a crossroad two miles southwest of our farm, Rush Point had a general store where one could purchase groceries and gasoline as well as beer and bait for fishing on nearby Rush Lake. Calvary Lutheran, a brown-brick church, stands on a hill east of the store. The parishioners, including many of our neighbors, descended from Swedish settlers who populated the area with names like Johnson, Mattson, Lindstrom, Swanson, Danson, Fredin, Olson, Hjelm, Sandstrom, and Mell. They were not like the strict Norwegian Lutherans we had known around

Kasson. In fact, we were one of the most devout Christian families in the area. But we were poor and lived off the land, and in that important way, we fit in.

After paying the mortgage each month, there was only $260 left for the expenses of daily living. To make ends meet I planted a large garden and began deploying the children to hoe and harvest the bounty. We feasted all summer on vegetables from the garden, while canning, freezing, and preserving enough to get us through the winter. And, with little delay, more children arrived in annual succession. Eunice Collette was born in February of 1959, Marlon Ole in April of 1960, and Milton John in August of 1961. In the fall of 1961, we had five children enrolled in school at Rush City. Each morning they rode the school bus seven miles to town and back home again in the afternoon.

About the time Marlon was born, Gordon began milking cows again, as David was eight years old and big enough to do chores once a day while Gordon was away at work. When seven heifers freshened that fall, Gordon installed a milk pump and bought a milking machine, which David learned to operate. It was a sorely needed financial boost when we began receiving milk checks. In 1962, however, money ran short again, and Gordon, who previously had refused government assistance, agreed to accept food stamps to keep enough food on the table.

After Milton was born, I had three babies in diapers, and life began to feel overwhelming again. In the wee hours one morning, Milton was awake and crying. I took him out of his little white crib, changed his diaper, and breast fed him in bed where we both fell asleep. Gordon got up at six and put Milton back in his crib. While Gordon was out doing chores, I got out of bed and began to prepare breakfast for eleven. At 7:00 a.m. I woke the children and called them to breakfast. While the other kids ate, I changed Marlon's diaper, put him in the high-chair, and fed him. Then I gave him a toy. Eunice woke up with sopping wet pants, so I changed her diaper also and held her briefly.

At 7:20 I issued the warning. "Hurry up kids! The bus is coming in ten minutes." Ideally they needed to be out the door by 7:25. "Elaine, what's the matter? You didn't eat your oatmeal." I broke up a fight between

Kenny and Carol and sent Kenny with the others to wait for the bus. The kitchen was a mess, and Carol was still crying. I held her and started cleaning up. Suddenly I realized Ernie had missed the bus.

"Run across the hayfield!" I yelled. "You can get on at Boese's corner."

"But I can't find my tablet," he whimpered.

"It's right where you left it in the dining room," I replied and hurried to get it. Ernie ran across the hayfield and got to Boese's corner just in time.

Gordon came in from the barn, and we ate our breakfast while watching the little ones. I dressed Marlon and Eunice while Carol dressed herself, and they all went outside to play. Gordon went out to do more work while I washed the breakfast dishes. Milton woke up, so I changed and fed him and laid him on the couch while I started preparing our noon meal. Suddenly I heard crying outside and went out to find the swing seat had hit Eunice on the head when Carol jumped off. I comforted Eunice and we all went back in the house to find Milton awake on the couch. Both Eunice and Carol wanted to hold him. Before long Gordon came in and asked, "Is lunch ready, Honey? I need to leave for work soon." His job in Cambridge started at one o'clock.

"It'll be on in a few minutes," I replied, holding Milton while I set the table. The children all sat down to eat, while I held Milton and Gordon fed Marlon in his high-chair. Eunice spilled her milk. Carol went to get a towel and punished her for making a mess. Marlon fell asleep in his high-chair, so Gordon put him on the couch before leaving for work. I got Eunice and Carol started on the dishes and then bathed Milton and laid him in the crib with a bottle of juice. Then I helped finish the dishes and put Eunice and Carol down for quiet time. I lay with them until they were asleep and then slipped quietly out to pick sweet corn and get the clothes off the line where they had hung since the last evening.

I was picking apples from under the tree when I heard Marlon crying. By the time I got in, all the kids were screaming, and so ended the quiet time. I attended to them, and one by one they stopped crying. Eunice and Carol went outside again. I put Milton in the swing and Marlon in the playpen and started making applesauce. Then I fried leftover meat and potatoes to go with the corn and applesauce. Soon the bus came and all the kids were home from school. We sat down to eat and listened to stories about the day's events, including how mean some kids had been on the bus and in the lunchroom.

After supper, Denny Nyblom came over to play with Kenny. Margaret did the dishes, and Elaine went out to pull Marlon and Milton in the wagon. David and Ernie went out to milk the cows and do chores while I cleaned the house. After sunset I played piano for a while, served the children a bedtime snack, and read them stories. I put Milton in his crib downstairs and went upstairs with the rest. When all were in bed and their clothes laid out for the following day, I went downstairs to clean up the kitchen and fold clothes. As I got ready for bed, Milton awoke and began to cry. I fixed him a bottle and sat with him in the rocking chair where we remained until Gordon came home from work.

One day that fall Gordon noticed that I was getting hyper after another night of little sleep. I was beginning to feel the same anxiety which twice before had engulfed me. This time Gordon took me to Rush City Hospital, where I convalesced from what Dr. Nelson diagnosed as nervous exhaustion. He treated me for low hemoglobin and prescribed sleep medication for badly needed rest. Most importantly, he gave me a listening ear and encouraging words, which boosted my flagging sense of self worth. "There is no need for any kind of shock treatment," he assured me, and I went home after eight days to resume the responsibilities of motherhood. Thanks to our neighbor Mrs. Amundson, an angel of mercy, my children were well tended in the interim.

Elaine seemed blessed and cursed. She excelled in school and had a very high aptitude for reading and writing. At age eleven she began writing a book. At first I had little concern about her isolation while she was writing in her room for long periods. She also wrote and directed plays in which she cast her younger siblings and neighbors. By sixth grade she was well on her way to mastering the piano. An A student in school, Elaine was also active in 4-H and in church. In 4-H she won the talent contest with her piano solo and won blue ribbons at the fair for her bread baking.

The book she began writing at age eleven turned into a twenty-eight chapter novel entitled *Three Years*, which was well written, interesting, and full of suspense. However, her intellectual and creative achievements could not conceal the emerging emotional and interpersonal problems that began to plague her in adolescence.

During the week of her fourteenth birthday, Elaine went to bible camp. She came home very disturbed, afraid that she was demon possessed. She thought we were all going to hell. The next day she came screaming down the stairs. "My room is red and orange!" she shrieked. "It's pure hell." Convinced that her room was hell, she could neither sleep at night nor concentrate during the day.

I called Dr. Nelson in Rush City. He referred me to the newly opened Braham Mental Health Clinic, where we went for an appointment right away. Elaine saw Dr. Ashley while I saw Dr. Williams and things began to improve. We continued this on a regular basis for nine months without significant disruption of Elaine's regular activities. Her hallucinations and delusional thinking subsided, and she continued to do well academically in school.

Seeking outlets for her creative energies, Elaine learned to play trombone and joined the high school band. She continued improving her piano skills and talked her father into purchasing a used violin. After a few lessons and a lot of practice, she learned to play it well enough to entertain the family. She continued writing stories, too, which she often read to her younger siblings. In addition to her music and writing, Elaine loved horses and could often be seen riding her mare Gypsy around the farm.

It was 1963 when our land came out of the soil bank. By then Ernie and David were old enough to drive the tractor and operate machinery. Gordon taught them to plow and disk the fields. He planted corn, soybeans, oats, and alfalfa. Ernie and David helped him clear more land. Gordon bought some pure-bred Holstein heifers from a local herdsman and began the long process of building a registered dairy herd.

At work, Gordon was promoted and got a raise. With the extra money, he bought some sows and went to work improving the old hog house. Before long, he was raising feeder pigs from the offspring. The boys, including Kenny, were quickly learning every aspect of the farming operation. The older they got, the more they worked. Gordon had the ambition to expand his farming operation and to keep his boys busy and challenged. When Gordon went off to his job, the boys carried on with the farm chores. They fed and milked the cows, tended the hogs, cleaned the barns, spread the manure, tilled the fields, and put up the hay.

Besides farm work, David, Ernie, and Ken each developed their own interests too. Gordon allowed the boys to purchase small caliber firearms, and they went off to the woods to hunt chipmunks and squirrels and eventually big game. David developed an interest in mechanics and built several go-carts before buying his own car at age fifteen. He and Ernie began taking part-time jobs, mowing lawns, and working for neighboring farmers. Ernie and Ken received bounty money from the township for trapping pocket gophers and made it a steady business in the spring and summer. With the income, they bought their first bicycles. David was interested in cars, motorcycles, and airplanes. Ernie favored camping, hunting, tree forts, swings, and sports. Ken liked to do whatever his brothers were doing, especially Ernie.

Meanwhile, I got pregnant after a two year respite and gave birth to Geoffrey George in November of 1964. Paula Marie, the eleventh and the last, arrived sixteen months later in March of 1966. The rest of our children were thriving too. With six boys and five girls, Gordon preferred to keep the work separate and specialized, so that the boys did most of the farm work and heavy labor, while the girls mostly did the house work, the cooking, cleaning, laundry, and child care. Although the girls settled for this arrangement, it was not without some resentment. They too wanted to drive the tractors and work with the animals. But the division of labor prevailed. Elaine, Margaret, and Carol all became adept at housework and childcare. When Milton, Marlon and Eunice were too young to contribute, they were happy participants and playmates whenever the older boys and girls included them in their activities.

All but the youngest children contributed to the gardening activities. In the late spring we planted a half acre of beans, corn, carrots, beets, cabbage, dill, peas, potatoes, radishes, cucumbers, rhubarb, squash, tomatoes, pumpkins, and watermelon. I planted a patch of strawberries in the middle and a variety of flowers along the edge, mostly marigolds, zinnias, and cosmos. The children specialized in certain areas such as picking peas, corn, and beans or digging potatoes, carrots, beets and radishes. All were expected to pick cucumbers, however, because we planted many rows which needed to be picked every day when ripening. I made dill pickles with some of them, but mostly we put the cucumbers into burlap bags, one hundred pounds each, and sold them at the sales barn for five dollars a bag.

When the produce reached maturity, harvesting and canning became a daily chore. I had a large pressure cooker and many dozens of quart jars. To fill all of them required the precision of an assembly line in the kitchen. One stood at the kitchen sink washing vegetables and several others were set up cutting and filling the jars, while I fastened the lids and operated the pressure cooker. The finished products were stored in rows on the basement shelves.

The apple trees we planted in 1958 were producing copiously by 1964. Besides canning the apples as they ripened, I frequently made apple pies, a big hit with Gordon and the children. During berry season the whole family went on the hay rack to pick berries. Gordon towed us on the tractor through woods and pasture to the thickets, where we picked raspberries and blackberries by the gallon. From these I made pies and berry jam to last the entire year.

The opportunities for recreation were virtually endless despite our limited financial resources. With several lakes nearby, swimming was a frequent summer ritual. We could choose among several beaches. The children took swimming lessons from an early age and became proficient swimmers. Ernie bought a used canoe and invited his brothers and friends to paddle down nearby creeks and rivers. In the wintertime the boys drove the car down snow-covered roads, pulling each other on skis and the younger kids on the toboggan. Before the snow got too deep, the nearest pond was shoveled clean for skating and nearby hills provided the children with ideal sledding opportunities. My children enjoyed these activities mostly on their own, and I worried occasionally about the potential for injuries. Other than the usual cuts, bruises and broken bones, however, none of them sustained life-threatening injuries.

In 1964 our financial situation had improved enough to remodel the house. We hired a carpenter to build new kitchen cabinets and install our first bathroom, complete with a steel tub and a flush toilet. In the back we added a porch with coat racks and in the front, a laundry room. We installed an oil burning boiler in the basement and baseboard heaters throughout the house. David and Ernie had saved enough money to buy a used television set, which they installed upstairs in their large bedroom. The whole family crowded into the boys' room to watch *Bonanza, Green Acres, Gomer Pyle,* and other favorites. Eventually, in need of privacy, they moved the television downstairs to the living room, where it stayed.

Upstairs there were four bedrooms. A hallway at the top of the stairs ran east and west. Down the hall to the left, the three older boys occupied the largest bedroom. Across the hall were two smaller bedrooms, one occupied by Elaine and the other by Milton and Marlon. The three younger girls occupied another large bedroom at the west end of the hallway. Gordon and I slept in the downstairs bedroom. Geoff and Paula slept in their cribs in the adjacent dining room. This was the arrangement in 1966 after Paula was born, which of course changed each successive year with the circumstances and necessities of our growing family.

As I mentioned before, Gordon and I had disagreed on the manner and severity of corporal punishment. Our children sometimes made trouble and needed to be disciplined. The punishment for swearing, for example, was washing out the child's mouth with soap. It was Gordon's belief that the children needed spankings for more serious misbehaviors. He kept a rubber hose hanging over the bathroom door and was capable of using it when necessary. Before he acquired the rubber hose, it was Gordon's practice to have the young offender fetch his or her own stick from outdoors, usually a sapling cut to a length of two or three feet. The spankings were made even more memorable by requiring the transgressor to pull down his pants allowing for a more stinging blow to the back side. After Elaine's first psychotic break, however, Gordon permanently ceased his practice of corporal punishment out of concern that it may have contributed to her emotional troubles. During one of her psychotic episodes, she had taken a stick on the school bus and threatened some of the neighbor kids.

Elaine continued to show signs of a troubled mind following her first psychosis, but otherwise she was physically healthy and attractive. Medium tall in stature, she had a beautiful face, deep blue eyes, long brown hair, and comely physique. Her behavior was unusual, however, and the close friends she kept before adolescence no longer desired her company. She was hurt by each rejection and became increasingly isolated as her peculiar behavior continued and worsened. Ernie noticed at school, for example, that she could be seen running alone at lunch hour to and from the stores on Main Street. This looked a little odd when her peers were strolling together in pairs or small groups. Two years after her first illness, Elaine's psychosis recurred. We took her to Dr. Nelson at Rush City Hospital, where she stayed for one week. After that she was able to resume her junior year in high school. She also resumed her counseling, driving herself each week to see Dr. Ashley at the Braham Mental Health Clinic.

When Elaine was a senior at Rush City, she set her sights on William and Mary College. The school counselor, however, who was familiar with her emotional troubles, discouraged the application and suggested she find something a little closer to home. Elaine was miffed. She insisted her grades would guarantee her qualification and refused to take no for an answer. She stayed up later and later at night to study. As I look back on it, there were other signs, too, of an impending relapse.

One evening Elaine walked over to see Billy Stich, a neighbor boy her age. Mrs. Stich came to the door and said, "Hello, Elaine, what can I do for you?"

"Is Billy home?"

"He's gone right now. Can I tell him what it's about?"

"I was wondering if he would want to go out with me."

By this time the whole neighborhood knew about Elaine's mental problems, and Mrs. Stich knew that Billy was not interested. "Elaine, I'm sorry," she said as kindly as possible. "Billy is not interested in dating you."

Elaine came home dejected and disconsolate. This kind of rejection had become all too familiar. Sometime after midnight, Gordon and I were awakened by Elaine pacing upstairs. I went to investigate and found her angry and agitated. "You're ruining my life!" she screamed. "Why do you always have to interfere?" She glared at me, her eyes flashing with hostility. Gordon came upstairs when he heard the commotion, and she began railing on him. As the other children began to stir, we tried to calm her and coax her down the stairs. When Gordon took her by the arm, Elaine's rage only intensified, and she screamed at him. I hurried downstairs and called Dr. Nelson.

"Bring her to the hospital immediately," he said.

Upstairs Elaine was screaming, "Dad is raping me!" I went to help get her down the stairs, out the door, and into the car while she continued to scream. When we drove past Stich's house she opened the window and hollered, "Billy! Billy!"

At the hospital the nurse was waiting with a hypodermic needle. Elaine began to calm down after receiving the sedative, and she was admitted willingly. When Dr. Ashley came to assess her the next day, Elaine was swimming in a world of hallucinations and delusions. No one could bring her back to reality. "I'm going to have a baby," she said. "Dad raped me in the music room. People can't exist without freedom in the music room. Jesus liked music? Ask forgiveness for your sins of adultery. Jesus is coming!"

Dr. Ashley recommended the University Hospital in Minneapolis, and Dr. Nelson made arrangements for Elaine's admission. It was late September when we drove her down and admitted her to Station 61, the locked psychiatric ward. Her diagnosis was chronic undifferentiated schizophrenia. She was not making any sense when we left her. With our written consent, she began electro convulsive therapy (ECT) the next month.

Confusing letters began arriving at home. At Christmastime we loaded up the kids and went to visit her. She was glad to see us but seemed a little vacant. In January they told us her capacity for abstract thinking was still zero. In February her letters started to make more sense. She sent this apology to Gordon: *Dearest Dad, You have gone through so much with me that wasn't good, and yet you still love me. Thank you. I love you so much, and I'm sorry I've made you feel so bad.*

By March Elaine had improved enough to continue her schoolwork in the hospital. Because of her previous precocity in high school, she had completed all but two of the required courses. By April she was well enough to come home. To her relief and to our delight she was allowed to finish school on schedule and graduate with the class of 1968. Her graduation was a happy occasion, but her dream of going away to college was over.

The following year Elaine wrote this explanation of her illness and the feelings she had regarding her dad and the accusation she had made:

> I got sick when I was a senior in high school. I imagined my dad was trying to rape me. I realize now it was just an extension of my longing for his attention, which I felt had been usurped by four cute baby sisters all born after me and by six brothers who helped him on the farm while I was not allowed to do farm work because I was a girl. I remember how much I loved and admired my dad when I was a little girl and he had time for me. I remember how resentful I felt later when the only time I saw him was at the table, and during a conversation that was much too short for me, he would always interrupt by suddenly standing up and declaring he had to go out to the barn. Gradually I came to experience deep feelings of hate and fear toward my dad. I had frightening dreams about him and began to imagine it was because he was really bad.

A couple months after Elaine's graduation, Esther and Harold arrived from Arizona with their boys, Danny, Jonathan, and Bruce. They drove to Minnesota in their station wagon and invited Elaine home with them to get a job in Phoenix and to live with Grandma Mikaelsen. Elaine was delighted. A letter arrived a week later with this report:

> On the way to Arizona the boys bought a whole bunch of fireworks. When we stopped to eat, Jonathan lit a smoke bomb in the toilet. Blue smoke came up from the roof. That gave Bruce ideas. He lit a smoke bomb in the telephone booth. Harold was furious. Their family has many, well, we'll call it heated discussions, out of respect.

Elaine moved in with her grandma and soon found a job at the Gruber Underwear factory. Thus began a series of fits and starts whereby Elaine ventured into the world only to experience rejection again and again. Her job at Gruber lasted only a few months.

Feeling isolated and lonesome at Grandma's house, Elaine decided to move back to Minnesota. She rented an apartment in Cambridge and a got a job at the state hospital where Gordon worked. That lasted only one month. I drove her down to the University of Minnesota, where she applied for a work study program and got a job in the food service department. She found a small apartment near downtown Minneapolis and rode the bus to her job at the university. Unfortunately, she was terminated at the end of the spring term. As luck would have it, she was able to find a job at a nearby coffee shop but was fired again after only one week on the job. Each failure was like another nail in her coffin. When she moved home in May, 1969, her behavior foreshadowed another relapse of her illness. She was anxious and discouraged. She refused to eat regular meals and took to eating popcorn, believing it was nutritious if she prayed for it.

Another round of disturbing interactions followed with her family and neighbors, and it was time to have Elaine recommitted to the hospital. This time Gordon and I were required to testify at a court hearing with Elaine present, to give reasons and evidence to justify hospitalization. Chief among these were the disruptions at home, her delusional thinking, and bizarre behavior. We did not feel capable of managing her, and she was not able to keep a job or function alone in the world. What else could we do? She clearly needed professional supervision, which at that time was available only in a hospital psychiatric unit or a state institution for the mentally ill.

The impact of Elaine's illness on the rest of the family was less obvious. The children coped in whatever way they could, including a mix of denial and dissociation, denial of the tragedy and dissociation from the anxiety brought on by the ever-present possibility of bizarre behavior and disruptions. Elaine sometimes behaved strangely in public too. The result for her siblings was often embarrassment and shame mixed with anxieties over what would become of their sister who formerly showed so much promise. Short of booting her out of the house, which we could never do, the only option available in 1969 was committing her to an institution.

After four months of treatment at the University Hospital, including ECT, Elaine was ready to come home again. The hospital social worker recommended she return to Arizona to continue working at Gruber, if they would hire her back. She had indicated the job at Gruber was a positive experience, and the social worker believed Elaine would do better away from home. This time Elaine was invited to stay with Esther and Harold rather than living with Grandma Mikaelsen again. Gruber hired her back, and this time Elaine succeeded. She also enrolled at Glendale Community College and took two fall semester courses.

For Christmas that year, Elaine came home to Minnesota and spent $200 of her hard-earned money on gifts for me, Gordon, and all her siblings. At last she seemed to be doing well. It was a grand reunion and we were filled with hope. Not to be outdone, Dave announced he was paying my airfare to Arizona that winter. He paid for my flight with money he earned the previous summer working on a ranch in Montana. I would go to visit Elaine and Esther and be with my mother on her eightieth birthday.

In February I flew with Ingeborg to Phoenix, where we enjoyed a glorious week in the sunshine. Content and competent, Elaine took me to visit the underwear factory and introduced me to her boss. My anxiety about Elaine, which had consumed me in previous years, gave way to hope. We had a good time together. The highlight of the trip was the birthday party for my mother, which Esther and Harold hosted.

It was not easy returning to the Minnesota winter and a house in disarray. Margaret, who had assumed more of the household responsibility after Elaine left home, did her best to take care of things during my absence. Sharing the same birthday as my mother, Margaret also turned fifteen while I was gone. Naturally she felt overlooked and underappreciated, and she resented the fact I was so focused on Elaine. Margaret came home one day and put to me like this: "Why don't you ever ask about me? Is Elaine the only one you ever think about?"

"I'm sorry you feel that way," I replied, and I tried to make it up to her. In retrospect, it is clear I let Margaret down.

When Elaine rented an apartment near Grandma Mikaelsen's house the following summer, she invited Margaret to come out and stay. I let Margaret go for a whole month and the two had a grand time together. Elaine was slender and beautiful again and had captured the heart of Chuck Burger, a young man she met at the factory. Chuck and his friends did their best to entertain Margaret during her stay. She returned to Minnesota tanned and rejuvenated.

At first I was relieved when Elaine wrote to tell us she was getting married. To have a husband caring for her seemed like a godsend to Gordon and me. We had been so worried about her future. It should not have been a surprise, however, that Chuck, though mentally stable, was wholly incapable of managing Elaine when she became ill.

Dave was the only family member to attend the wedding on November 29, 1970. He and his friend Dallas were on their way to California for the winter. When Dave got to Arizona, he noticed that Elaine was behaving erratically again, but the wedding went ahead as planned.

Before the honeymoon was over, Elaine was descending into madness again. At work the following week she began hallucinating and smashed her hand through a window. Gruber put her on involuntary leave pending a certification of wellness by a psychiatrist. Things went from bad to worse. Frustrated and scared, Chuck decided to bring her back to Minnesota. They arrived on the Friday bus in Rush City, the day after Christmas. We moved them into the small bedroom at the top of the stairs, and the relative calm of 1970 gave way to unmitigated turmoil in 1971.

Elaine had a manic depressive kind of schizophrenia that cycled from low to high and back again in a matter of hours. When she was high, there was not a corner of the house free from noise. She sat at the piano pounding away melodies she knew by heart, singing at a volume that could be heard in the barn. An hour later she would be in a suicidal depression. During one of these fits of depression, she found Ernie's deer rifle, carried it to Ernie, and begged him to put her out of her misery. Ernie and Ken quickly and quietly hid all their ammunition. Several times a day and all hours of the night Elaine and Chuck went to their bedroom, where Elaine could be heard screaming wildly in a manner revealing both pleasure and pain.

One evening while the family was watching television, Elaine came running naked down the stairs and went out the front door. It was only because Ernie caught a glimpse of her that anyone even knew she had left. Leaping to his feet, he went out the door after her. He stood and listened in the subzero darkness and heard footsteps going down the driveway. At the end of the driveway, he listened again and heard something down the road to the west. He ran in that direction and caught up to her at the bottom of the hill. She was completely naked, no shoes, no socks, on the snow packed road. Ernie scooped her up and carried her back to the house. The whole way, Elaine cried and wailed, "Please let me die! Please let me die!"

By Monday morning the entire household was tired and tense. Gordon and I coaxed Elaine into the car and drove her to the University Hospital once again. It is not necessary to burden you with all the gruesome details. Suffice it to say that she came home after several months of treatment, but she never seemed to fully stabilize after that. Though Elaine was no longer openly suicidal, she was still noisy and disruptive and went back to sleeping with Chuck in the upstairs bedroom. Chuck found a factory job in Rush City later that spring. It was a relief when he and Elaine moved into a small rental house in town. An atmosphere of normalcy gradually returned to our household, but another disappointment was waiting just around the corner.

This time it was Margaret who surprised us, a casualty of the family disruption that year. She became pregnant while seeing a neighbor boy three years older than she. We knew they were interested each other, but we were unaware of the extent to which they were involved. With my focus on Elaine, I was unable to stay attuned to Margaret, even though I relied on her for household chores. Still, we were shocked and disappointed that this happened in spite of our strict religious parenting.

That autumn at the age of sixteen, Margaret married John Mell in a small ceremony at Calvary Lutheran Church, just three weeks before Branden was born. They moved into a trailer home near Rush City. I took care of Branden while Margaret went to school. Paula, our youngest, had started kindergarten, so I had time available.

Another more ominous event occurred that summer, even before Margaret told us she was pregnant. Elaine was not to be our only child with a serious and persistent mental illness. Three months after Chuck and Elaine moved out, Ken began to hallucinate. One day just before his fifteenth birthday, Ken came indoors strangely agitated. "An airplane flew over," he said. "The pilot was shaking his fist at me! And Marlon was kidnapped." Marlon was at bible camp that week.

We did not know then that Ken was on his way to becoming a statistical norm. Researchers have found that when one sibling has schizophrenia, the other siblings have a one in ten chance of having schizophrenia, which compares to a one in a hundred chance for the general population. Although oblivious to the statistical norms, we were fully aware of the troubling possibilities for Ken when he started hallucinating.

Like Elaine, Ken had achieved academic success throughout his school years. He was not the straight A student Elaine was, but he was usually on the A or B honor roll. Good looking with deep blue eyes, Ken inherited his father's proclivity for hard work. He was a reliable assistant to Gordon as well as to Ernie and Dave, both of whom he deeply admired. Ken involved himself in their interests and activities, striving to excel in the things they did. Like a kind of apprentice, Ken emulated them, and they looked after him.

Ken was more reserved than Ernie and Dave and did not easily make friends. When left alone, he often spent his time honing skills that would allow him to duly impress or even defeat Ernie, his apparent idol. For example, Ken practiced basketball, shooting baskets for hours until Ernie arrived, and then he would challenge Ernie to a game of horse. But in sports Ken was rarely able to outdo his older brother. Ken could usually defeat Ernie in checkers, however. He did so with eager anticipation and then celebrated gleefully when he won, much to Ernie's chagrin.

Despite the competition for supremacy, Ken and Ernie were quite inseparable. They shared the same bed until Dave left home. They worked together in the barn and in the fields, fulfilling the diverse responsibilities required of dairy farmers. Ernie often confided his personal issues and ideas with Ken while they worked. When they weren't working together, they were often competing in games, target practicing with bows and arrows, camping, or hunting.

Around the time of Ken's psychotic break, this close relationship with Ernie began to change as Ernie became more involved in sports, more interested in girls, and less interested in hunting. While Ernie spent more and more time away from home, the responsibility for farm chores shifted to Ken when Gordon was away at work.

Ken's first psychosis was mild and short lived, the way it began with Elaine. Nevertheless, we went to see a psychiatrist in the Twin Cities, who wanted the entire family present. After two sessions, Dr. Shapiro announced his belief that Ken's psychosis was due to pathologies in the entire family system. Gordon was so disgusted he insisted we discontinue the counseling, which was too expensive anyway. The MMPI Ken took at Braham Mental Health Clinic came back normal. He refused to take the medication prescribed by Dr. Nelson, tossing it in the waste basket. "The fog seems to have lifted," he said, and before long he was fully functional and behaving normally again. Ken completed his sophomore year in high school without any delay.

In Rush City Chuck worked as a welder and came home every day to a jealous and insecure wife. Elaine's insecurity increased along with her weight gain induced by the antipsychotic medication. She learned that Chuck would hurry home faster if she turned the gas on in a mock suicide attempt, opening the gas valve on the oven without lighting the burner. Chuck would hurry home after work to find the house filling with gas. At his job he may have found sanity during the day, but at home he lived with the instability and uncertainty brought on by Elaine. This situation persisted, ebbing and flowing, for a about a year and a half. Gordon and I hoped for the best, while recuperating from the previous calamities. We prayed for a better future.

Ken and Elaine's mental problems affected our other kids as well. For example, Ernie came to me one night, unable to sleep. "Mom, I think I'm going crazy," he said.

There was nothing delusional in his thinking, only the anxiety.

"Don't worry," I replied. "If you think you're going crazy, you're not." Somehow he was comforted by that. The knowledge I gained from my own experience with anxiety and depression actually helped me in counseling my children.

It is not surprising Ernie left home shortly after graduating from high school. He spent the summer hitchhiking six thousand miles through the western U.S. and Canada, hoping to find refuge in the Rocky Mountains. Ernie planned to live off the land. His trip out West was a kind of odyssey for him, and he enjoyed the seeing the mountains and the Pacific Ocean. But he discovered the solitary existence did not work for him. He returned in late July, lonely and disillusioned, and decided to attend Anoka Ramsey Community College with Dave, who had already enrolled for the fall term. Without a clear direction or goal in life, however, Ernie floundered. The fall of 1972 was a dark and depressing time for him. Elaine was slipping again also, becoming more agitated and confused.

I took Elaine to see Dr. Nelson. He recommended another round of treatment at the University Hospital. Dave drove her down in early December. She came home for Christmas, but Chuck wanted her back in the hospital after that.

Early in January, Elaine asked me to bring Chuck down to see her. She sensed that he was distancing from her. Upon our arrival she seemed agitated with Chuck, although happy to see me. When we departed that day, she put her arms around me at the door, rested her head on my shoulder, and hung on for the longest time. I gently pried myself away and kissed her good bye. That was the last time I saw her alive.

The next time I saw Elaine she was in a casket, looking beautiful and serene. On January 11, 1973, she leapt from a sixth floor window on the psychiatric ward. When they called to inform me that she was dead, I was stunned. I cried for days and ceased praying. She was my beautiful first-born child, and God had taken her away from me.

My memory of the following year is blurred. The church was packed with over 200 attending Elaine's funeral, but I was too numb to appreciate it. I started going to a grief group, which helped me recover somewhat. My memories and photos of Elaine are treasures. I kept the 300 page manuscript of the novel she wrote. It is the colorful story of Lizzie, an orphaned adolescent girl, perhaps Elaine's alter ego, who manages to make her way in a rough and tumble world. On those beautifully written pages, the best of Elaine's imagination and intelligence are preserved. I hope it can be published someday.

1) Esther and me, Hartland, 1932.

2) Mikaelsen family, Hartland, 1935. Martin stands far left, John far right.

3) The road to Graettinger, Iowa. Ten miles southwest of Ringsted, March 1936. (courtesy of Verna Hanson)

4) I stand (center) with Esther and classmates at Pleasant View School, 1937.

5) Mikaelsen family, Ringsted, 1942. John is next to me; then Martin.

6) My senior picture, Ringsted High School, 1944.

7) With my pupils at Blue Bottom School, 1945.

8) My pupils playing outside Giffin School, 1946.

9) My pupils inside Giffin School, 1946.

10) Emil and Anna Mikaelsen visiting us at Ringsted, Iowa, 1946.

11) With Obert Quale, my first date, 1948.

12) My VBS children at Grover School, 1948. Near Peterson, Minnesota.

13) Kenley Boyum, 1948.

14) With my pupils at Toeterville School, 1948.

15) Enjoying Gordon's courtship, 1949.

16) Our wedding at Zion Lutheran Church near Dexter, Minnesota, October 16, 1949.

17) Our trailer home, 1949, right after the honeymoon.

18) Ready to pick corn in 1949, after our honeymoon.

19) The old Boyum farmhouse, 1951.

20) Gardening at the Old Boyum farm, 1951.

21) Family of six, 1955. Gordon holding David. Elaine holding Margaret. I'm holding Ernie.

22) At our farm near Thief River Falls, August 1956. I'm holding Kenny, who was born earlier that month.

23) Our train trip to Arizona, 1957. Just the tonic we needed.

24) Mowing the fields in 1962. Gordon made a cart so kids could ride along. Ernie and David are on the tractor, Kenny sits on the mower, Marlon stands, and Milton is sits in the cart.

25) Gordon and boys, with cousins Dan and Benji, 1963, putting up straw.

26) Family of eleven, Rush Point farm, 1963.

27) Elaine on Gypsy, 1965.

28) Our ten children in 1965. Paula arrived in 1966.

29) Rush Point farm, 1970. Photo taken by Ernie from the top of a tall pine tree in the neighbor's pasture.

30) Family of thirteen, 1968.

31) Ken milking cow, 1969.

32) Ernie took this photo on Easter Sunday in 1969. Elaine is far left. Ken is far right, holding Max.

33) Elaine and Chuck Burger, October 1972.

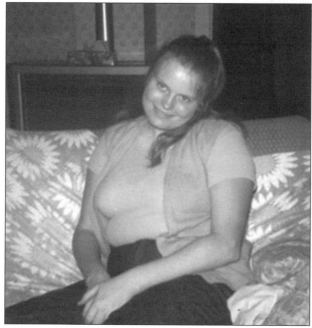

34) Elaine, 1972, in her Rush City home.

35) Ken, a junior in high school, fall of 1972.

36) With Gordon in Copenhagen, Denmark, 1979.

37) Our silver wedding anniversary in Mora, October 1974, Gordon and Ernie hugging me. Ken and Margaret sit at left end of couch. Carol, Eunice, Marlon, Milton, Geoffrey, Brandon, Paula, and Dave stand left to right.

38) Ken and Geoff with Liz and Kari, 1978.

39) Ken, 1981, after he took up weight lifting.

40) Square dancing with Gordon, 1987.

41) With Dr. Bob Rose, National Mall, 1990.

42) With Dave Durenburger and Paula Clayton, Russel Senate Office building, 1990.

43) With Dr. Paula Clayton on Capitol Hill, 1990.

44) With Dr. Erna Christensen at Chinese restaurant, Hartsdale, New York, 1990.

15

Ellis Island

Reverend Stringfellow concluded the communion, spread his arms, and prayed, "Almighty and everlasting God, we most heartily thank thee . . . The peace of God, which passes all understanding . . . Let us go forth into the world, rejoicing in the power of the spirit." Then came the organ and closing hymn. I wiped away my tears, which often came with memories of Elaine.

Although I still felt some grief, it was but a remnant of the anguish I felt in previous years. The tears I shed back then assuaged the pain and helped to heal my emotional wounds. I did not suppress the grief or carry it around like a sack full of stones. I had learned to feel it and let my tears wash it away.

When the final hymn concluded, I made my way to the hall where coffee was served and Reverend Stringfellow greeted the parishioners. I took a cup of coffee, shook hands with the reverend, and exited.

A chill was in the air, the sky still overcast. A steady stream of traffic was moving south on Fifth Avenue. At the street corner a vendor was selling everything from hotdogs to newspapers. I bought a bag of trail mix and went to the curb.

In New York City yellow taxi cabs are everywhere, more common than private vehicles, and the drivers can tell when you need a ride. All you have to do is stand next to the curb and hold up a hand, which is what I did next. A taxi pulled over within seconds, and I climbed in. "Can you take me to the ferry?" I asked. "The one to Ellis Island?"

"Yes, ma'am," the driver said, "that would be Battery Park," and he cruised off down Fifth Avenue. Of course the street traffic can only move at a very limited speed due to the frequent stop lights, and Battery Park is four miles south of 53rd Street. The ride consumed the better part of an hour, but I enjoyed it because the taxi driver was friendly, and I learned much more about the city. Fifth Avenue and Broadway are major routes with many landmarks, such as the Empire State Building, Greenwich Village, City Hall, the World Trade Center, and Wall Street. I would not have recognized any of these had the taxi driver not pointed them out to me. All I had to do was tell him where I was from and that it was my first trip to New York, and he spouted off like a tour guide.

Broadway leads right to Battery Park, which is where the driver stopped to let me out. The twenty-five acre park is at the southern tip of Manhattan Island. It is now a national monument named after of the artillery defenses located there during the colonial era. Castle Clinton, the military fort built just before the War of 1812, houses the gift shop and ticket sales for the ferry rides to Liberty and Ellis Islands.

I bought my ticket and strolled over to a staging area on the wharf where a crowd of tourists stood waiting. A white triple decker ferry boat, *Miss Liberty*, was moored at the wharf, disgorging its previous load of passengers.

The boat soon emptied; the crowd ahead began to move. I boarded along with a thousand other tourists, made my way to the third deck, and stood next to the railing. Thick clouds hung low over the harbor but still no rain, and little wind. Across the harbor to the west, I could see the New Jersey shoreline a mile or two away. A passenger ship was moving slowly north up the Hudson River, and several other ferry boats could be seen crossing the bay to the south. Much of New York Harbor occupies this bay, which is actually a widening in the Hudson River before it heads through the Verrazano Narrows and into the Atlantic.

When the ferry was full, the ropes were loosened, and the boat floated slowly away from the wharf. Somewhere below, I could hear the engines rumbling as the ferry turned southward and began to accelerate. Over speakers, a tour guide said, "Welcome to the Liberty Island Ferry. Ellis Island is closed for remodeling. This body of water is called Upper Bay . . ." The voice droned on, explaining various landmarks and historical events. It wasn't long before I could see the Statue of Liberty ahead. At first the greenish-blue statue was a small blur in the distance. As the ferry drew closer, however, Lady Liberty appeared to rise up from the bay until she towered overhead, the very sight which greeted my parents as they entered New York Harbor in 1926. I felt moved and humbled.

Ever since 1886, millions of immigrants entering New York Harbor have been greeted by this "mighty woman with a torch," as it was described by Emma Lazerus. Her world-famous poem, "The New Collosus," is engraved on the foundation.

Here at our sea-washed, sunset gates shall stand
A mighty woman with a torch, whose flame
Is the imprisoned lightning, and her name
Mother of Exiles. From her beacon-hand
Glows worldwide her welcome, her mild eyes command
The air-bridged harbor that twin cities frame.
"Keep, ancient lands, your storied pomp!" cries she,
With silent lips. "Give me your tired, your poor,
Your huddled masses yearning to breathe free,
The wretched refuse of your teeming shore;
Send these, the homeless, tempest-tossed to me,
I lift my lamp beside the golden door!"

The ferry pulled up along a pier and prepared for unloading. I followed the crowd off the ferry and down the walkway toward the statue. Close up, it did not have the same awe-inspiring effect as viewing it from the boat. When I had seen enough, I wandered back to the ferry, which was already reloading.

I found my way back to the third deck, and before long the boat began to back away from the pier. Ferries arrive and depart every half hour from Liberty Island and proceed a half mile north past Ellis Island, which remained closed for restoration until 1992. Like Liberty Island, Ellis Island is a national monument. The ferry boat puttered past the island while the tour guide told about the history and the $200 million renovation project headed by Lee Iacocca. It was funded entirely by private donations from people like me and my siblings, who contributed one hundred dollars to have the names of our immigrant parents engraved on the Wall of Honor. If you ever go there, look for Hans and Anna Mikaelsen on that wall.

As the ferry approached the island, I stared at the French Renaissance building where my parents and siblings passed their mandatory inspection. The low flat island is only slightly larger than Liberty Island, which isn't very big. It is mostly covered by buildings: the main processing building, staff housing facilities, and the barracks used to house those who were ill or awaiting deportation. I pictured my father and pregnant mother standing patiently in the processing line along with John, Martin, Esther, and all of their possessions.

The tour guide continued, "Beginning in 1892, over 12 million immigrants entered the United States here. Medical personnel watched the immigrants closely as they entered the building and climbed the stairs. If they were limping, laboring to breathe, or exhibiting any other signs of illness, they were subjected to a more thorough examination and usually not allowed to enter the country if determined to be ill. In the Registry Room, inspectors subjected each family or individual to twenty-nine questions including name, hometown, occupation, destination, and amount of money they carried." I had no idea how much money my parents had upon arrival, but I had learned a lot about the people and the land they left behind.

In midlife I finally acted on the longing to know more about my roots. Over the years I had heard many stories about my Danish relatives, but I had never actually met many of them or known them personally. All that changed in 1979 when Gordon and I flew to Denmark and became acquainted with a large extended family. Over there my horizons seemed to broaden, like I had finally discovered who I was. It only became possible for us after moving to Mora and becoming more financially secure.

16

Broadening Horizons

The year after Elaine died, Gordon decided it was time to quit his job and resume full time farming. In need of more land and a larger barn, he found a more suitable farm near Mora, twenty miles northwest of Rush City, as the crow flies. We moved on May 31, 1974, a few days after Ken graduated from high school.

Although the price was reasonable and the move went smoothly enough, Gordon was initially disappointed. He found structural and mechanical problems in the dairy barn and initially became discouraged. When he started talking about moving again, I told him, "If you move, it will have to be without me." Our sons came to the rescue and helped him make the necessary repairs and improvements in the barn.

It gradually became apparent to all of us that we had made a good move. For one thing, the farm was on a paved road less than two miles from town. The buildings were set into a hillside across the road from the Snake River. Out our front windows were a park-like yard and the forested valley beyond. With 128 acres, a big red dairy barn, a four stall garage, two corncribs, a pole-shed, and a granary, Gordon had everything he needed to support his farming endeavor and his family. The barn had a pipeline milking system, a refrigerated bulk tank for the milk, stalls for forty cows, and a barn cleaner for automated manure removal. Gordon gradually expanded his herd to fill the barn and fulfilled his dream of becoming a full-time dairy farmer. The commodious farmhouse was ideal, too, with four bedrooms, a spacious living and dining room, and a modern kitchen.

Being so close to town, we found it easy to be involved in church and school activities, a welcome convenience with six children still living at home. We joined a Lutheran church and a Bible study group and began to feel comfortable in the Mora community. Our move to Mora helped me get over the trauma of Elaine's death. I began to feel joy again as a sense of normalcy and stability returned to our lives. Gordon and I celebrated our silver wedding anniversary at our new home that fall.

Shortly after our move, my brother John traveled to Denmark to visit our relatives, the aunts, uncles, and cousins with whom my mother had corresponded since 1926. It was difficult for Mother to keep up with these correspondences, with her sight worsening and her mind slipping. I began taking up the slack with occasional letters of my own. Upon hearing John's descriptions of his trip and receiving letters from our relatives about his visit, I began to consider the possibility of visiting Denmark myself.

By 1976 Mother was no longer able to live on her own. John had applied for a room at a nursing home in Northfield, which became available in February that year. For the purpose of moving her back to Minnesota, I took a winter vacation to Arizona. After celebrating Mother's eighty-sixth birthday at Esther and Harold's, I brought her back to Minnesota to live in the nursing home. Among her things, I found a stack of letters from Denmark. Later, I replied to my elderly aunts who had sent them, and from then on I answered and saved all the letters from Denmark. It was like opening a door to my parent's homeland and to the many relatives whom I had never met.

One of the letters to my mother, for instance, was from Marie, her next younger sister, who lived in a nursing home near their childhood home. Here is an excerpt:

> My dear sister Anna, How far we are from each other. It was just our childhood and youth that we were permitted to be together. Now you are also in a nursing home. It is good you are close to John and Mary and our sister Ingeborg. Can you still sing? You sang so well when you were young…I don't have diabetes, but have gray spots in my eyes, so I don't write very well, but we have to take what comes from our Father's hand. He will soon take us home to Himself.

I was deeply moved. For the first time in my life, I understood the magnitude of my mother's loss in leaving her homeland. Perhaps it was my loss too.

Contributing to my interest in Denmark were visits by several of my Danish cousins over the years. They were always very interesting. I was impressed by them and entertained. While my mother still had command of her memory, I asked many questions about our family history. I was intrigued by the stories Mother and Ingeborg told me about Denmark and our relatives. Deep within, I longed to explore these family ties.

Gordon was also interested in visiting Norway. By 1979 our farm was flourishing. The kids were old enough to take care of themselves, and our sons were fully capable of operating the farm during our absence. With money in the bank, we decided the time was right. We ordered passports and began planning our trip to Denmark and Norway.

Our first view of Denmark, in late July, 1979, was looking out the window of a 747. On final approach at Kastrup Airport near Copenhagen, we saw ships and sailboats in the Oresund. It is difficult to describe the excitement and anticipation I felt upon that arrival, fifty three years after departing in my mother's womb. My cousins Knud and Inger, who had both visited us in Minnesota, stood waiting as we exited customs. When Knud offered in near perfect English to carry my suitcase, I replied in my best Danish, *"Nej tak, Jeg wille tager den kuffert."* (No thanks, I will carry the suitcase.)

"Your Danish is very good," he replied. He had told me this before. Younger Danes have studied English every year in school and typically speak it fluently, but it is very rare for an American who did not grow up in Denmark to speak Danish fluently. As the child of immigrants, I was an exception.

Knud Christensen was a professor of genetics at the University of Copenhagen, and his sister Inger was training to be a psychologist. Both lived in Copenhagen, where we headed next to find Inger's apartment on a street called Snorregade. *Gade* means street, and Snorre (Sturlusen) was the thirteenth century lawyer believed to be the author of an Icelandic saga. Up three flights of stairs, Inger's flat was small and cozy with a large bay window providing a view of Snorregade. I commented on the relative lack of automobile congestion in the city and the great number of bicycles both on the streets and parked in rows in front of the apartment buildings across the street.

"That's because Denmark has no oil," said Knud. "We put a high tax on gasoline to discourage consumption and spend the proceeds on public transportation – makes it cheap and easy to get around but expensive to drive a car. Best of all, it encourages conservation and bicycling, which reduces pollution, congestion, and noise."

"How much does gasoline cost then?" asked Gordon.

"Roughly four and a half dollars, American, per gallon. About three dollars of that is tax."

"Ufda!" Gordon exclaimed. "There would be a revolution in the States if they charged that much tax."

"Yes, but you will deplete your fossil fuels and the price of gas will go sky high anyway, which will ruin your economy. If Denmark is cut off from oil, we can still get around because the trains run on electricity generated in part by wind turbines. It is much cheaper to build and maintain railroads than freeways."

"Yah, well, I guess you have a point there," said Gordon.

After some refreshments and more conversation, Gordon and I were exhausted. We had missed a night of sleep on the flight over and were happy to accept the bed Inger offered us even though it was only noon.

Four hours later, we took a bus to Knud's apartment for supper, which he prepared. Afterward he took us to Tivoli Gardens, a carnival-like amusement park in the middle of Copenhagen, site of the world's oldest operating roller coaster and the world's tallest carousel. Knud took Gordon on the roller coaster; he took me on the Ferris wheel. It was hard to tell who had more fun, Knud or us. We walked back to Inger's apartment and went happily to bed, looking forward to the following day. Knud had scheduled his summer vacation around our visit. He had offered to take us to his parent's home in Vejrup, my father's hometown.

The next morning we did not proceed directly to Vejrup. Knud insisted first on a proper introduction to Copenhagen. We walked several blocks to see the iconic bronze mermaid in the harbor. Other than being famous on account of Walt Disney, it isn't that much to see. Nearby in the park, however, stands a much more impressive monument. "What about that sculpture over there?" I asked.

"That is the statue of Gefion," said Knud, as we strolled toward the dramatic sculpture and fountain. Mounted on top of a massive granite bowl are four larger-than-life bronze oxen pulling a plow driven by Gefion, the beautiful, whip-wielding goddess of fertility. Water shoots from beneath the plowshares, showering the sculpture in misty splendor, tumbling over a series of waterfalls below.

"Gefion is a monument meaningful to Danes," continued Knud. "It symbolizes the creation of the land we are on, Zealand, the largest island in Denmark. According to legend the king of Sweden promised Gefion all the land she could plow during the course of one full day. She cleverly turned her four sons into oxen and plowed up the land that became Zealand."

I was inspired by the beauty of the sculpture and fountain and felt a deep pride welling up within me. Behind us in the harbor a large cargo ship moved silently seaward. Across the water was an ancient-looking stone structure with a triangular truss protruding over the water. Knud said it was an old harbor hoist used for loading ships long ago. "It's a fitting symbol of Copenhagen, which literally means 'merchants harbor,'" Knud explained. "The hoist was recently restored and preserved."

It was an honor to be escorted by this erudite man who seemed knowledgeable about everything and therefore made an excellent tour guide. Gordon seemed to get along particularly well with Knud, maybe because they were both farmers at heart. Knud grew up on a family farm near Vejrup. At the time he was a professor and a researcher in agricultural genetics. His mother Sine was my mother's sister.

We strolled back south along the waterfront to Amalienborg Palace, Queen Margaret's residence. Guards stood like statues in black furry hats next to the entrances. A spectacular equestrian statue of King Frederic V stands in the center of a cobblestone courtyard surrounded by four identical palace buildings. Knud said the palace had been rebuilt in 1750 when the previous one burned down.

Two hours later we piled into Knud's Volkswagon and headed for Vejrup, 260 kilometers (160 miles) west of Copenhagen, not far from the western shore of Denmark. Copenhagen is on the far eastern shore. We took a freeway to the ferry, drove on deck and sailed to the main island of Fyn. The freeway continued seventy-five kilometers across Fyn and over a large suspension bridge to Jutland. A short distance farther, we exited at Kolding and headed back east to Agtrup, where my mother grew up and where Aunt Ingeborg had arranged to meet us at the train station.

We found Ingeborg, squeezed her into the Volkswagen and headed west along narrow paved roads. A valley appeared before us, checkered with fields and woodlots. "Johannes, your grandfather, worked on a threshing crew in this valley," Ingeborg said. "The threshing machine was run by a steam engine. It took all year to thresh the wheat, rye, and barley that grew in the area."

I was beginning to form an image of my grandpa as a real person instead of just a picture on the wall. My mother's birthplace and childhood home was nearby, but that would have to wait for another day, as we were scheduled for supper at Knud's parents' home in Vejrup.

A small town of several hundred people, Vejrup was my parent's hometown before leaving Denmark. When we arrived, the town I had pictured became the quaint reality before me: brick and stucco houses with small yards. Johannes and Eva, Knud's older brother and sister, still resided on and operated the family farm two kilometers west of Vejrup, while his parents had retired from farming a few years earlier and moved into town. His two elderly parents came out to greet us as we pulled up in front of their house. My aunt Sine and uncle Kristen, whose letters I had fetched from mailboxes for fifty years, now stood smiling before me. "We're so happy to see you," said Sine. "Please come in."

The dinner table was waiting with a colorful meal gathered mostly from the garden that day, including a large bowl of glistening strawberries. We sat down to eat, easily conversing in Danish. Knud translated for Gordon.

"How is Anna doing?" asked Sine.

"Not so well, I'm sorry to say. I moved her to the nursing home in Cambridge last fall, but she still can't figure out where she is. Her short-term memory is gone; she's nearly blind and very confused. I visit her twice a week. She keeps asking me to take her home and clings to me when I have to leave. It breaks my heart. I feel bad about leaving her there, but it would be overwhelming to have her at home. She's on a waiting list for the nursing home in Mora where I plan to move her when a room opens. I'm tired of the half-hour drive to Cambridge."

"I understand," Sine said. "Marie is in a nursing home in Bjaert. Knud will take you to see her. She is still mentally sharp but cannot see very well or get around." Aunt Marie was eighty-seven, two years younger than my mother Anna and the second of the six sisters in that family. Petra, the third sister, died as a young adult. Sine, the fourth, was seventy-nine. Hanne, the fifth, was seventy-seven, and Ingeborg, the youngest, was seventy-two at the time.

After supper we walked over to the church where my parents got married. It's a modest stone building, lime-washed white with a red-tile roof and a massive bell tower. Large wrought iron numerals mounted high on the bell tower indicate 1-9-4-3. "What does the date signify?" I asked.

"Your uncle August built the bell tower in 1943," replied Knud. "He was a bricklayer, you know." Beautiful in detail, elegant in simplicity, and nearly half the size of the church, the bell tower added considerable charm to an otherwise ordinary structure.

"When was the rest of the church built?"

"The sanctuary dates back to the twelfth century."

"Excuse me. Did you say the twelfth century?" I asked. It hardly seemed possible that a building could be that old and still look so good.

"Most of the churches in Denmark, including this one," Knud explained, "were built in the twelfth century after Denmark was Christianized."

The cemetery nearly surrounded the church leaving only a small church yard, which was surfaced with pea-sized gravel. We strolled into the cemetery and located the graves of August and Maren Mikaelsen. August, my dad's brother, was my only uncle.

"Where are my Michaelsen grandparents buried?" I asked. The name was originally spelled with a "ch," but August and Hans changed the spelling to Mikaelsen because, according to their pastor, that was presumed to be more biblically correct.

"Andreas and Maren Michaelsen were buried right next to August," said Kristian, "but the gravestones were moved over there." He pointed toward the stone fence surrounding the graveyard.

"Why did they move the gravestones?" I inquired, disappointed that I could not view the burial site of my paternal grandparents.

"The burial plots are leased. A rental fee must be paid every twenty-five years to preserve a plot. When the rental fee came due a few years ago, no one wanted to pay it," explained Kristen.

"What happened to the gravesite when the headstones were moved?"

"Someone else was buried in the same spot," Kristen answered. "We bury our dead in wooden boxes and do not embalm the bodies with preservatives. After fifty years the remaining bones can be exhumed and cremated, which allows the site to be reused by someone else. Otherwise, the cemetery would need to be enlarged every few years. As you can see, there is not any space available for expansion."

Looking around I could see he was right. To one side of the church was the street; to the other side were homes, and across the street was a barley field. "Couldn't they start another cemetery out in the country?"

"We put a high value on land. Extra cemeteries would take too much land out of production. Besides that, we value the biblical tradition of the body going back to dust."

"Oh," I said. What he was saying made perfect sense, but the concept of not embalming the dead seemed so foreign to me. I wondered why we do things so much differently in America.

Later that evening Johannes and Eva arrived at Sine's house to complete the family gathering. Eva had once visited me in Minnesota, but I was meeting Johannes for the first time. I liked him immediately. Affable and intelligent, he looked and behaved much like my brother Martin. After a long lively discussion, we took to singing Danish songs, the same ones my parents taught me. Many years had passed, but it seemed I was back among my own people after a long sojourn in a foreign land. Never before had I felt so completely happy and such a deep sense of belonging.

The following day Knud took us to Ribe, the medieval capital and one of the oldest towns in Denmark. The Domkirke, or cathedral, was originally established there by St. Ansgar, who came in the ninth century from Germany to establish a beachhead for Christianity. At the time, Denmark was populated by our pagan ancestors, the Vikings. Later, in the eighteenth century, Ribe was home to Bishop Brorson, who wrote many popular hymns adopted by the ultra-pietistic brand of Christianity that gave rise to the Inner Mission movement. Brorson's statue stands beside the cathedral. Inside I marveled at the artworks, which according to Knud were covered in lime-wash during the Reformation and then restored in the early 1900s.

On one wall was a sculpture of a mounted knight spearing a dragon. "What is that supposed to signify?" I asked Knud.

"That's St. George slaying a dragon to save the princess. St. George was a Christian in the Roman army. When he refused to recant his Christian beliefs, the emperor had him tortured and killed. It is believed that the dragon represents the Roman Empire and the princess represents Christianity."

I was still thinking about St. George and Brorson when we returned to Vejrup. After lunch we went to visit the Christensen family farm operated by Knud's brother and sister. A long, gravel driveway led into the farmyard. Eva was preparing coffee, and Johannes was working in the barn. Both emerged through separate doors as we parked the car. Gordon and Knud disappeared into the barn, and I went into the house with Eva and Aunt Sine.

In the traditional Old Danish style, their house is attached to the barn. The house looks like an appendage coming off the side of the barn. In fact a doorway in the back of the house leads directly into the barn. A machine shed is attached to the other side of the barn, creating a very compact cluster of buildings. While the men toured the farm, Eva took me to the back yard to see the kitchen garden. Sine invited me to sit with her in the flower garden while Eva returned to the kitchen. She told me about her life on the farm and her memories of Hans and Anna before they left for America.

"Do you remember when they left in 1926?" I asked.

"I remember very well. Actually Hans immigrated to America as a young man and lived in Wisconsin for seven years until World War One. To avoid getting drafted over there, he decided to come back in 1914 to serve in Denmark, which was a neutral country. He met and married Anna while serving in the military. August built them a beautiful brick house on the other side of town. Right after the war ended, Hans wanted to go back to America, but Anna did not want to leave. Hans insisted and they moved to a farm in Wisconsin in 1919 with one-year-old John. But Anna couldn't handle the isolation and the severe winter, so they returned to Denmark a year later and moved back to their old farm in Vejrup. That's where Martin and Esther were born."

"Knud pointed out that farm on our way into town," I said. "Tomorrow I would like to go over there and take a closer look."

"Ask one of the Mikaelsens to show you the old Andreas Michaelsen farm too, which is right nearby. And they can tell you more about the circumstances around Hans and Anna's departure. Anna has written us faithfully all these years, so I know that life in America was not always as rosy as Hans hoped it would be."

"Mother never really felt at home in America," I said. "In fact, she never learned to speak English. Life was hard for me sometimes, too, because I didn't feel like I fit in."

"You would have fit in around here. I can tell you that," Sine declared.

Eva called from the kitchen to invite us in for dinner. It was a meal fit for kings! Roast beef, potatoes, gravy and onions, all from the farm, were accompanied by bread and drinks, followed by currant pudding and coffee. After dinner the men went out to milk the cows, while I lay down for a nap. Later, after the chores were done, we returned to the living room and, again, sang the Danish songs we all knew by heart. I felt as though a broken string in my life was vibrating once more.

The next day Knud took us to see my aunt Marie at the *plejehjemmet* (nursing home) in Bjaert, fifty kilometers east of Vejrup. It is a very nice retirement home, good as the best in Minnesota. She had her own living quarters, but we found her in the activity room, making a pillow sham. Marie was 87 and resembled my mother. I recognized her immediately, a sweet, contented, gracious lady, whose given name my mother had intended for me and whose letters had often appeared in our mailbox over the years. She set aside her work and invited us to her room, a very homey and cheerful place. Marie showed me her photo albums while Ingeborg talked. All too soon it was time to leave.

From there, we drove on narrow roads to my mother's birthplace and childhood home in nearby Agtrup. Nearing a tee in the road, Ingeborg pointed to the house ahead and said, "There it is; that was our house." Only a narrow gravel shoulder separated the blacktop road from the simple but beautiful white stucco house. It's a traditional stucco house, rectangular with a hip-on-gable roof, typical in rural Denmark. Knud parked the car, and we all got out. I gazed at the house. I tried to imagine my mother and her sisters playing in the small yard. Ingeborg described the interior of the house. She knocked on the door, but no one answered.

It was only a short drive to the church where my mother was baptized and where my grandparents, Johannes and Karoline Kallesen, were buried. In nearly every aspect it was similar to the church in Vejrup, except that it had a dark asphalt tile roof and a main entrance through the bell tower. I was fascinated by the exquisite woodwork, altar, and pulpit. The baptismal fount is the same ancient piece in which my mother was baptized.

"What denomination would this church be then?" Gordon asked.

"This is the state-run Lutheran church, like most churches in Denmark," Knud explained. "The salaries and operating expenses are paid through taxes collected by the government."

"Well, don't they take up a collection on Sunday?" Gordon asked.

"Not for running the church," Knud said, "but occasionally for special missions."

Outside, Knud led us to my grandparents' gravesite. There, on a single granite headstone, were the names and dates of Johannas and Karoline Kallesen. My aunt Petra was buried next to them, and nearby was the grave of my great-grandmother, Johanne Langvad. Ingeborg took a photo of Gordon and me standing next to my grandparent's grave. "Anders and I traveled to Denmark in 1953 after Karoline fell ill," she lamented. "I was hoping to see her one more time, but she died the night before we arrived."

Later that day we toured Kolding Castle and then visited my cousin Tet, who lived nearby. This is where we parted with Ingeborg, who was leaving on the train the next day. The rest of us went back to Vejrup, this time for turkey dinner at my cousin Erna Fyhn's house.

Erna, one of August Mikaelsen's daughters, had also invited her brothers Alfred and Kristin and their wives. These Mikaelsen cousins, whom I was meeting for the first time, were full of stories about my father. Kristin explained, "When Hans returned from America, he wanted to farm like an American. He was the first to plant corn here and to build a silo, which amused the neighbors because no silo filling machinery was available. They were even more amused when he tried to build a ramp to the top of his silo. Hans was hard working, though, and ingenious too. The real problem, of course, is that the weather in Denmark is too cool for raising corn."

"Do you remember my sister and brothers?" I asked.

"Oh yes," replied Kristin. "I was born the same year as John. Our house was just across the field from your parent's house, so we were playmates. I saw him every day in school. Magna, my younger sister, was Martin's age. John was eight years old when your family moved to America."

"Did Hans write to you very much?"

"I think we still have some of his letters," Alfred replied. "Hans and Anna got to America just in time for the Depression. We didn't hear too much about it, just that he was surviving and raising his four children. John came to visit us in 1945 after the war. He told us you had some tough years. But at least you didn't have the Germans breathing down your neck."

"Crazy Germans," muttered Kristin. "I'll never forget the day they departed. They occupied Denmark five whole years, and then one day they were going south in convoys, just picked up their weapons and left. Many of them walked. Every Danish flag in the country was flying that day for the first time in five years."

After dinner, Kristin drove us out to see his childhood home. This is where our grandparents lived and where my father was born. "We know that oak tree by the house has been there over a hundred years," Kristin said. "August tore down all the buildings and rebuilt them as they appear now. Then he sold the place and moved to a larger farm in South Vejrup, where he lived and worked for twenty-three years. But he got tired of farming and moved back to town in 1939 to become a fulltime bricklayer."

"What do you remember about our grandparents?" I asked.

"Andreas died fifteen years before I was born, but Maren lived until 1931, so I knew her well. She was an avid seamstress, and I still remember the community costume she made and wore on special occasions."

"Oh my! Did you know her community costume was sent to us after she died?"

"She died the day after I turned fourteen," Kristen replied, "but I didn't remember what happened to her costume."

"I was five when we received it. My mother altered it so I could wear it to school, but I was embarrassed to wear it. Maybe if I had known my grandmother, I would have appreciated it more."

It occurred to me later that the big oak tree was a fitting symbol. The roots were like my ancestors reaching into the Danish soil, and the branches were like descendants, who have spread themselves across the world. In this moment of inspiration I decided to explore the family genealogy and compose a family tree which would include my ancestors and all my living relatives.

One by one, with clarity and force, the tales of my parents, cousins, and ancestors came alive. I felt like I had been reunited with the greatest family on earth, and I began to understand how my conscience took shape, how I acquired my personality and how the spirit given to me by God was hindered and nearly extinguished. I might have developed in quite another way had I been surrounded by all these cousins. I might have known who I was more clearly earlier in life had I also known my grandparents. The most important thing at the moment was the strong sense of acceptance and belonging I enjoyed with my relatives. Just to be among them for a short time seemed to inspire a surge of spiritual growth within me.

Two days later we boarded a train and headed for Struer in northern Jutland, where we had arranged to meet my cousin Emil Mikaelsen and his family. For several hours we glided across long expanses of pastoral countryside on a luxurious train, taking in the beautiful scenery through polished windows.

The landscape in Denmark is often very similar in appearance to parts of central Minnesota: rolling hills and valleys, scattered forests among farm fields, occasional lakes and many sloughs and bogs called fens over there. It is a small country with only one fifth the land area of Minnesota and only a slightly higher population. The countryside is populated with many of the same kinds of trees: maples, lindens, ash, spruce, and pine. Wildflowers common in Minnesota—such as tansy, plantain, mullein, curly dock, fireweed, red and white clover, Queen Anne's lace, and harebell—grow all over Denmark, althought they generally have different names.

Gordon noticed the farms were spaced throughout the countryside at about the same intervals seen in central Minnesota. Holsteins and Jerseys could be seen grazing in the pastures as well as plentiful numbers of sheep and horses. Barley, rye, and sugar beets appear to be the most common field crop. Cornfields are uncommon. Large wind turbines can be seen scattered across the countryside as well. We passed through a couple of tunnels and then, finally, came to a most magnificent view of the sea.

When we got off the train at Struer, Hanna was standing on the platform with her two older children. She took us to her summer home in the village of Thy, where her husband Holger was caring for their younger twins. During her college years Hanna visited us at Rush City. She still had fond memories of that visit. "Please tell me about Elaine," she inquired. This was a common inquiry among those in her family who had traveled to Minnesota and knew us. They were very interested in our family and very supportive.

The next morning Hanna's parents, Emil and Anna Mikaelsen, came to get us. We enjoyed the one hour drive to Thisted, their hometown, where Emil was a physician and owned a medical clinic. Holgor, a physician also, was in the process of taking charge of the clinic while Emil retired. Emil and Anna had visited my family at Ringsted in 1946 on their way to Berkeley and the mission field in China. Their younger daughter Rigmor, had also visited our farm at Rush City during her college years. She lived near the U of M when Elaine was hospitalized and made friends with her. I felt very close to this family, despite the great distance. Emil and Anna treated us to elegant meals, waiting on us and attending to our every need. Never have I been treated with more respect.

We toured Thisted that day with Rigmor and her husband Peter and spent the night at their house. The following day we went to church with them and then to the North Sea, sightseeing at the beach. Peter and Rigmor were both teachers as well as parents of two young children at that time. Rigmor taught at the local grade school and Peter taught Danish and French at a Gymnasium, the Danish word for high school. Their living room looked like a library. Both skilled musicians, they had two pianos and many other musical instruments. Much as we enjoyed the visit, Gordon and I were looking forward to the next leg of our trip, which would take us to Norway the following day.

Early on Monday morning, Peter took us to Hanstholm where we boarded the seven o'clock ferry to Norway. The boat ride across the Skagerrak was smoother than it usually is, and by noon we were in Kristiansand, heading for the train depot. It was one o'clock when our train departed for Oslo and soon we were rolling north through rugged wilderness landscape similar in appearance to the hills along the North Shore of Lake Superior, an utter contrast to the patchwork farm country of Denmark.

Vegarshei, the hometown of Gordon's paternal grandparents, is a small village two hours up the main railroad on the way to Oslo. We stepped off the train at Vegarshei rail stop and found ourselves staring at a rocky outcropping. Other than a few houses, the only building in sight was the train station, which we entered to inquire about lodging. "Is there a hotel in town?" asked Gordon.

"No," the man replied.

"Is there a restaurant?"

"No."

Gordon reached into his pocket and withdrew the list of names he had copied from his Aunt Carrie's will. When the man saw the name Bolsted, his eyes lit up. "There are two Bolsted families in town," he said, "but I don't know where they live. If you go to the grocery store, they can tell you."

At the grocery store, Gordon showed the list to a clerk. She looked at the name Bolsted and pointed to a house on the hillside nearby. We thanked her, went to the house, and knocked on the door.

A woman about our age appeared. Her fingers were all blue from picking blueberries. She did not understand a word of English, so Gordon showed her the list of names, copied from Carrie's will. That list included the names of Alma and Anna Bolsted, Carrie's two nieces in Norway and Gordon's cousins. She looked confused. I began to explain in Danish that Gordon was related to her aunt Carrie in America. The Norwegian language is similar to the Danish. She seemed to understand that we knew Carrie but still could not figure out who we were. After forty minutes of haggling, she suddenly comprehended that Gordon was the American cousin Carrie had told her about. Then she became very excited and invited us into the house.

Alma introduced us to her husband Olav and pulled a photo album off the shelf. She invited us to sit down in the living room and showed us the photos of Gordon and his parents, sent to them by Aunt Carrie. After serving us a delicious supper, Alma walked with us to the cemetery and showed us some graves of Gordon's relatives.

On the way back, we went to meet Anna, who was also thrilled to meet us. We learned that the men, Anna's husband and son and Alma's two sons, all worked for the railroad. When Gordon told them he milked thirty-six cows, it was almost more than they could comprehend. The one thing these folks had in common with my Danish relatives was their hospitality. Alma invited us to stay overnight at her house. She put sheets and blankets on the two living room couches and kindly left us a night pail so we would not have to find our way to the outhouse in the dark.

Before immigrating to America, Knud and Martha Gunderson lived on the Ufsvaten homestead about twelve kilometers southwest of Vegarshei. If time had permitted, it would have been fun to see the place, but we needed to head back the following day. We got on the 2 p.m. train and enjoyed the spectacular ride back to Kristiansand, marveling at our good fortune in Norway. Everything had fallen into place along the way. We had located Gordon's cousins with no information other than the name of a town and a list of relatives.

At Kristiansand we boarded the overnight ferry and slept all the way back to Denmark. The next morning we took the train south to Arhus, the second largest city in Denmark and the capital of Jutland. My cousin Magna, Emil's sister, met us at the train depot. We stayed overnight at her place before taking a bus back to Vejrup, where Sina and Kristen entertained us one more evening. My cousin Alfred came over to give me the letters they received from my parents in 1926 and 1927, family treasures stored away for fifty years.

On our last full day in Denmark, we took the train back to Copenhagen, stopping in Odense for a few hours on the way to visit two more cousins. Most of our visits and connections including this one had been arranged by my cousins who only knew of our desire to meet them and the length of our stay. I met fifteen Danish cousins and was overwhelmed by the displays of love, interest, and generosity throughout the trip. The information and history I gathered along the way was a potent beginning for assembling the puzzle of my past. I kept a trip diary the whole way, typed it up when I got home, and self-published a fifty-six page booklet entitled *Broadening Horizons*.

17

Choral Evensong

When the ferry docked at Battery Park, I waited in line as the crowd filed slowly off the boat. The cloud cover remained, but the air was warming up. With my stomach growling, I found a food stand, bought a hotdog, and went to a nearby park bench. While I sat there eating, an elderly man with a cane approached slowly along the walkway. The closer he got, the more he resembled my father, with his wool pants, brown tweed sports-jacket, and the same type of cap a farmer would wear. Transfixed, I swallowed the last of my hotdog as he passed by. Then I followed him on my way to the street and snapped a photo or two while he looked the other way.

With time to spare, I walked north along Broadway Avenue past Bowling Green, the oldest park in New York. A sixteen-foot-long bronze bull crouches there on the cobblestone median, supposedly to symbolize the stock market, head down and nostrils flaring as though poised to charge up Broadway. I came to Wall Street a couple blocks farther up. Someone said this was called the "Canyon of Heroes," the historic location of ticker-tape parades. On the right was a view straight down Wall Street into the heart of the financial district; on the left stood a stately old church and a cemetery. What an odd juxtaposition! I circled the cemetery, admiring the tulips, green grass, and ancient gravestones, and then went to the street and waved in a yellow cab.

"St. Thomas Church please," I said, sliding into the backseat." It's on Fifth Avenue at Fifty-third Street."

"Yes, ma'am. I know right where it is," the driver replied. He was a Negro with a strong Caribbean accent and a friendly manner. We drove past the twin towers of the World Trade Center and headed north toward Midtown Manhattan.

156

"Are you here on a tour, Ma'am?" he asked.

"Just for the day," I replied. "How could you tell?"

"You don't sound like a New Yorker."

"Do you live here?" I asked.

"I live in the Bronx—moved here from Haiti five years ago. Did you ever hear about Baby Doc Duvalier?"

"Sounds familiar, but I can't say for sure."

"Well, he's the dictator in Haiti. He murders people. That's why I came to New York. I have five children, and I can barely feed them on the money I make."

My heart went out to the man. "How old are your children?" I asked.

"The oldest is ten," he replied. "The youngest is two. Thank you for asking."

Although I was not in the habit of tipping taxi drivers, I gladly gave this fellow an extra dollar at the end of the ride, and he seemed pleased with that.

I stepped from the taxi at St. Thomas Church, went around the corner and up the steps for the second time that day. The four o'clock Choral Evensong would be starting in thirty minutes. Having enjoyed the morning service, I was interested in hearing the choir concert too. The narthex was empty and the choir, composed entirely of men and boys, was rehearsing in the sanctuary.

This time I went up the far left aisle to the Chantry Chapel, a smaller space supposedly used for baptisms and small weddings. The baptismal font and scenes painted above the altar depicted the baptism of Jesus and other biblical stories. I sat down for a few minutes and studied the brightly painted figures and exquisite carved wood.

At four o'clock I went back to the middle section of pews, where I had a good view of the choir. The organist concluded the prelude and played the first hymn. Then the congregants sat as the choir sang Psalms 141, 142, and 143. I followed along in *The Book of Common Prayer* and heard these words sung by the choir: "I cry with my voice to the Lord, with my voice I make supplication to the Lord, I pour out my complaint before him. When my spirit is faint, thou knowest my way . . ."

I remembered several times when my spirit had grown faint. Each time I had emerged a little stronger in myself and in my faith. And through each tribulation I had become wiser about my own self-care. It was this accumulation of wisdom, gained from counseling and life experience, that became my bulwark against calamity and crisis. I had learned the virtue of letting go and the value of simple trust. And I believed that all things would work out according to God's plan, which was rarely discernable ahead of time. The inner wisdom I came to possess was the voice of God speaking within me.

This did not mean my path was easy. It only meant that I was better equipped to handle the calamities that confronted me. Indeed, I had emerged only recently from the latest crisis and was still on the path of recovery. Elaine's death wasn't the only tragedy I endured. A more jarring trauma involving Ken was in the making even before Elaine died. Like Elaine, Ken recovered rather quickly from his initial instability, but thereafter he experienced periodic psychotic relapses, each growing progressively worse. With a tempered will and an accumulation of life experience, I endured my most difficult tribulation, which began to unfold in 1975 not long after moving to Mora.

18

Psychotic Relapses

With our move to Mora in 1974, Gordon fulfilled his dream of returning to full time farming. The rest of us were getting on with our lives as well. Dave began his career in trucking. Ernie went to St. Cloud State to study engineering. Margaret remained near Rush Point with her husband and son. Only two of our boys took an interest in farm work, Ken and Dave. Ken lived at home while he attended Pine City Vocational Technical School to get an education in farm management.

The rest of our children were still attending public schools in Mora with one graduating and leaving home every year or two. As the children grew up and became self-sufficient, I assumed responsibility for the financial aspects of the farm business such as bill paying, record keeping, asset management, and tax preparation.

There were many bright spots and happy occasions during our early years in Mora. Dave got married to Cindy. Carol married Lowell. Eunice went to off to college and married Mike. Marlon graduated number two in his class and went to St. Olaf College. Gordon won awards in milk production with his Holsteins. Ernie, our first to graduate from college, got his degree in engineering and found a job in the Twin Cities. By 1981 we were blessed with five more grandchildren. I could go on with all the good news and happy events, but the next memory I need to recount is not about success or achievement or happiness.

After completing his first year of trade school, Ken found a construction job for the summer. In his spare time, he helped Gordon with the farm work. Ken continued his farm management schooling in the fall of 1975, having declined an offer for permanent employment with the construction company. When winter arrived, however, he began to exhibit peculiar behavior. His thinking and movements grew sluggish. It was as though a thickening fog impeded his mind. One day his instructor called from Pine City to ask if he was using drugs, but we assured him that was not the case.

Shortly after Ken left for school on January 31, we got a call from the Kanabec County Hospital. "Your son was in an accident," the woman said. "We need you to sign admittance papers." Gordon and I hurried to the hospital and found Ken lying in bed with a large bandage over his nose. Although he seemed lucid and stable, we learned later he had a concussion and a fractured hip. Ken had run off the road on the way to town. He sped through the stop sign at Highway 6, plowed over a large snow bank, and smashed headlong into a tree. The car was demolished. The police said he was lucky to be alive.

We were hoping the mishap was accidental, but the evidence suggested otherwise. Asking Ken if it was a suicide attempt was not something we were able to do. Fearing the worst, we did not ask. Years later he told Ernie that it was a suicide attempt, although the intended target had been a concrete bridge on the way to Pine City. He could not explain why he drove into the tree instead.

The doctor told us Ken was hallucinating when the accident occurred. As the days progressed following the accident, Ken became more disturbed, confused, and delusional. They moved him to a private, lockable room and summoned a psychiatrist from Braham. The next day he was transferred to Golden Valley Mental Health Center in the Twin Cities, which was better equipped to deal with him. During our second visit there to see him, the attending psychiatrist recommended ECT because Ken was not responding to medication. We approved, and they commenced with shock therapy.

Ken's hallucinations and delusional thinking gradually subsided. After two months, he was stable enough to come home, but he did not return to vocational school. Instead he went to work helping Gordon on the farm. Hard labor was one thing Ken did especially well, particularly when it did not involve a lot of personal interaction. This quality also caught the attention of a local dairy equipment dealer, who offered Ken a job installing dairy equipment in the spring of 1976. After a few weeks on the job, his boss reported that Ken was reliable and hardworking.

At home Ken was usually obedient and helpful. He could also be lively. He enjoyed debating or playing the devil's advocate. Sometimes he instigated arguments with his younger siblings with a curious kind of oppositional humor. Sometimes he was resentful of their successes, and sometimes he was disrespectful or unkind to them. One day, for example, Ken smashed a model airplane which Marlon had just spent several days assembling. Geoff remembered that Ken would wrestle him into submission when they had disagreements. One night while Eunice and her boyfriend were kissing on the livingroom couch, Ken went outside and poured water in the fellow's gas tank.

Socially Ken was marginalized; in fact, he had practically no friends at all except Margaret's husband John with whom he hunted occasionally. Ernie, his closest brother and childhood playmate, was long gone and only rarely came home to visit. Although they were not close any more, Ernie occasionally invited Ken to go camping or canoeing. Usually Ken was busy helping Gordon with the farm work. Ken seemed to derive satisfaction and self-esteem from his work.

The dairy equipment job went well for Ken. A few months later, however, Ken got an offer from the Dairy Herd Improvement Association in Kanabec County to take the milk testing position. Trained and well suited for the work, Ken accepted the job. He also moved to town and rented a boarding room at the Lake Hotel. The social worker at Golden Valley had encouraged him to try independent living. Ken's life seemed to be getting back on track. His new job and living arrangement went well for almost a year. Then Ken's condition began to deteriorate again and the telltale signs of a relapse began to appear.

First he withdrew socially. He made no eye contact, even with family members. His affect was flat, his movements slow and deliberate. His comprehension was sluggish. Several neighbors and friends, whom Ken had seen for milk testing, told us he seemed confused and was not functioning well. Before anyone confronted him, however, Ken began a two week vacation just before his twenty-first birthday in August.

Psychotic Relapses

While Ken was on vacation, his landlord called from the hotel. He said Ken had disappeared without paying his rent. I telephoned friends and family members but found no one who knew where he was. In a state of alarm, I went to city hall and filed a missing person report with the police department. Eunice helped me move Ken's belongings out of the boarding room.

A week later, Ken was still missing. No one had called, and nothing had come up anywhere regarding his whereabouts. Dave decided to do some investigating on his day off. He went to the Mora police department and asked if they had heard anything.

"Not a thing," he was told.

"Have you initiated any action to search for him?"

"Posted a missing person bulletin last week. We don't normally search for anyone unless there's a lead."

Next, Dave went to the Lake Hotel. Several people were lounging on the veranda as he went up the steps. "Any of you folks know my brother Ken?" he asked.

"I do," replied a middle-aged woman.

"When did you last see him?"

"Can't remember," she said. "But a while back he was talking about living off the land - said he was thinking about trying it someday."

Just then a man emerged from inside. "Lookin' for Ken?" he asked.

"Yeah. Do you know anything?"

"The last time I saw Ken," the man said, pointing west, "he was headed that way walking on the railroad tracks. That was about a week and a half ago."

Dave drove back to the police department and told the dispatcher, "Someone at the hotel saw him walking west on the railroad tracks. Is there anyone who could go along on a search?"

The dispatcher radioed a patrol car and requested help. Then he told Dave, "Someone will meet you on the west end of town in ten minutes."

Dave drove to the farthest street crossing where the railroad tracks headed west out of town. Before long a patrol car pulled up, and two deputies stepped out to meet him. The three men walked west on the railroad tracks about a half mile to the Snake River bridge, where a large

162

wooded lowland begins across the river. Walking over the bridge, Dave spotted something in the trees south of the tracks. "There's something white over there in the trees," he said.

"I'll check it out," said one of the deputies. Dave and the other deputy continued west. They hadn't gone far when a shout came from the woods. "I found him!"

Dave hurried back to the bridge and watched the deputy lead Ken out of the woods, dirty, emaciated, and gaunt. He was found sitting up against a tree, wearing only jeans and a white tee shirt, having eaten nothing but a few berries in ten days. The three convinced Ken to go along to the hospital where he was bathed, fed and examined. I got the call from Dave right after they arrived. Paula ran happily out to the field to tell Gordon the news. By the time we got to the hospital, Ken was clean, lying in bed, and chewing on a granola bar. Gordon broke into tears and hugged him. I hugged him too and told him we loved him. We were both very relieved.

The doctor recommended Ken's return to Golden Valley Mental Health Center. Ken went willingly with Gordon the following day. Again he was treated with ECT and held for about one month. During Ken's stay at Golden Valley, Ernie, who lived and worked nearby, went to visit him regularly. One day Ernie scheduled an appointment to see Ken's psychiatrist. "What is your prognosis for Ken?" Ernie asked.

"Ken has chronic paranoid schizophrenia," replied Dr. Clark. "Because of the early onset and suicidal behavior, the outlook is grim. It is only a matter of time before he attempts suicide again, and next time he will be more determined and probably more effective, like jumping in front of a train, for example. I have seen other cases like him, and that is what you can expect. If I had observed Ken in his childhood, I could have predicted this. The signs are usually there at a young age." This was Dr. Clark's calculated answer and attitude in a nutshell. He maintained little hope for Ken.

When discharged in September, Ken seemed happy to be coming home. He smiled when we arrived to pick him up and seemed pleased we had driven down in his car. The clarity of mind, however, and the good humor Ken presented the first few days at home was but a fleeting respite. He refused to take the antipsychotic medication and insisted that he was fine. Less than a week passed before Ken announced one day that he was going to the Museum of Science in Chicago to take a spaceship to Pluto.

I tried to reason with him. "Why do you wanna go to Pluto?" I asked.

"For publicity," he replied, and then he sped off on his motorcycle.

Having told me he needed to stop at the courthouse to pick up his new driver's license, I called to warn them that Ken was coming and that he was delusional. I asked them to try reasoning with him. It wasn't long before a man called back and said they had talked him out of going. He asked me to come and get Ken as they were going to keep his motorcycle until Ken's thinking cleared up. By then it was well known at city hall and in the neighborhood that Ken was mentally deranged.

When I brought him home, Ken went reluctantly out to help Gordon with silo filling. As the day progressed, Ken became more and more agitated and oppositional, and that night he did not settle down. On my way upstairs to bed, I encouraged him to get a good night's rest.

At 1:30 a.m. we got a call from the police. "A neighbor of yours called to report that your son is walking down the road toward town," the man said. "A squad car is on the way to pick him up. They'll take him to the hospital. We'll call you back if they need you to get involved."

At 2:30 a.m. they called back and asked Gordon to come in and sign admittance papers at the Mora hospital. Feeling incapable of dealing with Ken at home, Gordon went in to sign the papers. The following morning the doctor called and told us Ken had been transferred to Moose Lake State Hospital.

"Why not Golden Valley?" I asked.

The doctor explained almost apologetically, "We consulted Ken's psychiatrist at Golden Valley. Dr. Clark said there was nothing more they could do for him. He recommended that Ken be sent to Moose Lake."

"Can we go up there to see him?"

"No. He's violent and had to be put into restraints," the doctor said. "The social worker in charge will be calling you."

Having worked for the state hospital system, Gordon knew all about Moose Lake. At the time, only the hard core mentally ill were sent there. It had the atmosphere of a prison. We felt very worried about Ken and went the following day to sign papers for his temporary commitment pending a court hearing in two weeks.

"By then," the welfare official said, "maybe he'll calm down."

I felt terrible and irresponsible for not knowing how to help Ken and for not preventing his incarceration at Moose Lake. Gordon and I were busy with fall harvest and milking 36 cows twice a day. With four other dependents still under our roof, we just didn't know what else to do.

Ken's records from Moose Lake tell the story. To summarize, Ken became combative when the sheriff came to take him up there. He broke out some lights at the Mora hospital and then threatened to break out the lights at Moose Lake too, which is what he did upon arrival when they put him in a locked cell. Then he broke the window out of the door, so they put him in a secluded room in four-point restraints; that is, with a team of eight men they pinned him on his back to a sturdy bed, cuffing his hands and feet to the corner posts. When Ken refused to take his medication, the doctor in charge ordered forced injections of Haldol to be given each time he refused medication. Several times a day they injected him in the buttocks with this powerful anti-psychotic drug while he lay strapped to the bed.

At mealtime, Ken's wrist restraints were removed so that he could eat, when willing, and he was taken several times a day in a straight-jacket to the toilet. Three times on the way to the toilet, he bolted for the door, and each time the accompanying orderlies wrestled him to the floor and dragged him back to seclusion. When he refused to eat for several days, they put him on an IV.

The case notes by staff workers indicate that Ken pleaded daily to be released so he could walk home. He claimed to know the way. He spoke often of wanting to be in a coffin, and according to the notes, he planned to jump off the silo to kill himself. When asked why, he said, "I've been treated several times for mental illness, and I don't see any hope."

I am quite sure that if Ken had been treated with respect and gentle persuasion by the authorities after they found him on the road that night, or if he had been sent back to Golden Valley, all of this could have been avoided. Before that night, Ken had not been a violent person. I'd like to know what they did to him. Did they treat him roughly because they knew he was mentally ill or feared he might be dangerous?

After ten days in restraints, many injections of Haldol, and intravenous feeding, Ken's resistance was broken. The fight went out of him, and he began to cooperate with his caregivers. The staff psychiatrist saw him at this time and made an interesting note in the record. It was his opinion that Ken was suffering from catatonic schizophrenia, not the paranoid schizophrenia diagnosed at Golden Valley. The forced injections were discontinued, but he was kept in the four-point restraints when unattended until his departure for the court hearing.

It so happened that Carol, Ken's next younger sibling, had scheduled her wedding that fall on the first of October. Aware of Ken's incarceration, yet unaware of the grisly details, it was with regret for his absence and concern about his predicament that the rest of us gathered in Rush City to celebrate Carol and Lowell's wedding. To the Nelson family and an audience of friends and relatives, I made no secret of the fact Ken was at Moose Lake. Present that day among our guests was Gordon's niece Janet and her husband Dr. Sam Lotegeluaki, a psychologist at St. Mary's Hospital in Rochester. Alarmed at the news, Sam drove straight to Moose Lake after the wedding to visit Ken. However, Ken was still strapped to the bed in isolation and not allowed to have visitors. Before leaving, Sam scribbled a note of encouragement, promising Ken he would attend the court hearing.

Ken was taken to the Kanabec County Courthouse on October 13, where he was locked up behind bars. Gordon and Sam went there before the court hearing to greet him and offer him words of encouragement. I saw Ken for the first time in over two weeks when he was escorted into the courtroom by two burly deputies. Attending the hearing with us were my brother John from Northfield and Sam Lotegeluaki, who wanted to prevent Ken's permanent commitment to the state hospital as recommended by the county attorney.

The two doctors who examined Ken said he was permanently disabled, that he would never recover, and that he should be institutionalized. Citing these opinions, the county attorney suggested that Ken be returned to Moose Lake and that he should not be allowed to go home with us. That's when Sam stepped forward and presented his credentials. He volunteered to take Ken into his custody so that he could counsel and rehabilitate him. The judge agreed and Ken, a pen stroke away from permanent commitment to the state hospital, was free to go with Sam.

Janet and Sam Lotegeluaki lived on a farm near Kasson and both worked at St. Mary's Hospital in Rochester where they had met. An immigrant from Arusha in northern Tanzania, Sam was a practicing psychologist, thirty-eight years old at the time. Whether it was a simple act of altruism, a result of his personal integrity, an opportunity to practice his trade, or a reflection of familial ethos rooted in the Maasai culture of his homeland, Sam's generosity was a personal sacrifice of high order. Using no force, no threats or restraints, and no medication, Sam personally supervised and counseled Ken, giving him indoor responsibilities as well as outdoor chores. He dedicated hours of his personal time each day over the span of five weeks. In his written evaluation, Dr. Lotegeluaki rated Ken's conceptualization I.Q. not less than 130 and his comprehension at 112 despite his diagnosis of schizophrenia.

"He can still function in society if it does not greet him with hostility," Sam wrote. "It is the responsibility of his family to create a generous, forgiving, supportive, receptive, and loving atmosphere for him," which is exactly what we did when Ken came home to Mora a few days before Thanksgiving. We welcomed him home and showed him all the supportive love and kindness we could muster.

As a consequence of his involuntary commitment and treatment at Moose Lake, Ken developed a deep antipathy and distrust toward all doctors and lawyers, including Doctor Sam who rescued him. Because Ken had been declared disabled, he qualified for social security income. Soon he was receiving monthly social security checks, considered a permanent benefit unless he found employment. Never one to loaf around, however, Ken went back to assisting Gordon with the farm work. And gradually his competence and former ambition returned.

As if to prepare himself for future self-defense, Ken took up body building as a pastime and a passion. He acquired barbells and began weight

Psychotic Relapses

lifting every day. Before long it started to show. His neck thickened, his shoulders and biceps bulged, and Ken took on the look of a muscular body builder without an ounce of fat. When his brothers came home to visit, he took pride in demonstrating his strength, either in arm wrestling or handstand pushups, ten in a row with his feet propped straight up against the wall. His feats of physical prowess seemed to give Ken a needed boost in self-esteem after the terrible humiliation of his insanity and his treatment at Moose Lake.

Ken continued living at home and helping Gordon with the farm work. What he lacked in interpersonal skills and emotional stability, he made up for with hard work and dependability. We came to rely heavily on his assistance in many aspects of the farm operation. For example, Ken operated the feed grinder which ground the corn into feed. He fed the cows, cleaned the dairy barn, cleaned the calf barns, hauled manure, chopped the bedding, dehorned the calves, baled hay, filled the silo, unloaded the silo, harvested the oats, mounted the corn picker on the tractor, picked the corn, helped put up corn cribs, removed the mounted corn picker, fixed the machinery, oiled the machinery, cut the firewood, split and stacked it in the basement, and carried out the ashes. These are just some of the many tasks he performed for us, willingly and reliably.

Each Sunday Ken went to church with us, but he seemed stiff and uncomfortable in a crowd. I was glad when they asked him to be an usher at church. He agreed and did quite well at it. Sam had suggested, and I agreed, that Ken should get counseling at the Braham Mental Health Clinic. After going once, however, he refused to go back again.

"He needs to be in counseling," I told Gordon.

"Ken should not be forced to go if he doesn't want to go," Gordon replied.

Next I went to our pastor to ask his advice. "You and Gordon could go together back to Braham and talk to Ken's counselor," he suggested.

At Braham his counselor said, "If Ken doesn't want to go, the counseling wouldn't do a whole lot of good." Eventually I gave up trying to maneuver Ken into counseling and hoped for the best, but I could not help but foresee a grim future.

About a year after the debacle at Moose Lake, the county welfare office called to ask if Ken would be interested in applying for a job opening at the Fingerhut Company in Mora. They were looking for a material handler. Although Ken seemed mostly recovered at the time, I felt nervous about his ability to function in a job that required interaction with others. As a vulnerable adult, he was susceptible to the inconsiderate and potentially provocative responses from others who did not understand his illness. Nevertheless, he wanted the job, even if it meant losing his social security income.

The job at Fingerhut went better than I expected. His workmates seemed to give him a measure of respect, perhaps owing to his powerful-looking physique, which he continued to hone daily. When he was not weightlifting, Ken continued working for us too, giving us two hours labor each day in exchange for room and board. For any time beyond that, we paid him a decent wage. Ken often worked well in excess of the two hours agreed upon even though we did not require it.

At Fingerhut Ken was promoted from materials handler to materials coordinator and from that to fork lift driver. He received several pay increases along the way. His job, however, was not without a few disturbing interactions with his coworkers and superiors. Ken was a hard worker, but at times his behavior was noticably odd. Others could easily observe his peculiarities, which occasionally invited criticism or ridicule from thoughtless or irritable coworkers.

Although it has genetic etiology, schizophrenia is thought to be triggered or exacerbated by stress. For persons afflicted by schizophrenia, the relatively calm periods characterized by more normal functioning, or baseline behavior, can often be maintained for years between recurrent psychotic episodes. Many people with schizophrenia can live fairly normal lives with the benefit of medications, the guidance of a social worker, and helpful, compassionate family members. But the disorder comes in a variety of shades, types, and intensities. No two cases are exactly alike. Unfortunately, the stress one might experience in the course of employment or even in the normal passages and transitions of life, such as leaving home or losing a girlfriend, can become triggers for decompensation in schizophrenia. Although we were not educated in proper psychiatric lingo at the time, we were well aware of these concepts and the possible risks facing Ken in a cruel world. It was with this tension we coexisted with Ken more or less trouble free for a period of seven years.

It was during this period that Gordon and I went to Denmark and observed many other memorable family events. Geoff and Paula graduated from high school. Milton got married to Robin Hall. My mother died at the age of 90. I flew with her body to Arizona and buried her next to Dad. Ernie endured ten months of chemotherapy for Hodgkin's disease and got married to Jane Souhrada, all within a year. Ken was a groomsman in the wedding. Marlon went off to Stanford University to get his MS in electrical engineering. There he met his future wife, Julie Bunn. Things went along quite smoothly until 1984, when both Ken and I suffered major setbacks.

In August I was diagnosed with endometrial cancer and had a total hysterectomy followed by four weeks of radiation therapy at the University Hospital. Five days a week, I had radiation treatment for about an hour, so I had lots of time to do as I pleased while staying at Ernie and Jane's house in Minneapolis. One day it occurred to me to look up Elaine's hospital records since I was at the University Hospital every day anyway. First I had to get permission; then I went each day to the records library, found a secluded place, and sat down with the stack of Elaine's records.

As I perused the reams of patient notes, I was disheartened to find many critical comments in the personal history and summary of Elaine's home and parents. Here are some of the comments I found, which I recorded in my notebook:

1. Childhood was generally unhappy in adverse home environment.

2. Elaine was the focus of much undesirable altercation. Her mother made many unreasonable demands, constantly degrading her performance.

3. A fundamentalist Christian background, in addition to her mother's demands and reproof, instilled an ever-present feeling of sinfulness and guilt.

4. Nursing staff must work intensively with Elaine to achieve a more positive role model than her mother presented.

5. There evidently has been little communication between her parents with an atmosphere of emotional coldness prevailing.

6. Pathological home situation indicates a psychotic or near psychotic mother, an indifferent, punitive, and uninvolved father, and a family of many children without accompanying emotional and financial security. Very religious background with home environment producing feelings of guilt, shame, and inadequacy.

I was shocked and saddened. I had always considered myself a good mother, doing the utmost for my children. The indictment on my integrity as a mother was clear and powerful. I felt guilty as charged. Hoping to find exoneration and comfort during the remaining days of my treatment, I went to other libraries. I read books on schizophrenia by authors such as Werner Mendel, M.D., and jotted down many pages of notes. At that time, however, it had not been concluded that schizophrenia is a disorder of the brain, so it was difficult to find comfort in the academic texts. When my cancer treatment was completed, I remained heavy hearted and went home to regain my health as well as my self-esteem.

Ken's setback was that he got fired from his job that fall. A coworker had repeatedly taunted and provoked him. Ken finally lost his temper, picked the guy up and tossed him into a dumpster. The fellow sustained no injury, but Ken was fired because he had broken the rules. It was just the thing I had often feared. The only silver lining was the timing, which was favorable because I was out of commission for many months as a result of my cancer surgery, and Ken became available to help Gordon when I could not.

Dave, our only other son who took an interest in the farm, had taken a break from his trucking career earlier that year to work with Gordon on the farm. He was considering taking over our dairy business when Gordon retired. The idea soured, however, when Dave discovered, as he put it, "his day off was when he only had to work eight hours." When Dave went back to trucking, Ken was available full time again to work for Gordon, who was grateful for the help and companionship after Dave's departure. Ken busied himself with the farm work, and things went along quite well that way for nearly a year.

Psychotic Relapses

When Marlon and Julie got married in Pasadena the following September, Gordon and I left Ken in charge of the farm while we vacationed for a week in California and attended the wedding. At the same time Ken was developing an interest in Vicky, a friend of Cindy's. Dave had introduced the two. While Ken tended the farm during the week we were gone, Vicky came to help with the chores and said she had a blast. By the time we returned from California, a romance had developed.

At first this appeared to be a positive development for Ken. During the week, Vicky drove up from Isanti, a half hour drive, to visit him. Each Sunday Ken drove down there and went to church with Vicky and Philip, her eight-year-old son. Before long Ken and Vicky got engaged and things seemed to be progressing rather well. As the days of autumn shortened, however, Ken began to exhibit the ominous signs of another psychotic relapse.

19

A Stroll Down Fifth Avenue

When the Evensong ended, I exited St. Thomas Church and strolled south along Fifth Avenue. I decided to walk over to Grand Central Station—nine short blocks down to 42nd Street and two long blocks over to Park Avenue. I had two hours to get back to Hartsdale and only a forty-minute train ride, plus I needed the exercise.

By then I was somewhat familiar with midtown Manhattan. Fifth Avenue, as it turns out, boasts some of the most prominent landmarks in the city, and it is one of the premiere shopping streets in the world. On the basis of square footage, Fifth Avenue often claims the world's most expensive retail spaces, which is why it is called the most expensive street in the world.

Three blocks south of St. Thomas, I came to the forty-five foot tall bronze statue of Atlas, bearing the world on his shoulders. The largest of many sculptures featured at Rockefeller Center, Atlas stands directly across the street from St. Patrick's Cathedral. I continued south another block where a promenade opens to the dazzling central plaza of Rockefeller Center. The promenade, replete with fountains and flower gardens, leads one to the towering GE building, the centerpiece of Rockefeller Center, home of NBC studios, the *Today Show,* and *Saturday Night Live.*

A plaque by the sidewalk says Rockefeller Center was one of the foremost architectural projects in America, in terms of scope, urban planning, art, and landscaping. Built between 1931 and 1939, it provided jobs for thousands of laborers during the Great Depression. One might wonder how such a large project could have been financed during the Depression when many banks were collapsing and most folks were

173

struggling just to keep food on the table. Rockefeller Center was built by the Rockefeller family, financed by the personal fortune of John D. Rockefeller, the family patriarch, the first American billionaire, and the richest man who ever lived. No American since then has even come close to amassing the fortune accumulated by John D. Rockefeller, due mostly to his near monopoly of the developing petroleum industry. To his credit, Rockefeller's ability to amass personal wealth was matched generously by his penchant for philanthropy.

Continuing south, I strolled past the flagship Saks Fifth Avenue store across the street. I noticed an increasing number of jewelry stores with names like Chilano, Sephora, Jewelers on Fifth, and Treasurly. At Forty-Seventh Street I passed the Diamond District. Over 2000 independent diamond traders and jewelers work on this one block alone. In fact, ninety percent of the diamonds in the United States enter through New York, the result of an influx of Orthodox Jews from the European diamond business who fled the Nazis by the thousands before and during World War II.

Block after block, I passed banks and upscale retailers such as Phantom of Broadway, Fossil Jewelers, Bank of New York, and Morgan Stanley. Ten blocks ahead, I could see the Art Deco tower atop the Empire State Building, the world's tallest building for over forty years after its completion in 1931. Many of the great buildings in midtown Manhattan were built in the late 1920s and 1930s when Art Deco styling was popular. A notable exception is the New York Public Library on the corner of Fifth Avenue and Forty-Second Street, a Beaux-Arts monolith with seventy-five miles of bookshelves.

I crossed Fifth Avenue and walked east along Forty-Second Street past Citibank and Price Waterhouse. Directly ahead was the stainless steel crown and spire atop the Chrysler Building, an Art Deco classic with exterior details resembling hood ornaments and radiator caps. I strolled past the remaining store fronts and entered Grand Central Terminal at 6:00 p.m. through the familiar southwest doors. This time I bought the three dollar senior ticket to Hartsdale.

The 6:30 train to Hartsdale was already waiting on track 27. I boarded the train and plopped into the padded seat, resting my weary legs.

Although it had been a long day, it was an unforgettable experience finding my own way around New York. It felt good to be on my own and make up my own mind about where to go and what to see. I opened my journal and began writing about Ellis Island and the streets of New York. I was writing about St. Thomas Church when the commuter train started rolling north.

As I watched the city passing by, my thoughts returned to Ken, the tragic life he lived, and the violent manner in which it ended. Four years and three months had passed since that frightful day in January, yet the images were still fresh.

20

Blessed Are Those Who Mourn

In the fall of 1985, Ken was facing crucial decisions and challenges regarding his future. He was engaged to be married but was still unemployed. Vicky did not have a job either, and Ken wanted to provide financial support for her and Philip. With this goal in mind, Ken began searching for a job and a place where he and Vicky could live when they got married. Although Gordon was planning on retiring in a year or two, Ken was neither interested in nor capable of managing the farm or the dairy operation, even if comfortable in his role as Gordon's assistant.

A week after Marlon and Julie's wedding, the newlyweds came to Minnesota for a hometown reception. During the celebration and a weekend of family festivities, some of Ken's siblings noticed that he was exhibiting more than his usual peculiarity. He seemed to isolate himself and had that rigid catatonic look. Ernie in particular was concerned and decided to do something about it.

The following Monday, Ernie called the Braham Mental Health Center and made an appointment for the entire family, including Ken, to see a psychologist. Ken refused to attend, but many of us showed up for the appointment to talk about the situation and to learn about any resources available to Ken. Ernie was the main spokesperson, explaining Ken's history. When I asked the psychologist if there were any services available for Ken, he told us that Social Services in Mora could send out a health nurse to talk with him. He also told us about the Area Vocational Professional Services (AVPS), which would help persons with mental illness to find jobs.

The attempted intervention may have produced some positive feelings and a little hope among us, but the results were incremental at best.

Ken continued his lonely struggle with schizophrenia. He was either too proud or too stubborn to accept the public assistance and was unable or unwilling to admit anything was wrong with him or to seek treatment or take medication.

The closest anyone came to getting through to him was Ernie. In October Ernie invited Ken and Vicky to his cabin in northern Wisconsin. Ken and Vicky took Phillip along and car pooled with Dave and Cindy. While spending the weekend together, Ernie invited Ken to go for a walk. They headed west on the footpath along the Moose River, chatting occasionally along the way. A half mile down the trail, Ernie turned and put his hand on Ken's shoulder. "I have something to tell you," he said. "I want you to know I love you, no matter what has happened in the past, regarding your illness and treatment. It doesn't matter to me."

Ken stood perfectly still, remaining silent, eyes fixed on the ground.

Then Ernie asked, "Can you tell when your illness is relapsing?"

Keeping his downward gaze, Ken slowly nodded his head. This was the first and only time Ken actually admitted to a family member that he was aware of his illness.

"Is there anything I can do to help you?" Ernie asked.

Ken slowly shook his head.

Ken's odd behavior was perhaps more noticeable to others who did not live with him. Some thought it was a little strange, for instance, that he drank sumac tea. Ken gathered the sumac, boiled it, strained it, and kept it in his thermos. I asked him about it one day. He claimed it was a recipe he had read about somewhere. Maybe it wasn't so strange, I thought. However, Ken really caught my attention when I saw him putting coffee grounds on his sandwich.

"Why are you putting coffee grounds on your sandwich?" I asked.

"A person needs food of every color," he replied. This was typical of Ken's thinking when he was decompensating.

At social gatherings Ken was ill at ease. He often avoided crowds and gatherings, even those among his own family. He did not communicate very well with me either. I tried to make conversation with him, but there wasn't the rapport there should have been. It was easier to talk with everyone else. However, we peacefully coexisted in our kitchen. He had his special places for his things, and we got along fine. He read the newspaper while he ate, and he read books in the evening.

I tried to overlook Ken's peculiarities and to see his many strengths instead. When Marlon and Ernie were concerned about Ken's withdrawal from the family, I pointed out all the things that he was doing well. Maybe it was my helplessness in knowing what to do for him or the fear of potentially disastrous outcomes that kept me in denial. He seemed to be taking care of business matters logically and continued his employment search methodically, calling about job openings he found in the want ads. Gordon and I had gradually developed an acceptance of his peculiarities. As long as he was functioning as well as he was, we let things slide along. We hoped perhaps Vicky could persuade him to get counseling before they got married.

Meanwhile, Ken was taking instructions on becoming a member of Vicky's church, Elim Baptist in Isanti. Without telling us, he got baptized by immersion one Sunday in December. When he came home that night, I asked, "How was your day?"

"Wet," he said.

"Wet?" I inquired.

"Yeah, I was immersed."

"I would like to have been there," I said. "I've never seen that done."

"I'm going to move to Isanti to be closer to Vicki," he said.

"Well, I can understand that," I replied.

The first week in January was very cold, and the cold snap was followed by a few days of thawing weather. Ken informed us he would be going to town three mornings the following week to search for job openings at the employment agency and told us he would be moving out in two weeks. We thought he was making progress and didn't want to hinder him from achieving the independence he desired. We felt he and Vicky should work things out for themselves and hoped they would find employment and a place to live. One day the two of them sat on the couch together, studying a list of job opportunities. My heart went out to Ken, and I hoped he would pursue something that would materialize.

Gordon found a man to help him who would be available part-time when Ken moved. The man came right over the next morning, after Gordon called, apparently eager to have a job. With my health and strength on the mend, I also felt able to help more with the barn chores. We accepted the fact that we would soon be empty nesters and began discussing retirement options. We went about our usual January business working on income taxes, going to meetings, and going to Tuesday night Bible studies. Whenever Ken left home, he was courteous and thoughtful to tell us, even calling long distance sometimes to tell us when he would be home. He was very private about his affairs, otherwise, and I generally did not pry or ask questions.

A week before he left us, Ken wasn't home one evening for supper as usual. Gordon had an ominous feeling that something was wrong. Then Ken came in from the woods after dark, having cut a month's supply of firewood. We were relieved and decided we couldn't rely on that kind of foreboding.

On January 21, Ken went about his own business. He had caught up with the feed grinding and bedding in the barn and replenishing the firewood in the basement. He made several trips to town, some on business for Gordon. We went to the annual lunch meeting of Kanabec County Cooperative Association. Afterward, it was beginning to snow and blow as the weather was turning bad. Ken arrived home shortly after we did. He went up to his room with an application of some kind, and then went back to town. Before long he called from town.

"Do you think I should move out?" he asked.

"I don't think you should move out until you find a job; otherwise your savings will be depleted," I replied.

"Oh, okay," he said and hung up.

The snow was coming down heavily, and soon it was time to begin the evening chores. Because Ken was not home yet, I went to feed the cows while Gordon started the milking. Normally Ken handled the silage, but I was able to do it also, whenever Ken was gone. I turned on the silo unloader

Blessed Are Those Who Mourn

and hauled the silage to the mangers, one wheelbarrow at a time. When the cattle were fed, I went to the house just as Ken returned from town. The wind had calmed and the stars were shining down on the newly fallen snow.

"I fed the cows," I said. "Do you want your supper now?"

"Okay. I'll be right back," he replied and went to his room. Five minutes later he was at the table eating the leftovers I had prepared for him.

It was hard for me to know what to say sometimes. He was quiet, and I tried lamely to make idle conversation. "When you find a job," I said, "perhaps it will easier to find a place to live, a place that's convenient for getting to your job. And don't worry about us; we'll get along okay without your help. I can help Gordon with the chores when the hired man can't come."

I only wanted Ken to feel free to pursue his own interests and not feel obligated to help with the farm work. In retrospect, I fear he got the wrong message and thought we did not want him anymore. How I wish now that I had expressed my appreciation for all he had done to help us or complimented him on how strong and able he was.

That evening Gordon and I watched a television program, which caught our interest, and soon we were absorbed in it. During a commercial break, I noticed Ken sitting on the floor next to the warm air register.

"Are you cold?" I asked. "Should I put more wood in the furnace?" "I'll take care of it," he said and went to the basement to stoke the furnace. Then he went upstairs.

We did not know it then, but Ken had called Vicky that afternoon to cancel the engagement. He had told her he was mentally ill and couldn't find a job.

After the 10 p.m. news, I went upstairs to bed. Ken's door was open, the light was on, and he was sitting in his chair looking through some papers. Nothing appropriate came to mind so I said, "Goodnight Ken," and didn't wait for an answer if there was one. Soon I was snuggled in a warm bed and fast asleep.

Sometime in the early morning, I remember hearing a crack but thought it was just the usual ice contraction we hear from the roof on cold winter nights. It did sound a little different though. I awoke later to the sound of Ken's alarm clock when it did not stop. Sleepily, I went to his room thinking he must have gotten up and forgotten to turn off the alarm. I went back to bed for another hour and then got up and went downstairs to face the new day.

In my morning prayers I asked God's blessing on all my children naming each one and asking for specific blessings as I thought about each of them and their needs, especially Ken and his need for a job and a place for himself and his future family. I prepared breakfast as usual and then, waiting for Ken and Gordon to come in from the barn, I went to the piano and played "Swing Low, Sweet Chariot."

At 8:45, Gordon came in from the barn just as the phone rang. It was Vicky calling for Ken, and Gordon told her, "Sure, just a minute, I think he's upstairs."

"He's not in his room," I said.

"He didn't come out to help me," Gordon replied.

"Well he's not in the house," I said.

Gordon told Vicky we didn't know where he was at the moment. Vicky suggested that maybe Ken was outside cutting wood again.

"Oh, that might be," Gordon replied.

"Tell him I'm coming over this morning," Vicky added.

"Okay, we'll see you then," Gordon said and then hung up the phone.

Every other morning, Ken got up at 6:30 to clean the barn. He usually came in for breakfast with Gordon, and if not with him, he came in shortly afterward. That morning, as usual, I had set a place for Ken at the table. Gordon and I ate without him and read our morning devotions. Afterward, I decided to go on my skis and follow his tracks that I was sure to find in the fresh snow.

I dressed warmly, braced for the cold air, and prepared to ski out to the farthest woods, if need be, to find Ken and let him know Vicky was coming. Starting out on my skis, I noticed his footsteps leading into the garage. I skied around the garage expecting to find his footprints leading from the back door, but there were none. So I went back around to the front and took off my skis. The garage door stood partially open. I opened the door and looked in. There he was lying before me, face down in a pool of blood in a most gruesome and unnatural way! What I saw darkened my life for years and will forever be imprinted on my mind. I turned in horror and ran to the house. "Ken shot himself!" I exclaimed. "Ken shot himself!" Gordon stood, shocked and immobile, while I grabbed the phone and dialed 911. Someone answered immediately.

"Our son shot himself," I declared numbly.

"Where is he?"

"In the garage," I replied.

"What's your name?" the kind woman asked.

"Mary Gunderson."

"Where do you live?"

"On a farm," I said, "a mile and a half north of Mora on Highway 8."

"Are you alone?"

"No, my husband Gordon is right here."

"I'll send a deputy. He'll be there soon. Do you want to stay on the phone?" she asked. "Are you all right?"

"Yes, thank you, I'm shaking but okay."

"It should only be a few minutes," she said.

Again, I thanked her and hung up phone.

Just then Vicky drove in. I went out and met her as she got out of her car. She knew something was wrong as Gordon was coming out right behind me. "Ken shot himself," I told her.

Immediately she began crying, "Oh, I should have come yesterday. I wanted to tell him I knew about his illness and that it makes no difference to me."

Shortly, the deputy sheriff drove in. We knew him from church and greeted him. "I don't want to take a second look," I said, "but Ken is right inside that door."

He went in and came out about as fast as I had.

"He's out cold, isn't he," I said.

The deputy nodded.

"I can't bear to go in there," I pleaded, "and I don't want Vicky or Gordon to see it either." They agreed.

"I need to call the coroner," said the deputy, and he called on his two-way radio.

The chief of police arrived next. He asked us to wait in the house while he and the deputy inspected the scene in the garage. Five minutes later the chief came in, introduced himself, and said he was sorry we had to meet under these circumstances.

"Do you know where his gun is?" he inquired.

"I don't know," I replied, wondering which gun he might have used and whether it could have been an accident. In my heart, however, I knew it was not an accident. "His guns are all up in his room," I continued, "but he doesn't own a pistol unless he bought one recently."

"We may find it beneath him," the chief said, "but I'd like to check his room."

I showed them to Ken's room. Meanwhile, the coroner and funeral director came and soon found the shotgun underneath Ken's body and the sawed off end of the barrel still clamped in the vise. They asked what time it happened. I said it must have been between 5:30 and 6:00 while I was asleep, and Gordon was in the barn.

Then Dave drove in. Gordon had called him at work. We embraced and wept together. All of us began incriminating ourselves for things we hadn't done or things we should have done.

I asked myself, why didn't I counsel him? Why didn't I put my arm around him as he was sitting there looking so sad the night before, and tell him that everything will work out? Even if he could not find a job, he could still get married. He and Vicky would have been welcome to live with us. Why didn't I offer that to him? Why didn't I offer to type the letter he needed that day? Why didn't I applaud his strength and his capabilities more than I had? Why didn't I . . . ? Why? Why?

Likely aware of his deepening slide into psychotic confusion, unable to find another job, without hope, and probably in need of another hospitalization, Ken gave up his struggle on that cold morning in January. Gordon and I were in shock for days after it happened. We agonized for months over our last interactions with him, trying to identify all the possible errors we might have made and all the possible actions we might have taken to prevent his suicide. I wrote a long letter to Ken, filling an entire journal, to say everything I should have said before he died, rehashing the final months, days, and hours of his existence.

In writing this letter, I reconstructed the scene and the events leading up to it, hoping in vain to relieve the pain, but I was only at the beginning of the grieving process. Not only was Ken our last one at home, he was Gordon's companion and right hand man on the farm. More than a shocking end to our son's life, it was also our abrupt transition to the empty nest. Of course, Ken's suicide also brought back the memories and grief from Elaine's death. After the funeral, I sank into bitter regrets and self-reproach, which was fueled by the doctor's comments I found in Elaine's records. For a long time I bore a cross of shame and self-blame.

To cope with the pain, I joined a grief group at a local church, where the facilitator invited people to talk about their losses. At first I listened and didn't share a whole lot; the memories were still too intense. When I finally began to speak about Ken and Elaine, I mostly wept, but everyone seemed to understand. The overwhelming response was one of deep sympathy. Several months later, still in a lot of pain, I decided to attend an Emotions Anonymous meeting at the Mental Health Center in Braham. There I learned about Recovery, Inc., a community-based, non-profit organization run by volunteers. I liked the concept and began attending the meetings, where I also found helpful books on mental illness.

Gordon, sixty-four that year and close to retirement, lost his ambition to continue farming. Everywhere he looked, he saw reminders of Ken. My assistance in feeding the cattle and the hired man were not enough to replace Ken. When the 1986 federal dairy buyout program took effect, Gordon sold his entire herd of dairy cows. Many of our better producing cows went to a farmer in Manitoba, and some of the heifers were exported to China. The dairy buyout was a godsend for us because it guaranteed us a premium price for our dairy cows during the "farm crisis" when prices were generally plummeting. That year was a very depressed year for farmers nationwide. The price of farmland, which peaked in 1981, plummeted 60 to 75 percent by 1986 as the "farm crisis" climaxed and many farmers went broke.

As if to assuage our pain in the months following Ken's suicide, three happy events occurred. Two more grandchildren arrived, Ellie and Soo. And Paula, our youngest, graduated from vocational school and got married to Brad, her high school sweetheart.

I continued on the road to recovery, attending the group meetings and reading books and articles about mental illness. The more I searched, the more I found that other folks were suffering too. There seemed to be a pervasive need for help among other families experiencing mental illnesses. Six months after Ken died, I attended a meeting of the Five County Consortium for the Mentally Ill at the Braham Mental Health Center. Among other things, I learned of their plan to open a community support program in Mora which would offer daytime treatment twice a week for the mentally ill. When they asked for volunteers to help organize the effort, I raised my hand.

This was the beginning of my volunteer work to help others avoid the terrible pain I had endured myself. As long as I lived, it would be my mission to see that no family in this community would ever have to suffer the way my family had.

The community support program in Mora died on the vine when it did not win necessary county and municipal approval. However, with encouragement from Carol Hass, the local facilitator of Emotions Anonymous and an alliance member in Mille Lacs County, I agreed to organize a Mora chapter of the Alliance for the Mentally Ill (AMI), affiliated with the State and National Alliance for the Mentally Ill. The first monthly meetings were held at Zion Lutheran Church in the fall of 1986. I ran notices in the local paper and on local radio, and by year's end the meetings were attended by up to a dozen individuals well acquainted with the experience of mental illness in their families.

Although I did not pursue this volunteer work for personal gain, it was the sharing of my loss and my effort to help others that really began to assuage my own pain. When others shared in my grief, it reduced the burden, which I could not carry alone. Focusing on the grief of others around me and joining hands with them, I received a satisfaction and comfort that overshadowed my own grief.

Blessed Are Those Who Mourn

The mission of the AMI, as stated in our first brochure, was to "better the lives of mentally ill people and their families by helping to create needed services, to improve public perception of mental illness and the people it affects, and to provide information and support." The more I pursued these goals, the more I learned about the inconsistency and lack of public support for the mentally ill. After the deinstitutionalization of mental health services in the 1960s and 1970s, county governments were given block grants to deal with mental health problems in whatever way they pleased. Although some counties used this money to provide services, many counties such as ours did little or nothing.

In November I was disappointed when a building permit for a group home was unanimously denied by the Mora City Council. The home was intended for rehabilitation of emotionally and mentally challenged persons. It would have provided a twenty-four hour crisis care home for the mentally ill, a residential treatment center that would also provide vocational guidance and local job opportunities. It was exactly the kind of place that might have prepared Ken for his return to independent living after his treatment in Golden Valley. I sent a letter to the editor of the local newspaper, which was published the following week. Among other things, I responded to this calloused remark made at the hearing: "We don't want that kind of people running up and down our streets."

"This hurts me," I wrote, "because I am that kind of people." It was in this frame of mind I began my letter writing campaign. I had been awakened to the disregard shown by local officials toward the mentally ill and vulnerable people. With assistance from the state alliance, I learned about the mental health issues and the legislative calendar regarding mental health policy. I began writing articles for the newspaper, letters to my legislators, congresspersons, and every official who had any influence on mental health policy. I attended the annual meeting of the Minnesota Alliance and met the state and national leaders as well as other local chapter leaders. In March 1987, I attended the mental health rally at the state capitol and wrote an article for the Minnesota AMI newsletter about my experience and participation.

At the time there was debate in the state legislature over a mental health bill championed by Senator Linda Berglin and supported by Governor

Perpich. The bill would mandate uniform and consistent services for the mentally ill in all eighty-seven counties using the existing federal block grants already intended for these purposes. In support of this bill, the Minnesota Comprehensive Mental Health Act, and in strong opposition to a competing "do nothing, don't change the status quo" bill, I wrote letters to a half dozen legislators from the five county area and organized a letter writing campaign among the Alliance in Kanabec County. I was elated when the bill passed. I felt that our AMI group had made an impact, a small contribution to the successful implementation of a comprehensive mental health policy.

With encouragement, resources, and funding from the state AMI and plenty of enthusiasm among our ranks, we elected a board of directors. I was elected president. We also started the process of incorporating as a non-profit organization, which facilitated the fundraising we needed to do. We moved our meeting location to the medical library at Kanabec County Hospital, as some thought that would be a more suitable venue. To publicize our existence and activities, I wrote an article for mental health month in May, which ran in the local newspaper. "The Mora area Alliance for the Mentally Ill," I stated, "has organized together with many other county groups. The state and national AMI organizations provide the information and working tools so together we can affect change and improve the way mentally ill people have been treated in the past."

Because of my earlier AMI organizing efforts, I was invited that year to serve on the County Advisory Board for the Mentally Ill, which I did on a volunteer basis for several years. In 1987 I received the Volunteer Certificate of Recognition signed by Governor Perpich and presented to me by the Community Support Program director. The attached letter from the program director stated, "You are an important role model to your community in reducing the stigma of mental illness and helping to meet the needs of long-term mentally ill persons."

Gradually my own pain and grief subsided. Although I still mourned at times, I also felt blessed to be alive and to be a part of an important movement. The satisfaction I received from helping others was a comfort to me, which did more to promote my own healing than anything else.

21

White Plains

At Scarsdale I put away my journal and gathered my things. Approaching Hartsdale Station, the train began to slow and gradually rolled to a stop. I stepped into a cold north wind and crossed the foot bridge to the parking lot, longing for the ninety degree heat of the previous day. The wind chilled me to the bone as I entered the parking lot where Erna was waiting in her car.

I hurried over, opened the door, and slid into the warm seat. "Thanks for coming, Erna. I wasn't sure if you'd be here."

"I thought you might be on the earlier train," Erna replied as she turned toward home, "but that's okay. You're back safely now. Did you have a good day?"

"Yes, did I ever!" I replied. "It was quite an adventure. You were right about St. Thomas Church. It was much better than the cathedral. And the Ellis Island cruise was interesting too."

"And you never got lost?"

"Nope, not at all," I replied. "How was your trip to the theater?"

"We had a grand time as usual. It helps that we get along so well. Everyone liked the play."

Back in her apartment, Erna baked a pizza and prepared a salad for dinner while I set the table. Then we sat down to eat.

"Now tell me again about this organization you're involved in," Erna said.

"Okay, yes. It's the National Alliance for the Mentally Ill, NAMI. They're headquartered in Arlington, Virginia. They have a state office in St. Paul, which assisted me in starting a local chapter in Mora."

188

Mary Gunderson

"But how did you get invited to New York?"

"Well, it's a long story. Actually I was invited first to a mental health forum in Marshall, Minnesota, sponsored by a consortium of mental health groups, one of which was the National Institute of Mental Health. They asked twenty-seven consumers of mental health services, including me, to testify about their experiences. When it was over, they invited me to Washington for a day of lobbying. It's Jim Cromwell at NAMI who is trying to get me a spot on the *Today Show*. I need to call him tomorrow morning to find out if and when I'm on."

"What is it they want you to say?"

"NAMI wants me to tell about Ken and Elaine. You see, there's a lack of services for the mentally ill, particularly in rural areas. The American Psychiatric Association and the National Institute of Mental Health are trying to raise public awareness about this and get Congress to do something about it. They want money for research and more services for the mentally ill. Apparently they felt my story did well to spotlight the consequences of inadequate services."

"How are the rest of your children doing?"

"They're fine, mostly. They all have good jobs, several have college degrees, and most of them are married and have children. In fact I now have eight grandchildren and four more are due this year."

"That's wonderful. You have much to feel good about too. It never ceases to amaze me how people can recover from the most devastating things."

We finished eating and kept talking while clearing the table and cleaning up the kitchen. "Before we continue, what's your plan for the week?" asked Erna. "I need to go to work tomorrow from ten to three."

"First I need to call in the morning to find out whether I'm scheduled for the *Today Show*. If so, I might be heading back into New York; if not, I'd prefer to spend my time at the library if there's one in the neighborhood."

Erna said she could drop me off at the White Plains Library. Then she invited me to the living room, where she pulled several photo albums from a shelf. I was eager to see her photos of my Danish relatives.

"Did you visit Laurids and Greta in Washington?" she asked. Laurids was our cousin from Denmark who was counselor to the Danish ambassador in Washington.

"No, I didn't. They left for Denmark before I arrived. I was disappointed because it was my one chance to visit them, and they weren't there. The last time I saw Laurids and Greta was about three years ago at the Mikaelsen family reunion in Denmark. That was before they moved to Washington."

For two hours we shared family stories. Erna and I often conversed in Danish, which came easily for both of us. At 10:00 p.m. she excused herself, and I went to bed very tired and went quickly to sleep.

The following morning I called Jim Cromwell at NAMI and learned he had not heard back from NBC studios. "I'll probably hear from them today," he said. "I'll call you this evening."

After a light breakfast, Erna drove me to the White Plains Library. She escorted me on a brief tour. "The Galleria is right next door if you need to do any shopping," she said. "Meet me right here in the lobby at 3:00 p.m."

I went to do some shopping, bought some snacks, and returned to the library, where I found a comfortable seat near a window. A fig tree with glossy green foliage stood under a skylight a few feet away. I had four hours to read, write in my journal, and contemplate my themes for the televised interview.

Reflecting on my conversations with Erna, I remembered the stories she told me about traveling in Denmark. She seemed well acquainted with Emil Mikaelsen, who had visited my family twice in Iowa and whom I had visited twice in Denmark. Two of his daughters, Hanna and Rigmor, had come to Rush Point to stay with us on the farm. It was Emil's son Laurids who lived in Washington. The last time I saw them was three years earlier at a family reunion in Denmark. It is one of my favorite memories. After that trip, I was a changed person. That was when I really started to live and enjoy life again.

22

A Time to Dance and a Time to Speak Out

In the midst of my AMI organizing activities, a year or so after Ken died, I received a letter from my cousin Signe in Denmark inviting me to attend the biannual Mikaelsen family reunion in May. Sufficiently on the mend and eager for a diversion, I decided to go alone as Gordon would be in the middle of spring planting. He still enjoyed crop farming, even without his dairy herd.

On May 20, 1987, I boarded a plane in Minneapolis and flew to Copenhagen. This time I took the connecting flight to Billund, an airport town near Vejrup, where I was greeted by my cousin Alfred. Thus began a glorious fourteen-day tour of Denmark. Once again I was escorted by relatives around the country and saw many of my cousins and their families. The highlight of the trip was the family reunion.

The *familiefest*, as the reunion was called, was held at the Morkenborg Kro, a restaurant on the large island of Fyn near the center of Denmark. It was hosted by Signe and Bent who lived in nearby Odense. This was the traditional Ascension Day gathering of the descendants of my only uncle, August Mikaelsen, whom I never met. Ascension Day, a national holiday in Denmark, was on Thursday that year. Twelve of us carpooled from Vejrup, two hours across greening farm country and the big suspension bridge to the island of Fyn. More than just the highlight of this trip, the *familiefest* was one of the most important and memorable occasions of my life.

Morkenborg Kro is located on a country estate near the town of Stillebaek. An ancient manor house converted to an inn, it overlooks a pond surrounded by trees, grassy pastures, and grazing animals. We were the first to arrive, just before noon. Another forty or so began arriving soon after. The children played in the yard among friendly ponies and goats while the adults gathered, watched, and visited. When all fifty had arrived, we went inside to a large private dining room with two, long, beautifully set tables. I was seated between Emil and Anna Mikaelsen, my cousin and his wife from Thisted. Bouquets of fresh cut flowers adorned both tables.

Arranged in front of me were three plates in a stack, two goblets, several sets of silverware, and a bread plate on the side. Anna kindly instructed me in the proper use of each plate and utensil. A fish entrée was served first on the top plate. One goblet was filled with water and the other with a choice of beverage, citron in my case. However, I noticed most of the adults were drinking beer, wine, or *snaps* (schnapps). A bread basket went around the table several times along with butter. They called it lunch, but I thought it was more like an elegant dinner. Between story telling and singing we visited.

"It's nice you could come," Emil said.

"Oh, I'm so thrilled to be here," I replied.

"You look really good. How are you feeling?"

"I am feeling fine, thank you. I was so sorry to hear about Hanna."

"Thank you," he replied, "and I was very sorry to hear about Ken."

Emil and Anna's oldest daughter Hanna had died of cancer the previous year. During her college days in 1963, Hanna visited us in Minnesota and ever since then had kept up a correspondence with me. She left her husband Holgor and four school age children when she died.

When the fish was gone, the waiters collected the top plates and placed pork rolls on the second plate. Between courses the adults stood up one at a time to tell stories or recite poems prepared ahead of time. Songbooks were passed around, too, and we sang several traditional songs in typical Danish fashion. Every time I looked around the table, Signe flashed me a beaming smile. The waiters and waitresses moved about the room silently and efficiently.

Then Emil got up to speak. The room went politely silent. "I want to tell you about the first time we met Mary," he said. "Anna and I were on our way to California in 1946. We called ahead from New York to tell Hans and Anna we would be passing through Omaha on the train. Think about this: Omaha is a three hundred kilometer drive from Ringsted where they lived. Mary drove six hours with her parents and waited over twenty-four hours, while our train was delayed, just to see us for a half hour in the middle of the night. I will never forget looking out the window upon our arrival and seeing Mary on the platform. She looked just like my sister Lydia, and I knew she must be my niece."

As Emil spoke, I felt waves of pride and joy mingled with the sadness that I was separated physically by half a world from these relatives. All eyes were on me as I looked around the room. Across the table, Emil's younger son Laurids winked at me. One year later, he and his wife Greta would move to Washington.

With a twinkle in his eye, Emil continued, "Headed for Berkeley and then China, we were not sure if we would ever see Mary again. One month later, however, I received a letter from Hans with an invitation and the money for a bus ticket to Iowa. During our summer break we traveled there with little Thomas and Hanna and stayed two weeks."

Thomas smiled across the table. He was just six years old when they came to Iowa. As an adult he became a teacher and, later, the school superintendent in Ringe, not far from Morkenborg Kro.

Then Anna stood up. "I had only one dress along on that trip," she added. "so Mary loaned me one of hers. She and I were the same size. Twenty years later, both our daughters traveled separately to Minnesota and stayed with Mary's family. Thank you, Mary, for keeping up the communication and for coming here today."

The food, the song, and the humor lasted three hours. The bottom plate, I learned, was for the assorted cheeses, which came last as a kind of dessert. I will never forget the respect, courtesy and etiquette observed throughout the celebration. The cohesiveness of this family is remarkable. I familiarized myself with all of them, wrote down all their names, and took many photos.

After the meal, all were invited over to Signe and Bent's house, a fifteen minute drive from the inn. The tables were set on their patio, coffee was on, a large birthday cake and assorted coffee and nut breads awaited everyone. It was Signe's birthday a few days earlier and her grandson Peter's birthday that very day. Soon the whole group was seated including the children and everything was in perfect order. Everyone sang happy birthday to Peter followed by, "Hooray! Hooray! Hooray! Hooray!" The cake was served, song sheets were passed around, and more singing followed, accompanied by organ music.

During the entire trip I collected the stories, letters, and history of the Mikaelsen family. What could not be photocopied, I recorded in my notebook, including the names of my relatives and ancestors back to 1800. My inquiries were met with enthusiasm by many relatives who were also interested in the family history. The information I gathered became the foundation for my book, *History of a Danish Family*, which I later self-published. I did not want my children to live their lives not knowing who they were or where they came from.

I stayed at Signe's several more days and took photos of the elaborate flower gardens in her neighborhood. I wanted to incorporate that kind of beauty in my yard at home. Signe took me on a tour of the Hans Christian Andersen house, now a museum in Odense. To my surprise, I discovered that both Andersen's mother and grandfather died in mental institutions and Hans himself was very troubled in his youth. His story of the ugly duckling, in fact, is thought to represent his own life, and to some extent I identify with the story also.

When it was time to leave, I took a bus to the Island of Lolland, where I visited the Ernst Mikaelsen family before heading to Copenhagen and flying home to Minnesota. I carried home a large stack of notes, photos, and information on my family history.

Upon my return to Mora, I felt like a changed person. With renewed zeal, I tackled my yard, gardening, and home improvement projects, as well as my AMI goals and objectives, old and new. As president of the Mora area AMI, I was determined to increase our publicity. We set up a booth at the Kanabec County Fair and constructed a display. We continued posting meeting notices in the local papers. In the fall we hosted a fundraising concert at Zion Lutheran Church and raised over a thousand dollars, half of which came from a matching grant from the Aid Association for Lutherans. We invited a group of musicians from Minneapolis who were consumers of mental health services, and they stayed at our farm. Tony

Wentersdorf played his autoharp, Doug Williams played the organ, Shelley Burns played the piano, and Dolly Koch sang the vocals. Their music was a witness to the talent, beauty, and grace which emotionally challenged persons have to offer. Mental illness need not be debilitating.

On the farm, Gordon and I adjusted to life without milk-cows. With money in the bank and a monthly social security check, we began a new era of financial security. We decided to make needed improvements like refinishing the floors, residing and painting the barn, and repainting the house. Although Gordon continued his field work, and I my gardening and volunteering, the two of us also began enjoying more leisure activities. Taking trips to visit friends and relatives became a regular pastime. I took an interest in exploring Gordon's family genealogy in addition to mine. In August Gordon and I traveled to Alberta, where we met nearly all of his twenty-seven cousins.

Besides traveling and spending time with our grandchildren, Gordon and I decided to take up square dancing. I had long since rejected my childhood taboos and allowed my own children to go dancing. So why shouldn't I take up dancing too? Gordon supported the idea, especially after visiting his relatives in Canada and learning that they were avid dancers. In the fall of 1987 we joined the Rum River Squares and began attending weekly dance lessons and monthly square dance rallies. After six months of dance lessons we were awarded a *Bachelor of Square Dancing* diploma by the Square Dance Federation of Minnesota. From then on we were regular attendees at the monthly square dances.

To augment my interest in writing, I took a woodworking class in town and built a large writing desk with several shelves. As I dedicated more time to writing, others began to take notice. A local reporter came to interview me one day about support groups for the mentally ill. In a subsequent article published in the *Isanti County Times* and the *Chisago County Press*, this is what he wrote:

> Mary Gunderson, of rural Mora, mother of eleven children and wife of Gordon Gunderson, has written memories of her childhood, her growing up in Iowa, her experiences as a teacher, her life on farms in Iowa and Minnesota, her own mental illness and that which took the lives of two of her children when they succumbed to suicide.

When you walk into the Gunderson farmhouse, a warm feeling envelopes you. Offering a cup of coffee, Mary rises from the table to put on a fresh pot of brew.

Mary experienced mental illness in her own life and was treated in hospitals for depression. Although she learned to cope with her thoughts and feelings and has been free of illness for many years, it did not prepare her to deal with the problems related to the schizophrenia and suicide deaths of her two children, Kenneth and Elaine.

The article went on to describe my organizing activities with AMI and the positive effect it had on my healing process. I had responded to a call and found a purpose, which I pursued with a passion I had not felt before.

Of course all my volunteer activities, including my trip to Denmark, required Gordon's acquiescence, which he generously extended. A marriage enrichment retreat made all the difference. When Gordon sold the cows in 1986, I had already begun to spread my wings. A sense of purpose and individuality was stirring in me. I no longer felt willing to bow to my husband's interests, and to his will, at the expense of my own. Here is a statement I wrote for the marriage enrichment retreat:

I don't want to be just someone's wife or someone's mother; I want to be me, and to be recognized as me. If I don't find recognition as a wife, I must find it elsewhere. You may not like who I am and try to suppress me, but if others accept me, I can still flourish. How much easier it would be to give me the attention and recognition I need. It would cost you so little to lay aside your own needs a wee bit to recognize mine. I exist. I cannot be suppressed. I have felt victimized by always having to yield to my husband, to do as he wants, think as he wants, and believe as he wants, isolated and alone forever with him. When I tried in the past to break out of this stifling mold, I was met with rebuff, so I silently resumed my seclusion because I was afraid to lose my one source of earthly security. But that was then, and I am a different person now.

Gordon accepted my desire for independence, bless his soul, and he allowed me to go my own way and pursue my own activities and ambitions. His willingness to bend and allow me some independence was a major step. He respected my deep convictions and allowed my individual pursuits and expanding time commitments with AMI and the Mental Health Advisory Board. Therefore, with Gordon's approval, I made arrangements in April of 1990 to attend a national hearing on mental illness in Marshall, Minnesota.

The hearing, one of three held that year across the country, was cosponsored by the National Mental Health Leadership Forum and the National Advisory Mental Health Council, both established by Congress. The purpose of the hearing was to assess the need for improvement in the treatment of mental illness and to measure the level of public awareness with regard to the issues. The focus of this particular hearing was on mental illness in rural America. Marshall was selected because of its distinctly rural setting, sixty miles from the nearest psychiatrist. Susan Cohen, the public relations specialist for the hearing, was interviewed by the *Marshall Independent* and had this to say about the meeting's purpose: "It will be a time to listen, a time for experts to listen and learn and get information. They'll be collecting this information to provide recommendations to Congress on how to shape future policy." The proposed venue was Southwest State University.

A month before the hearing, I received an invitation to submit a written testimony about my experience with the stigma of mental illness. I had been recommended to the sponsors of the hearing by my colleagues at Minnesota AMI headquarters as one who had experience with mental health services in a rural community. I was enthused about the opportunity and began composing my testimony on stigma. Out of the hundred plus testimonials submitted, I was one of twenty-seven participants chosen to appear as a speaker. Each speaker was assigned to a predetermined panel and asked to give a five to seven minute oral summary of his or her written testimony.

With reservations at the Country Inn in Marshall, my daughter Carol and I drove down the evening before the hearing. At daybreak on April 12, I wrote a note to Carol and slipped quietly out of the room. I went to the student center on campus, bought some breakfast, and found a table where I could work on my speech. At 9:30 I headed for the gymnasium and claimed two empty seats near the front. The proceedings started at 10:00 a.m.

A wave of nervous anticipation came over me as the university president welcomed the crowd and the hearing got under way. I had never addressed such a large audience before or one consisting mostly of mental health professionals and legislators. Dr. Fred Goodwin, one of the opening speakers, apprised the audience of the issues before us. "People in rural areas cannot escape the serious mental illnesses that affect twelve percent of our population," he said, "and they face trying circumstances that seem to have worsened in the past decade." He was referring to the farm crisis of the 1980s which precipitated economic and social hardships and added to the stress of rural Americans. This was not causal for Ken or Elaine, but it was true in general.

The panel on stigma was not scheduled to begin until two o'clock in the afternoon, but I was in no hurry and found the speakers interesting. Dr. Lewis Judd—chairman of both the cosponsoring organizations and the National Institute of Mental Health—spoke next. "Teen suicide is now the second leading cause of death among adolescents throughout America," he said. "Effective prevention and treatment are often more difficult to provide in rural areas. The testimony from this hearing will serve a vital function in helping the National Institute of Mental Health build the mental health needs of rural America into its agenda."

I felt honored, if a little jittery, to be giving my testimony for this purpose. Was it possible that my past suffering could make a difference in national mental health policy? What mattered most was the mission. Regardless of the potential outcome and despite my jitters, I had a story to tell, and I was prepared to tell it.

Several hundred chairs covered the gymnasium floor in rows with two aisles up the middle. In front, a podium stood at the center. Two long tables stretched to either side with chairs facing the audience. Microphones were mounted on the podium and in front of each chair. On the eight-foot-high backdrop behind the podium, a large banner read, MENTAL ILL-NESS IN AMERICA: A SERIES OF PUBLIC HEARINGS. A woman stood next to the podium hand-signing to the deaf. Dr. Judd was concluding his speech when I spotted Carol making her way toward the empty chair next to me. We smiled at each other as she took her seat.

The hearing co-chair, Dennis Jones, introduced the panel on teenage suicide next. Seven panelists went forward and took their chairs. Following introductions, they went to the podium one at a time to give their testimonies. A yellow light came on after five minutes, and then a red light came on when the speaker's time was up. Each speaker was allowed seven minutes, which was strictly enforced. This procedure was repeated with each of the four panels, lasting one hour apiece. At noon the panel on mental illness in rural America was introduced.

Other than a short lunch break, Carol and I watched and listened to every panel. The time flew by. At one o'clock the panel on depression commenced, and finally, at two o'clock, the panel on stigma was invited forward. I made my way to the front and took my chair. A name tag was placed in front of each panelist as the co-chair introduced him or her. The first two panelists got up to speak, but I barely heard what they said. Then it was my turn. I went to the podium, placed my script in front of me, and looked at the crowd before me. Had I not felt this was my mission, I might have frozen there in fear, but I gathered my courage and spoke into the microphone:

"She's had a nervous breakdown!"
"Don't pay any attention to her, she doesn't know what's going on!"
"Wouldn't it be dangerous to marry someone like that?"
These were stigmatic remarks about me, which hurt at the time.
"We don't want that kind of people living here," community residents said when a local agency applied to open a half-way house in my neighborhood. Less than four years ago, our local zoning commission met to consider a variance necessary to allow a large residence within the business district to be used as a residential treatment facility for the mentally ill. The variance was unanimously denied. I overheard someone say, "We don't want that kind of people running around on our streets." It hurt because I am that kind of people.

Twenty years ago, I followed Senator Thomas Eagleton's candidacy for vice president. He was rejected on the basis of his past hospitalizations for mental illness. I went down with him in the eyes of the public, because I have been hospitalized three times and treated with electric shock therapy and tranquilizers and have had to admit that I was mentally ill. If others would accept mental illness as they would any other illness, it would help, and some do, but concepts formed early in life are hard to change. The feeling that you have a weakness or a mental handicap is there.

Stigma is also what we as parents feel when judged by professionals. It saddened me beyond measure to see myself through the eyes of the psychiatrists who treated my oldest daughter. The nursing staff was ordered to work intensively with her "to achieve a more positive female role model than her mother presented." I had always considered myself a good mother, doing the utmost for my children. When I looked at the record later and saw how they described her past, I was disheartened indeed. "Her mother made many unreasonable demands, constantly degrading her performance and attainment . . . A fundamentalist Christian background in addition to her mother's demands and reproof instilled an ever-present feeling of sinfulness and guilt." The blame for her condition lay squarely on me. I felt guilty as charged. It was as if an arrow had pierced my soul, and it is still there. This is the burden I carry.

The doctor summarized her situation as "resulting from a pathological home environment, a psychotic or near psychotic mother, an indifferent, uninvolved, and punitive father, a lack of emotional and financial security, and a religious background producing feelings of guilt, shame, and inadequacy." What I don't understand is how such a set of parents could have managed to raise nine other wonderful children who are all getting along in the world. It must be a miracle. How am I to explain why, when given the antidepressant Vivactil, my daughter's behavior was improved? There were no more peculiar gestures, no more religious preoccupations, her studies went well again, and she expressed high regard and appreciation for her parents.

Twice her delusions and agitated behavior were eliminated by multiple electro-shock therapy which had beneficial effects both times. The last time she was hospitalized, her doctors refused her request for additional shock therapy. Her agitation was so great, she made threats of killing herself one week before she died. Instead of treating her, they cut her medications and suggested she be discharged. I maintain they share the guilt I was made to feel. She had terrible feelings that she would never get well. On the eleventh of January 1973, she jumped from a sixth floor window at the University Hospital, a victim of chronic undifferentiated schizophrenia. The coroner wrote, "The psychiatrists didn't think she was as sick as she was." We are left with a memory of a beautiful, talented, vivacious daughter, whose skills as a writer had reached "a very mature level," according to her teachers, and who "was doing as well as could be expected as anyone learning the trade of typesetting," her employer told us. Our neighbors, friends, and relatives grieved with us.

When our son first became delusional, the psychiatrist in Minneapolis who saw our family said, "Why pick on him? The whole family is sick." By the time we got an appointment at our local mental health center, our son seemed to be doing okay, and nobody suggested treating our family then. What was the matter with us? I really would like to know.

When my son had an accident, the doctor told us he was hallucinating. Our insurance coverage determined how long he could be hospitalized. The court-appointed lawyers maintained his environment was to blame. When released from the hospital, there was no place for him to go but home with us, and nothing more was said about his unsuitable environment. For ten years of his adult life, our son lived with us. Most of the time he functioned quite well. Sometimes we wondered about his queer notions but overlooked these and tried to focus on the many things he did well. He had the negative symptoms of schizophrenia: uncommunicative and socially withdrawn. But he was a willing worker and very adept at all the skills required of a farmer. He seemed to thrive when busy working and would choose work instead of socializing with his brothers, sisters, and parents. How I wish someone could have taught us a more effective way of communicating with him.

After an altercation with a coworker, our son was fired from the job he had held for six years. We felt he needed psychological help but could not convince him to go with us to the area mental health clinic. The county social service told us there was nothing they could do as long as he would not cooperate. Cooperating meant being put in an institution. For a farmer that is not an attractive alternative. They told us he could apply for aid if he had less than $750. Besides his job in town, he had been doing a lot of work for us. We were paying him a wage, and he had over $40,000 in assets.

Just then, the red light came on. I stopped, looked at the chairman, and said, "I have two paragraphs remaining; should I quit here?" He urged me to finish, so I resumed my testimony.

In the busy silo filling season and in the middle of the night, he was picked up by the police because they knew he was mentally disturbed. Walking down the road toward town, he was harming no one. He was forcibly taken to a mental institution and fought like fury to free himself. They put him in isolation in physical restraints. They brought him back two weeks later and put him in the county jail to wait for his court hearing. This was humiliating and demeaning for a sensitive soul such as he was. He came home like a scared rabbit: licked, rigid, and grim. I always thought a person in our country was innocent until proven guilty. Not so with the mentally ill. They are given the same punishment as someone who has been proven guilty.

When farming was no longer profitable, he wanted to be independent, find work, get married, and earn a living for a wife and family. The Area Vocational Professional Services taught him job-seeking skills and noticed he was very withdrawn. They called to offer condolences after he shot himself. On January 22, 1986, our son gave up his struggle with life and left us broken hearted. A thoughtful son, strong and physically healthy, a good-looking man with a gentle nature and Christian virtues left this earth for a better land.

When I finished, the auditorium erupted in applause. As I returned to my seat at the table, the whole crowd was standing and continuing to applaud. I did not realize until later what an impact I had made. I received many compliments on my testimony and felt affirmed and supported. The following day I clipped an article from the *Marshall Independent*, which put it like this:

> Throughout most of the day, long testimonials were discouraged, with one exception. When Mary Gunderson, a Mora woman who lost two children to suicide, voluntarily stopped speaking because her time was up, chairman Dennis Jones of the Texas Department of Mental Health urged her to complete her tear-filled testimony. Her speech on stigma drew applause from the panel, the audience, and the media. When the applause died down, Jones tried to speak, then paused and cleared his throat before introducing the next speaker.

Besides the *Marshall Independent* I was quoted in several other regional newspapers including the *Rapid City Journal* and the *Willmar West*

Central Tribune. I was asked to share the entire text of my testimony with the monthly publication of Minnesota AMI, the *Mental Health Advocate.* A few days later I received a letter from the hearing co-chair, Dennis Jones, in which he wrote:

> Your willingness to publicly share the emotional challenges of your private life and the crushing unfair stigma which you faced, brought a truly invaluable perspective to us in understanding the unique problems for mental health in rural America. But it also brought a message of hope to those who may now be feeling overwhelmed and hopeless. Your contributions to the success of the hearing cannot be overestimated.

The next week, I got a letter from Laurie Flynn, the executive director of NAMI in Arlington, Virginia. "Thank you for your wonderful presentation," she wrote. But the biggest surprise was a phone call I received from Dr. Halter of the National Institute of Mental Health. He said my testimony was by far the most compelling. Then he asked if I would be willing to come to Washington and tell my story to law makers on Capitol Hill. "If so," he said, "we will try to get you a spot on the *Today Show,* and we will pay all your expenses."

"Yes, of course," I said. "I would appreciate that."

"Would you be willing to spend a few extra days in New York, if we can get you on the *Today Show?*"

I could hardly believe what I was hearing. Ever since learning about Erna Christensen on my last trip to Denmark, I had wanted to go to New York to meet her. "Yes," I answered, "I would like to spend a few days in New York, especially if I could visit a relative of mine who lives in the area."

"That's no problem," said Dr. Halter. "You can do anything you like. We can book an open-ended return flight. You can stay as long as you like."

"Thank you," I replied. "I look forward to seeing you."

A few days later my airline ticket was delivered by Federal Express along with a schedule of planned events and appointments. I was to accompany lobbyists on visits to Minnesota congressional delegates at the Capitol. They wanted me to tell my story to the law makers. The primary purpose of the lobbying was to procure increases in funding for mental health research.

I am still amazed by the reaction to my testimony. All these years I had carried the scarlet letter of shame about my own mental illness and blamed myself, too, for Ken's and Elaine's. When I finally revealed it to the world, I received not ridicule, nor scorn, nor blame, but applause, high praise, and an invitation to the Capitol, all expenses paid.

23

Last Evening in Hartsdale

By half past three we were back at Erna's apartment. Erna offered suggestions to improve upon several pages of remarks I prepared at the library, but it was a lost cause. At half past four Jim Cromwell phoned from NAMI headquarters.

"NBC studios called," he said. "They were noncommittal; it could be two weeks or two months before they schedule you for an interview. So, I guess it's off for now. I'm sorry we got you all excited for nothing."

"It's okay, Jim. I've had a good trip up here, visiting my cousin and touring New York, so don't you worry about me. I'll head home tomorrow unless you have anything else for me to do."

Jim thanked me for coming to Washington. I thanked him for paying my expenses, and that was the end of it. My mission to New York was over. I said goodbye, and began preparing for the trip home.

For dinner that evening, Erna took me to an Italian restaurant in Greenburgh. Waiting for our entrées, she told me about the time her mother met the king and queen of Denmark. Erna loved telling stories about Christine.

"I was a member of the American Scandinavian Foundation headquartered in New York," she began. "King Frederic and Queen Ingred were visiting and there was a reception for them at the Metropolitan Club. I had only a single invitation, but my mother was staying, and she was more excited about it than I was. After a few phone calls and a little persuasion, I was able to get another ticket for her. She was 88 at the time."

"Wow! Did you actually get to meet them?"

"I'll tell you. My mother got all dressed up—she loved nice clothes —and my friends got in on the act too. When we arrived there were many VIPs, like Ralph Bunche and Adlai Stevenson, all over this huge dining

205

Last Evening in Hartsdale

hall. We were ushered into the main dining area. The king and queen sat with dignitaries in a cordoned-off area in the front. After dinner there were speeches and presentations, and then everyone stood around talking. I wondered if there would be an opportunity to meet the king. So I went to inquire and found that because the crowd was so large, there would be no receiving line. Well, I knew Mother was going to be very disappointed because she was counting on meeting the king. She had met Frederic in Philadelphia when he was a crown prince.

When I returned, Mother had disappeared. I thought I'd never find her in such a big crowd. I suspected she might have ditched me because I wouldn't let her violate the protocol. You have to be presented to royalty, you know. Well, the crowd thinned, and there I saw my mother standing between the King and the Queen engaging them in conversation. They were over by the door waiting for their car to come. King Frederic was a great tall man, and he was bending down and looking very interested in Mother. Finally their car came, and they went, and Mother sort of floated across the room and sat down at the table. I asked her, 'Who presented you?'

'I just went over and presented myself,' she said.

'But how did you get over the ropes?'

'I just moved them a little.'

Then Mother gave me a verbatim report on their conversation. She had a fantastic memory, you know. The king and queen were very interested in older people. They had gone to rest homes in New York and Chicago and visited the elderly Danes. The king said most of the old folks, though still conversant in Danish, had lost some fluency. But he told my mother, 'You speak perfect Danish, and you've been over here all these years.' That's all I can remember of their conversation. I only wish I could have taken a photo of them together."

"What a great story," I said. "I wish I could have known Christine."

The waitress came with our food, and soon we were dining on pasta entrees.

"I can't thank you enough for everything you've done," I said. "Gordon and I would love to have you visit the farm if you ever come to Minnesota."

"Well, thank you," Erna replied, "I have a lot of very dear friends in the Midwest whom I never get to see because there just isn't time or a convenient flight into the area."

"Well, remember that you're welcome if you ever visit Minnesota."

"Thank you, Mary. I'll keep that in mind. And if you need to come back to New York for the *Today Show* or for any reason, you're always welcome at my place too."

"It's possible they'll want me back in Washington sometime in the future, and who knows, maybe in New York too."

"That reminds me. I was going to ask you about your day at the capitol. You told me about your testimony at the mental health forum, but I haven't heard much about your lobbying trip. How did that go?"

"Well, thank you for asking. I'd love to tell you about it." I recalled the scenes and scenarios of the previous week on Capitol Hill. It seemed like I could remember every detail.

24

Capitol Hill

On April 25, 1990, with Gordon's blessing, I flew to Washington with Dr. Paula Clayton and Dr. Robert Rose, two of the nation's leading mental health researchers and advocates. Paula Clayton, head of the University of Minnesota Department of Psychiatry, was a professor of psychiatry and the first woman to chair a department of psychiatry in the United States. Bob Rose was a psychiatrist at the University of Minnesota medical school. They were working on behalf of the American Psychiatric Association (APA) and the National Institute of Mental Health (NIMH) for two days of planned advocacy and lobbying on Capitol Hill. Without their guidance and companionship, I would have been lost.

Upon our arrival at Washington National Airport, the three of us piled into a taxi and headed for NIMH headquarters in Wilmington, Maryland. There, we had lunch and a briefing with Dr. Judd and Dr. Goldman. Lewis Judd was one of the opening speakers at the hearing in Marshall. After the initial greetings and introductions, he looked at me and said, "Thank you for your excellent testimony, Mary." Turning to Dr. Clayton and Dr. Rose, he asked, "Did Mary tell you about her testimony at the Marshall hearing?"

"We heard about it, but we'd like to hear more," replied Dr. Clayton.

Dr. Judd turned to me again and said, "I'm very sorry about your daughter and son. And I appreciate your willingness to come here and tell your story. It's important that our lawmakers know what is going on out there."

"Thank you," I replied, "and thanks for inviting me. I'm glad to be involved. I've been working on this cause ever since my son died four years ago, and I started a chapter of AMI in my hometown."

"Well that's great," he said. "We could use more people like you. Now, regarding tomorrow, are you comfortable going with Bob and Paula to tell your story again?"

"Yes, I am," I replied.

"Good, but you need to shorten it a little because we only have twenty minutes for each appointment." Dr. Judd then informed us about the financial needs for proposed research projects and handed us our itinerary and instructions for the following day.

After the lunch meeting, we drove a half hour to the Capitol where NAMI and NIMH were hosting an orientation for lobby day participants and a reception afterward which included senators and representatives and their aides. On the ride over there, Dr. Rose asked, "Can you tell us more about your daughter and son?"

Reaching into my handbag, I said, "Here's an extra copy of my testimony. I can rewrite it tonight to shorten it a little, but you are welcome to read this in the meantime." I handed it Dr. Rose. "It's mostly about the stigma of mental illness, but it's also about my son and daughter who both had schizophrenia and both committed suicide. A few years ago, I went to the records library at the University Hospital and read the patient notes on my daughter who died in 1973 while being treated there. The testimony will tell you what I found. Basically they had concluded that Elaine's illness was due to a pathological home environment and poor parenting."

"Schizophrenia is no longer believed to be caused by the home environment or parenting," said Dr. Rose. "They might have thought that back then, but it has not been supported by the research. Schizophrenia is a brain disorder with genetic etiology. Other disorders can result from bad parenting but not schizophrenia."

"Do you mean they were wrong?"

"Yup, they were wrong," he replied.

I looked at Dr. Clayton. She smiled and nodded in agreement.

Ever since I read those damning words, they had been etched in my mind, haunting me: "pathological home situation; atmosphere of emotional coldness prevailing; much undesirable altercation; psychotic or near psychotic mother." In that moment, a great weight lifted away. Dr.

Rose and Dr. Clayton had exonerated me, removing the arrow and festering tissue from my soul.

On Capitol Hill, I stepped from the cab with a renewed sense of self-worth and confidence. The orientation hosted by NAMI and NIMH was intended for all those who had come to Washington, several from each state, to participate in the planned lobbying effort the following day. Introductions were made, and Dr. Judd was given an award by NAMI. Then several speeches were given about the importance of our lobbying mission, the problems and deficiencies of mental health care in America, and the proposed and pending legislation. Afterward everyone was invited to the reception held at the Hart Senate Office Building nearby. I walked over there with two NAMI woman I met at the orientation.

The reception was attended by mental health professionals, elected officials, their aides, and regular folks like me who had been recruited for lobbying. At the center of the reception hall stood three elegant tables full of food and hors d'oeuvres. Drinks were served at bars along each side. I got a diet Coke and mingled with the guests. One NAMI member from New York told me how to get to Hartsdale. "Get on the Amtrak right here at Union Station," she said. "Go to Penn Station in New York City, take a cab to Grand Central Station, and take the commuter rail to Hartsdale."

"Well that sounds easy enough," I replied.

A man next to us saw my nametag and said, "With a name like that you must be from Minnesota."

"Mora, Minnesota," I replied. "Good guess. Where are you from?"
"Well, I grew up in Iowa; my father still lives there, but I live in Chicago. The name is Lindberg, Donald Lindberg. I teach psychology at Northwestern University."

It was easy talking to people, knowing they were all there for the same purpose. I spoke with several others who were active in NAMI, all with stories of their own to tell. An older gentleman from California told me about his 29-year-old son who had paranoid schizophrenia and was in an institution for the mentally ill. I felt glad it was not Ken sitting dejected and unloved in an unfeeling place. Between conversations, I made several trips to the food tables to sample the hors d'oeuvres. Bob Rose and Paula

Clayton introduced me to some congressional aides we would visit the next day.

By early evening I was feeling tired. I said goodbye to Bob and Paula and a few others, picked up my packet of information, and went outside where the air was still warm. The sun was sinking in the west. Following Constitution Avenue, I headed west down the hill. The evening air was full of the sweet aroma of spring. Daffodils and tulips, red, orange, and yellow, graced the gardens along the mall and boulevards. The cherry blossoms were gone, but the dogwoods, redbuds, and azaleas were in full bloom: pink, fuchsia, and red. I was enchanted by the sights and sounds and aromas permeating the spring air. Robins chirped and sang. A mockingbird chattered its repetitive phrases. I continued west, strolling past stately buildings, statues, and shimmering pools. The sun was setting when the White House came into view between the trees across a vast manicured lawn. Behind me towered the Washington Monument, a perfect obelisk penetrating the deepening sky.

It was dusk when I hailed a cab. The driver took me across the Potomac to the Comfort Hotel in Arlington, Virginia. It was a nice medium sized hotel just two blocks from NAMI headquarters. Jim Cromwell from NAMI had booked my room and delivered my luggage to the hotel. A hotel gentleman carried my suitcase and showed me to my room. I collapsed into a lounge chair, rested my weary feet, and reflected on the day.

Upon arrival in Washington, my first reaction was one of intimidation perhaps, like I had landed in a jungle. Later, however, it felt like heaven on earth because glory came down that day and filled my soul. Mental health experts, including people from APA, NAMI, and NIMH, were well represented in Washington that week. I was treated like one of them and perhaps, indeed, I was. The only thing I lacked was a degree and credentials.

I reviewed my testimony, circling the parts I wanted to include the following day. Then I prepared an outline. Before bedtime, I took time to write in my journal and concluded thusly, "Here I am, Lord. If you can use me on earth, that is where I want to be. If you can use me in heaven, then I'll be glad to go there." Utterly blessed, I went to bed and to sleep feeling loved, valued, and supported.

Capitol Hill

The following day dawned clear and warm with a high of ninety degrees in the forecast. I awoke to the trill of a cardinal, Virginia's state bird, outside my window. After breakfast at the hotel, I took a taxi back to Capitol Hill to rendezvous with Bob Rose and Paula Clayton. The taxi dropped me off in front of the Cannon House Office building, a mammoth limestone and marble edifice on Independence Avenue that houses the offices of several hundred representatives. I went to room 106, Minnesota Representative Vin Weber's office, and waited for Bob and Paula to arrive.

We had been scheduled to meet with four of Minnesota's congressional delegates, Vin Weber, Rudy Boshwitz, and Martin Sabo in the morning and David Durenburger in the afternoon. The plan was for us to talk five minutes apiece and limit our visits to twenty minutes. Because senators and representatives are often in committee meetings or in session, they are not always available to meet with constituents. This was the case on all three of our morning visits in which Bob and Paula presented their proposals to the congressional aides, and I told my story. All four visits transpired in a similar fashion. Therefore, I will describe only the last of our visits, the one with Senator Durenburger.

We crisscrossed Capitol Hill in the morning, walking from the Cannon House Office Building to the Hart Senate Office Building and back to the Rayburn House Office Building via the tunnel system underneath the Capitol. After the visit with Martin Sabo's aides, our third call of the morning, we left the Rayburn Building and headed on foot to the Waterfall Cafeteria downstairs in the National Gallery of Art. Already it was very warm with the temperature in the high eighties. Cumulus clouds drifted like large cotton balls slowly across a pale blue sky. We stopped on the way to admire the Ulysses Grant Memorial. Grant sits astride his horse, facing Lincoln three miles away, like bookends at opposite ends of the National Mall.

After lunch we walked up the long hill to the Russel Senate Office Building. With the temperature pushing ninety, it was a relief to step inside the air-conditioned hall. We found our way to suite 154. Tom Bour and Lu Olsen, Durenberger's aides, greeted us in the reception room and spoke to us while we waited. Before long, the senator emerged from his office.

"Welcome to Washington," he said, smiling broadly. "Please come in, come in."

His office was quite large. A long leather couch faced a semicircle of upholstered chairs arranged living-room style around a coffee table. The creamy white walls were decorated with modest artwork and several framed awards and honors. An ornate, marble fireplace added to the genteel quality of the room. Dr. Clayton, who already knew the senator, introduced us.

"Please sit down," the senator said. "Coffee or tea anyone?"

"Tea would be great," replied Paula.

"Have anything cold?" Bob asked. He and I requested iced tea.

The two aides prepared and served drinks while the senator engaged us in small talk about the weather in Washington versus the weather in Minnesota. Then he inquired, "What brings you here today?"

"We need your support for increases in funding," began Dr. Clayton. "Important mental health research is on hold for lack of funding. In 1982 government grants covered 40 percent of the national mental health research budget. This year the government grants cover only 16 percent, and that's declining fast. We'd like to get $675 million next year and that only brings us back to 40 percent."

"Research funds don't go as far as they used to," added Dr. Rose. "With the addition of new technologies we could do so much more, but the costs are eating up the budget. Right now we have research on schizophrenia on hold because we don't have the money for MRI technology. Neuroleptic medications still need improvement and more testing. Meanwhile millions of Americans are suffering from mental illnesses."

Dr. Rose pressed his case with other examples of research sidelined for lack of funds. Dr. Clayton suggested the extra grant money and research dollars would help boost enrollments at medical schools, which had been lagging in recent years, particularly in psychiatry. When the complexities of research and various medical technologies were discussed, I understood little of what they were talking about. That I have barely more than a high school education, however, seemed immaterial that day. Mr. Durenburger was personable and listened well. I liked him from the start.

Capitol Hill

"We want you to hear from Mary next," said Dr. Clayton. "Her story is emblematic of the problems in mental health care, particularly in rural America where resources are minimal. She gave a testimony at the Mental Health Leadership Forum in Marshall, Minnesota, and we'd like you to hear it."

"I was actually in Marshall that day but couldn't attend the testimonials," replied the senator. "I attended the town hall meeting with Vin Weber instead, and then I had to leave early."

"Yes, I saw you there," I said. "I wanted to speak with you then, but this is even better." For some reason I felt entirely comfortable. That would not have been the case even a few months earlier, but I had discovered that others were moved by my story. "My husband Gordon and I live on a farm near Mora in central Minnesota. Gordon recently sold our dairy herd, but he still farms the land. We raised eleven children. Two of them, Elaine and Ken, had schizophrenia and committed suicide. Elaine was treated several times at the University of Minnesota, and she died there by jumping out a sixth floor window. Comments I found in her records led me to believe that I was responsible for her illness. I read things like, "a family of many children without accompanying emotional and financial security; near psychotic mother; pathological home situation; fundamentalist Christian background; mother constantly degraded her performance . . ." This hurt all the more because I have experienced three bouts of mental illness in the past, involving debilitating anxiety and depression. Twice I was treated with shock therapy. Throughout my adult life, I have lived with the stigma of being mentally disturbed. . . ."

I told my abbreviated story as succinctly as I could in five minutes, passing photos of Ken and Elaine to the Senator and pausing occasionally to wipe my eyes. As much as I had grieved this and retold the story, I still could not get through it without weeping. One of the aides passed a box of Kleenex. I blew my nose and regained my composure.

"For the next eight years," I continued, "Ken lived at home with us. He got a job in town and also helped us on the farm. He was a good looking man, physically healthy and strong with a gentle nature. In 1985 he met a woman and wanted to get married. Unfortunately, he also lost his job and his mental condition deteriorated. On the morning of January 22, 1986 he shot himself. I found him dead in the garage."

When I finished, the room was silent. Senator Durenberger reached out and placed his hand on my shoulder, "I'm so sorry," he said.

I smiled and said, "Thank you." Then I handed the senator a packet from NAMI and concluded, "I want to tell you about the positive things that are happening too. First, I have nine other healthy children, making their way and doing fine. Second, I started a local chapter of Alliance for the Mentally Ill in Mora. We had fundraisers and got a matching grant from AAL, the Aid Association for Lutherans. I want other families with mental illness to know they do not have to face it alone like we did, and I support the additional funding proposed here. Treatment methods and medications need to be improved. And mental illness must be given the same insurance coverage as physical illnesses. At NAMI we call it mental health parity."

Our time was up when I finished. I asked if I could get a photo before we left.

"Of course," Mr. Durenburger said. "I'll sit between the two of you." He moved to the couch and sat between Paula and me. Bob was in the chair.

I handed my camera to one of the aides, and he took a picture of the four of us. Then we shook hands again with all of them, thanked them for their time, and departed with a good feeling that our mission was completed. Bob and Paula went their separate ways, and I went back to my hotel in Arlington.

The following day I walked to NAMI headquarters just two blocks up the street. First, I met with Jim Cromwell in his office. He was thoughtful and concerned about my welfare. "How did it go yesterday?" he asked.

"We went to four different congressional delegates . . ." I gave Jim a full report of the day, glad that I had my notes to help me recall the names and places. It was nice he was so interested.

"That's precisely the kind of information we wanted," he said. "I appreciate the report and everything you have done."

Capitol Hill

Next I met with the executive director of NAMI, Laurie Flynn. She thanked me for my Alliance work in Mora and asked me to come back once a year. "They need to hear it again," she said.

When I was finished at NAMI headquarters, I went back to my hotel room to make phone calls and travel plans for my trip to Hartsdale. The next morning I went to Union Station and took the Amtrak to New York.

25

The Journey Home

"That's quite a story," Erna said. "You've done a great service for the cause of mental health. You should be proud of yourself."

"Well, thank you, and thanks for listening," I replied.

Erna suggested we head home. The restaurant was nearly empty and would close shortly. I paid the bill and the two of us went out into the evening chill. Back at Erna's apartment, I went to sleep on the foldout bed one more time.

When I awoke the following morning, May Day, bright sunshine lit the curtains. By the time the aroma of coffee drifted in from the kitchen, I was packed and ready to leave. Erna and I shared some parting thoughts over breakfast. Then she repeated the instructions for getting to Penn Station.

At 7:45 I thanked Erna again, said goodbye, and went out the door. In bright sun and the morning chill, I carried my suitcase to the bus stop. This time I rode the express bus all the way down to 34th Street and got off next to the Empire State Building. In the shadow of skyscrapers, I took a taxi back to Madison Square Garden and entered Penn Station. I needed to ride the Amtrak back to Washington to catch my return flight, scheduled to depart from Washington National Airport late that afternoon.

It was 10:45 when the partially filled train rolled slowly out of Penn Station and crossed over the Hudson. I closed my eyes and tried to picture all the places I went and people I met in New York, Hartsdale and Washington. The whole week was a wonderful culmination of my adventure that began in Marshall on April 12.

In some important way, I felt like a changed person with a renewed sense of pride and purpose. My former sense of shame was gone. I found

217

The Journey Home

it easier to treasure my good memories of Ken and Elaine and to cease agonizing over the tragic manner in which they had suffered and died. I felt like my emotional wounds had healed. Unlike earlier years when lesser traumas overwhelmed me, I had learned to cope in healthier ways. I had become comfortable expressing myself and speaking freely to others about the tragic events. I kept no more secrets, which could eat away at my inner peace and strength. My anxieties and my preoccupation with failure were mollified; mostly joy and a deep sense of peacefulness remained. As a result, the full force of my energy was available for creative pursuits and helping others who suffered from mental illness. These pursuits would be my ongoing work and purpose.

My newfound joy, however, was not entirely free of concern for some of my surviving children, most of whom were busy raising families or pursuing careers, or both. They seemed to be doing quite well, but a few were struggling and clearly troubled. I had read enough to know the trauma of schizophrenia in the family does not stop with a suicide. The ones I had neglected, while my energies were focused on Elaine and Ken, would likely experience repercussions. Dr. E. Fuller Torrey (1983), in his seminal family manual, *Surviving Schizophrenia*, declared, "Schizophrenia is a devastating illness not only for the person afflicted but for the person's family as well. There is probably no other disease, including cancer, which causes more anguish" (p. 154). Studies of the effects on siblings of schizophrenic children were just beginning to emerge.

I had already observed some of the repercussions among my surviving children. For example, in high school Ernie sometimes feared he was going crazy, too, after his sister and brother had psychotic episodes. His flight from home after graduation and his desire to live alone in the mountains might have been responses - not unlike PTSD (post-traumatic stress disorder) - to the tragedies unfolding at home. For several years after Ernie moved to St. Cloud and the Twin Cities, he felt a reluctance to return and came home to visit only on major holidays. He worried about Ken's condition and future prospects. Ernie's reluctance to have children of his own, even after he got married, might also be traced to the experience of chaos in our home. These and other coping behaviors are common reactions among siblings of schizophrenic children, which have been observed and documented in recent years by mental health researchers.

For the moment, I busied myself writing thank you letters, watching the scenery go by, and napping briefly. All too soon I arrived back in Union Station, where I made my way to the street and found a taxi. At 2:30 p.m., I stepped up to the ticket counter at Northwest Airlines and checked my luggage. The flight home was smooth and uneventful. It was dinnertime when I called Ernie at his home in South Minneapolis. He left immediately to pick me up at the Lindbergh Terminal and found me waiting at the curb, happy and smiling.

"Hi Mom, how was your trip?" he asked, loading my suitcase into his truck.

"Things went even better than I expected," I replied, "except I didn't get on the *Today Show*. Did you get the message about that?"

"Yeah, Dad called to tell me."

"But it was a wonderful trip anyway, and I took a lot of pictures. How was your week?"

"It's been a busy week at work, big project, a lot of pressure as usual. Jane and I are going to the cabin this weekend though. We went to dinner at the pastor's house on Sunday. That was cool. How did you like New York?"

"New York is just huge. It took me almost an hour just to go five miles in Manhattan and the skyscrapers are gigantic. But it was a lot of fun seeing it. Mostly I enjoyed visiting Erna. I stayed at her apartment three days."

By the time we got to Ernie's house, he had sensed the change in me. "Mom, you seem different," he said. "You've changed. What happened?"

"What do you notice that's different about me?"

"You seem more relaxed and present. Before, it seemed like you were off in another world and didn't always hear what people were saying."

"I guess my computer got cleared. I used to have a lot of things on my mind."

"I'd like to hear about that sometime."

The Journey Home

"It's all in my journal. You're welcome to read it. Everything else I collected will go in the scrapbook. You can look at it next time you come home."

"Okay, Mom. I love you."

"I love you too, Ernie."

Epilogue

Before the close of 1990, Mary welcomed four new grandchildren into the family. Her grandchildren provided her with a deep sense of purpose and joy. She continued her leadership in the Alliance for the Mentally Ill for several more years, organized letter writing campaigns, and helped other families cope with the difficulties of mental illness. By 1992 Mary researched, wrote, and self-published her eighty-six page *History of a Danish Family,* including a family genealogy back to 1800. She printed twenty-five copies and gave them to her children and relatives. By 1995 she completed a two-hundred page unpublished memoir, which became the basis for this book.

Mary was never invited to appear on the *Today Show,* nor did she return to lobby in Washington. In 1996, however, Ernie accompanied Gordon and Mary on a tour of Washington, D.C., Gettysburg, and Lancaster County, Pennsylvania.

Throughout the 1990s, Mary continued to pursue the things she loved, including vegetable and flower gardening, tending her house and her yard, church activities, daily letter writing, traveling with Gordon, and spending time with her children, grandchildren, and relatives.

In 1999 Mary was diagnosed with late stage colon cancer. She died peacefully on January 23, 2000, in her home at the age of 73. Among an overflow crowd at her funeral were Gordon, nine surviving children, sixteen grandchildren, and one great grandchild, Carly Ann Mell. Here are three excerpts from Marlon's eulogy:

> . . . This is a bittersweet moment for the Gunderson family. Bitter to lose Mother's physical presence in our lives, but sweet to see her legacy all gathered together to celebrate her remarkable life and her passing into God's loving hands. She brings her family together today for a celebration as she has countless times before, but this one for her last time.

Epilogue

Mom has endured her time in the valley of the shadow of death and today we know that she dwells in the house of the Lord. But she is also with us today in this house of the Lord. I feel her comforting presence around me; if I didn't I would not have the strength to speak to you today. And I want to speak to you today because, while it goes without saying that Mary was a very precious woman, I need to say it. I want to remember and tell you who my mother was, even though many of you know.

Mom was a prolific writer, and one of her great gifts to us children is a written record of her life and the lives of her relatives. She has made it easy for us to know who we are. And she has made it easy for me to tell you about her because much of what I have to say in the following is in her own words, because I could not say it better.

To understand Mom, you have to understand a family uprooted from the soil in Denmark and transplanted here in America in 1926. She was the youngest of four, and the only one in her family born here. Mary's mother always yearned for the old country and never came to feel at home in America. I remember the forlorn funeral service for my grandmother in this church twenty years ago with only about the first four pews occupied; she hadn't lived in any one place for very long her whole life, until she was elderly. It sometimes takes more than a generation for roots to take hold. . . . Look how we've grown.

. . . My grandparents' gift to our mother was their steadfast faith in God. What Mom had to struggle with and find for herself was a sense of belonging in this new country. Mom's mother had never found her place in America and was unable to help Mom find hers. The pressure of the melting pot was to assimilate and be American, but that was a challenge for a Dane with no English starting out in a school of second generation Swedes, Norwegians, and Germans. It took half of Mom's life, including several bouts with depression, exhaustion, and hospitalization, before she felt she had found her place in life. But the trials that Mom went through to find her identity, and the loss of her cherished brother to polio, and the tragic loss of two of her children to schizophrenia ultimately made her a very strong woman. I know no one who worked harder than my mother. She was humble but capable and incredibly generous.

. . . Mom was a letter writer and gift giver. I would receive cards and letters from Mom at Easter, on my birthday, on my anniversary, at Thanksgiving, at Christmas, and after any event in which I had done anything for her. Every year for the past fourteen years since my wedding, on my wedding anniversary, she wrote to thank me and tell me what a thrilling vacation she had with us on our drive from San Francisco to L.A. along the coast during the week before our wedding. She gave gifts to her young grandchildren at Easter, on their birthdays, and at Christmas. Multiply that letter writing and gift giving times eleven kids, 16 grandchildren, and at least 30 friends and relatives, many in Denmark with whom she kept a close correspondence, and it astonishes how she managed to do all she did.

Mom used to say that she had been as poor as a church mouse her whole life. Our family may not have been wealthy by material standards, but WE WERE WEALTHY in family love, and in opportunities, and in parental devotion. Her children were blessed to have the parents they did, growing up in loving hands, connected to the bounty of the good earth that provided our livelihood, shown the value of honest work daily. They not only raised us, but they showed us how to live right. And we especially thank Mom for providing our children with all these wonderful aunts, uncles, and cousins…

May she rest in peace above knowing that she lived and loved right.

In accordance with Mary's bequest, she was buried at Rush Point next to Elaine because "she was closer than any friend." Gordon grieved for two years, and his family thought he might never be happy again. Then he met Ellen Underdahl, whom he married on his eightieth birthday. At the time of this publication, Gordon and Ellen are still living on the farm near Mora. Gordon is 89, and Ellen is 85, the same age Mary would have been.

Mary and Gordon's nine surviving children are, as Mary said in her testimony, getting along fine in the world. In 2010, Dave retired from his job at Gunderson's Motors and became a licensed flight instructor and a tour bus driver. He is still married to Cindy and has three grown children and five grandchildren.

Ernie got divorced in 1997 and retired from a 24 year career in engineering at the end of 2000. He received his master's degree in social work from the University of St. Thomas in 2011 and began his new career as a volunteer counselor at Catholic Charities.

Margaret got divorced in 1980 and raised her two children as a single mom. She works for the State of Minnesota and helps care for her six grandchildren.

Epilogue

Carol recently completed her bachelor's degree in psychology and is still married to Lowell Nelson, an electrical contractor and jack-of-all-trades. They have three grown children and two grandchildren.

Eunice got divorced in 1986 and raised her two children as a single mom. In 2005 she earned her master's degree in human development, and she continues to pursue her avocations in singing and songwriting. She produced her first CD, *True North*, in 2007 and performs at coffee shops around the Twin Cities.

Marlon earned his master's degree in electrical engineering at Stanford University in 1985 and is presently employed at Micron Technology. He was a campaign organizer for his wife, Julie Bunn, a two-term Minnesota state representative until the end of 2010. Their daughter Lauren is a senior in college.

Milton is an electrician for East Central Electric; his wife Robin is a vice president at Kanabec State Bank. They have two sons in college and two children in Mora public schools.

Geoff, still single, is a retired air traffic controller. He lives on a hobby farm north of Mora and likes to plant trees and restore old trucks.

Paula is still an account manager for Old Republic Title. Her husband Brad is a computer programmer. They have two sons, one in high school and one in college.

Acknowledgments

In the fall of 2005 I, Ernie Gunderson, enrolled in the School of Social Work at the University of St. Thomas and the College of St. Catherine. This book is a result of that beginning, thanks to Leola Furman, my human behavior professor who read my life cycle history paper and suggested I write a book. Thanks also to Mari Ann Graham, my advisor, who later approved a one year leave from the MSW program so I could pursue that goal.

I owe a debt of gratitude to my partner Becky Hanson, the grammar and style wiz, who encouraged me and donated many hours of her time to editing. Special thanks also to Becky's mother, Verna Hanson, who published her book *Snapshots* in 2007 and provided the essential catalyst. In Verna's manuscript I recognized the name of her hometown, Graettinger, Iowa, which was near the country school where my mother taught in 1945 – 46. Blue Bottom School was just three miles from Verna's home and ten miles from Ringsted. One of Mary's pupils was Verna's cousin. Verna arranged a tour with Ray Ohrtman, who showed me the Ringsted area and Mary's childhood home. For the first time, I set foot on the ground where my mother was raised, the farm and two country school sites. I was deeply moved. Not only was this the jump start I needed to begin the research, it truly inspired me to write the book.

Thanks to Ray Ohrtman for my introduction to the Ringsted community. To Rob Sorensen for providing names and information about characters in the Ringsted area. Special thanks to my father Gordon and Aunt Esther, who contributed many hours recollecting and recording their memories of life with Mary. To my sisters Margaret, Carol, Eunice, and Paula, who preserved the written materials which make up the collection of Mary's work. To Rigmor Wemmelund for sending me valuable descriptions of family

Acknowledgments

customs common among our Danish ancestors. To Carol Hass for encouraging and supporting Mary's mission. To Knud Christensen for connecting Mary with her relatives in Denmark and for facilitating my education about the places and people there. To NAMI and NIMH for inviting Mary to lobby Congress and for paying her way. To Howard Kranz, Tony Wentersdorf, Amy Sabrina, Jesse Watkins, Mari Ann Graham, Tamara Kaiser, Geoff Gunderson, Eunice Collette, Carol Nelson, and Libby Nelson, all of whom read my first draft and suggested many essential improvements. And to my instructors and colleagues at the LOFT literary center, who illuminated a variety of issues and problems inherent in writing someone else's memoir.

And finally, thanks to Libby Nelson who skillfully transcribed several hours of taped conversations between Mary and Erna Christensen. Thanks also to Marlon Gunderson for contributing his eulogy. And thanks most of all to Mary who raised me lovingly, who wrote so often and saved it all.

Ernie Gunderson, MSW, LGSW, 2011

To offer feedback or purchase books, visit www.erniegunderson.com

Bibliography

Casson, Lloyd S. *Sermon for 8th Sunday after Pentecost*, Retrieved on 1/18/2010 from http://dfms.org/sermons_that_work_11684_ENG_HTM.htm?menupage=23285.

Gulliford, Andrew. (1996). *America's Country Schools.* (3rd edition). Niwot, Colorado: University Press of Colorado.

Hansen, Thorvold. (1992). *Church Divided: Lutheranism Among the Danish Immigrants.* Des Moines, Iowa: Grand View College.

Heyrman, Christine, L. (2007). *The First Great Awakening.* Divining America, TeacherServe: National Humanities Center. Retrieved 10/13/2008 from Http://nationalhumanitiescenter.org/tserve/eighteen/ekeyinfo/grawaken.html.

Minnesota Climatology Working Group. 1936 temperature and precipitation data. Retrieved 2/15/2009 from http.//climate.umn. edu/doc/historical.htm

National Park Service Brochure. *Statue of Liberty and Ellis Island*, Statue of Liberty National Monument, New York, NY.

Nouwen, Henri, J.M. (1972). *The Wounded Healer.* New York, NY: Bantom Doubleday Dell Publishing Group, Inc.

Pallesen, Tim. (2007). *Happy and Sad Danes Unite.* The Lutheran, Vol. 20 (10), 36-37.

South Zumbro History of Ole Bergh. Retrieved on 9/25/2008 from http://freepages.genealogy.rootsweb.ancestry.com/~mbiker3/bergh-5/text.

St. Thomas Church. (1990). *Sunday Bulletin* for April 29, 1990, Morning Prayer and Choral Eucharist.

St. Thomas Church. *Order of Service*, Morning Prayer and Choral Eucharist. Obtained by Mary from St. Thomas Church on April 29, 1990.

Torrey, E. Fuller. (1983). *Surviving Schizophrenia: A Family Manual.* New York, NY: Harper Row, Publishers.

Bibliography

Wikipedia, the free encyclopedia. Various topics including Art Deco, Asclepius, Beau-Arts architecture, Broadway, Charging Bull, Demographics of Denmark, Diamond District, Empire State Building, Episcopal Church, Fifth Avenue, Gilded Age, Grand Central Terminal, John D. Rockefeller, Manhattan, New York Public Library, Pennsylvania Station, Rockefeller Center, Ulysses S. Grant Memorial, Union Station, Saint George, White Plains. Retrieved between 11/1/2008 and 1/15/2010 from http://www.wikipedia.org.

Williams, Alfreda, A. (1994). *This is Greenburgh*. Greenbergh, NY: Town of Greenburgh Publication.

World Factbook, Denmark, Retrieved 5/19/2009 from http://www. cia.gov/library/publications/the-world-factbook/print/da.html.

Wright, J. Robert. (2001). *Saint Thomas Church Fifth Avenue*. Grand Rapids, MI: William B. Eerdmans Publishing Co.